Unpacking Queer Politics

For Ann Rowett with gratitude for her love and her clear lesbian feminist vision which support me in my writing and my political work.

Unpacking Queer Politics

A Lesbian Feminist Perspective

Sheila Jeffreys

polity

First published in 2003 by Polity Press in association with Blackwell Publishers Ltd, a Blackwell Publishing Company.

Editorial office:
Polity Press
65 Bridge Street
Cambridge CB2 1UR, UK

Marketing and production:
Blackwell Publishers Ltd
108 Cowley Road
Oxford OX4 1JF, UK

Published in the USA by:
Blackwell Publishers Inc.
350 Main Street
Malden MA 02148, USA

ISBN 0-7456-2837-0
ISBN 0-7456-2838-9 (pbk)

A catalogue record for this book is available from the British Library and has been applied for from the Library of Congress.

Typeset in 10.5 on 12 pt Berling
by Kolam Informations Services Pvt. Ltd., Pondicherry, India
Printed in Great Britain by MPG Books Ltd, Bodmin, Cornwall
This book is printed on acid-free paper.

Contents

Acknowledgements

The ideas in this book owe a great deal to all those good discussions I have had over the years that the book has been brewing. Feminists and lesbian feminists in Australia, the UK, the USA, Canada and many other countries have contributed to the development of my thinking, particularly those involved in the international struggle against sexual exploitation. Ideas that come out of a political move-ment are not the result of one person sitting in an attic, but emerge from a collective process. My sisters and friends in the Coalition Against Trafficking in Women Australia and all those with whom I am fortunate enough to discuss ideas here in Melbourne have sustained me, particularly Carole Moschetti and Kathy Chambers. I am grateful to young lesbians and feminists in Melbourne who have kept me informed of how difficult it is these days to maintain lesbian feminist vision and politics within a queer culture. I am fortunate in having the resources and encouragement of my department, Political Science, at the University of Melbourne, to put into writing what so many other lesbian feminists have been thinking for so long. My undergraduate and postgraduate students have helped me develop my ideas and have contributed their knowledge and understanding of what is happening in the parts of lesbian and gay culture in which they seek to live and thrive.

I am particularly grateful to Ruth Margerison and John Stoltenberg who read this book in manuscript and offered valuable insights. Both John Stoltenberg and Christopher Kendall have inspired me in their written work on gay male sexuality and gay male pornography. I am aware that men who stand out against the dominant values of queer sex culture do not have an easy time, and I am grateful that they continue to do so.

Introduction

In the 1990s a phenomenon developed within sectors of the lesbian community known as 'packing' (Volcano and Halberstam 1999). This entailed the wearing of a dildo down the trouser leg to suggest the existence of a penis. This practice signalled that, for the lesbians who adopted it, the worship of masculinity had triumphed over the lesbian feminist project of ending gender hierarchy. At the same time a cult of transsexualism developed amongst similar groups of lesbians. Some of the lesbians who had demonstrated their commitment to achieving male power and privilege by assuming a 'butch' identity, by packing and holding 'drag king' contests to see who could most convincingly look like a man, and particularly a gay man, moved toward the mutilating surgery and hormone consumption which promised 'realness' in their quest (Devor 1999). The change from the heyday of lesbian feminism in which we understood, as Adrienne Rich said, that 'The meaning of our love for women is what we have constantly to expand' (Rich 1979: 230) to a situation where, in some influential and much publicized parts of the lesbian community, masculinity is the holy grail, could not be more profound.

Why did this happen? I shall argue here that the most significant reason was the influence of a powerful male gay culture which, from the late 1970s onwards, rejected the gay liberation project of dismantling gender hierarchy and chose 'manhood' as its goal. Through sadomasochism, gay male pornography, sexual practices of public sex and prostitution that celebrated masculine privilege, dominant areas of gay male culture created a hypermasculinity and said this was gayness, and this was good. In the last decade several US books by gay men have launched broad-ranging critiques of gay men's sexual freedom agenda. These critiques are inspired primarily by the continued extremely high rate of HIV infection in the USA, but also by a perception that gay commercial sex culture impoverishes lives and relationships (Rotello 1997; Signorile 1998a). Some male gay theorists have employed feminist understandings to launch swingeing critiques of the gay male cult of masculinity (Stoltenberg 1991; Levine 1998; Kendall 1997; Jensen 1998). This work by gay men is a most useful starting point from which to embark on a lesbian feminist examination of gay and queer culture today. It is the recognition of the very harmful impact of the gay male worship of masculinity on the lives of lesbians that impels me to examine gay male culture and politics in this book.

The harmful practices that have developed in this period have all been given theoretical justification within queer theory and politics. I argue that when queer politics in the 1990s attacked the principles of gay liberation and lesbian feminism, which required the transformation of personal life, there was a backlash against the possibility of radical social change. The new politics was based, quite explicitly, upon a repudiation of lesbian feminist ideas. Queer politics enshrined a cult of masculinity. I will argue here that the political agenda of queer politics is damaging to the interests of lesbians, women in general, and to marginalized and vulnerable constituencies of gay men. The notion that queer politics could represent the interests of lesbians as well as gay men arises from a mistaken idea that lesbians and gay men can form one unified constituency with common interests. Lesbian feminism was created out of the feminist understanding that lesbians are women, and the interests of women in mixed political organizing are regularly excluded or even directly contradicted. This understanding has been lost in queer politics, and this book is written to bring the interests of women and lesbians once more into the forefront of lesbian and gay political discussion.

The welcome outpouring of books on lesbian and gay political and legal theory in the 1990s seems to start from the premiss that lesbians and gay men form one unified social category which has a homogeneous agenda to serve unified interests (Evans 1993; Wilson 1995; Vaid 1995; Stychin 1995; Bell and Binnie 2000). Much of this new writing seeks to integrate lesbians and gays into the theorizing of citizenship with the creation of new categories of sexual or queer citizenship. Diane Richardson is one of the very few voices pointing out that lesbians cannot be simply subsumed within such a category (Richardson 2000a, b). The general absence of such a feminist viewpoint in relation to 'sexual citizenship' is a puzzle. Books by feminist theorists on women's citizenship do analyse the contradictory interests of women and men. They point out that the idea and practice of men's citizenship have been created precisely out of the subordination of women (Pateman 1988; Vogel 1994). But this feminist understanding seems to disappear in the theorizing of 'sexual' citizenship. In fact, lesbians and gay men are far from a unified category with unified interests. Lesbians are women, and lesbian theories of citizenship must continue to examine the contradictions between the interests of women and men, particularly in relation to the contradictions between the interests of gay men and the whole constituency of women.

No necessary community of interest

Lesbian feminists, who have chosen to organize and live their lives separately from gay men, have long been keenly aware that there was no necessary community of interest between lesbians and gay men. The poet and writer Adrienne Rich wrote in the late 1970s, when lesbian feminism was at its peak, that the interests of lesbians were threatened by both heterosexual and gay men's cultures.

> Lesbians have been forced to live between two cultures, both male-dominated, each of which has denied and endangered our existence. On the one hand, there is the heterosexist, patriarchal culture . . . . On the other hand, there is homosexual patriarchal culture, a culture created by homosexual men, reflecting such male stereotypes as dominance and submission as modes of relationship, and the separation of sex from emotional involvement – a culture tainted by profound hatred for women. The male "gay" culture has offered lesbians the imitation role-stereotypes of "butch" and "femme," "active" and "passive," cruising, sado-masochism, and the violent, self-destructive world of "gay" bars. Neither heterosexual culture nor "gay" culture has offered lesbians a space in which to discover what it means to be self-defined, self-loving, women-identified, neither an imitation man nor his objectified opposite. (Rich 1979: 225)

Lesbian feminism has offered lesbians the necessary space in which to create lesbian feminist values and express their love for women. The lesbian feminist philosopher Marilyn Frye has written incisively about the shared values that exist between gay and heterosexual men and the need for lesbians to separate to create their own community and politics (Frye 1983). The AIDs crisis and the birth of queer politics led to many lesbians moving back to work with gay men whilst burying their anxieties about the values of dominant male gay culture. This is despite the fact that some influential gay writers and activists have not been shy about expanding upon their hostile feelings towards lesbians and women. One good example of this is the cheerfulness with which some gay men have been prepared to talk about the 'ick factor'.

The existence of what has been called the 'ick factor' might well be considered to stand in the way of any easy assumption of there being a unified lesbian and gay category within a pluralist citizenry. This term is employed in gay male writings to describe the extreme revulsion experienced by some gay men at the thought or sight of women's naked bodies. It has become quite well known since workshops on the topic have been held yearly at the US National Lesbian and Gay Task Force conferences. Eric Rofes, a leading member of Sex Panic, has been involved in organizing the workshops which lesbians and gay men are supposed to attend to hear what each thinks of the other. He explains that he is very lesbian- and feminist-identified and greatly troubled by the 'ick factor' he experiences. He writes of walking through sunbathing lesbians at a gay beach who were topless. He experienced great discomfort: 'When we finally walk beyond the women's section and male torsos appear, my breath eases, my skin stops sweating, and my heart stops racing' (Rofes 1998b: 45). He explains his reaction thus:

> I am a gay man with long-term friendships with lesbians and a strong commitment to supporting lesbian culture. Yet I'm one of many gay men who share what I call "the ick factor" – a visceral response ranging from dislike to disgust when confronted with lesbian sex and bodies. Over almost twenty-five years of involvement in gay male cultures, I've witnessed many men express their revulsion at lesbian sex and women's bodies. I've heard countless "tuna" jokes, seen men's faces turn sour when lesbian sex appears in movies, and watched gay men huddle together in small groups voicing disgust at topless women in political demonstrations. (p. 46)

'Tuna' jokes arise from the habit amongst gay men of calling women 'fish' after what they consider to be the repulsive smell of their genitals. Some gay men cannot bear to be near lesbians because of the way they smell. Rofes quotes one man as saying he could not become physically close to lesbians 'because of the odors he believed their bodies emitted' (p. 47).

Though he has no evidence from which to calculate this, Rofes considers that one-third of gay men are thus repulsed. For a while at least, the term 'ick factor' was common currency. For instance, a piece by a US male gay writer published in the Australian male gay magazine *Outrage* in 1997 called 'Getting a grip on the ick factor' describes gay men going to a mixed sex party in order to try to get over being 'grossed out' by female genitals. The author comments that 'the ick factor in gay male culture' is 'not unusual among gay men' (Strubbe 1997: 44).

Racism in the UK in the 1960s often focused on the supposedly different smell of Asian British citizens. The feelings of those gay men who find women's bodies so difficult to cope with remind me of that kind of visceral racism. Men and women, whatever their sexual orientation, are raised in a male supremacist society which teaches that women's bodies are disgusting, whereas penises confer honour and pride. The mental health of lesbians who are seeking to recover from this woman hatred so that they may love and respect the bodies of women may not be well served by any level of community with men who harbour such deep-seated misogyny. Rofes feels guilty, and wishes to overcome his extraordinarily negative feelings towards women, but what is surprising is that he feels able to speak of them so readily, when similar feelings on the basis of race would probably not be considered quite as acceptable to relate. In the face of such feelings it may be unreasonable to expect any straightforward community of interests between lesbians and gay men.

Lest this picture of gay male misogyny should look too bleak, it is important to point out that there was one gay man in the same anthology, *Opposite Sex*, which contained the 'ick' factor piece, who utilized a lesbian feminist perspective and showed genuine sympathy with the experience of women. Robert Jensen explains how lonely it is to take such a position in a sexual libertarian gay culture in which political questioning of sexual practice is simply disallowed on all sides: 'For me, being gay means not only acknowledging sexual desire for men but also resisting the norms and practices of patriarchy.... Such a commitment is difficult to make good on in a world of male privilege, and I have found few role models for how to live ethically as a man – straight or gay – in a patriarchy' (Jensen 1998: 152).

Jensen utilizes the work of radical feminist lesbian theorists such as Marilyn Frye to support his refusal to make a public/private split. He does not allow gay male sexual practice an immunity from political criticism: 'it is these practices themselves that mimic heterosexuality in their acceptance of patriarchal sexual values: the disconnection of sex from affection and emotional interaction with another, the heterosexual equation of sex with penetration and domination and submission, and the commodification of sex in pornography' (Jensen 1998: 156). In direct opposition to the liberalism of public gay politics, he considers that 'There are political and ethical implications in all aspects of everyday life.... There is no escape from judgment, nor should we seek such an escape' (p. 154).

Gay masculinity

Since I will suggest in this book that it is the promotion and celebration of gay male masculinity that creates the most fundamental difference of interest between the malestream gay male agenda and the interests of lesbians and other women, it is important to explain what I mean by masculinity. My understanding of masculinity is that it refers to behaviour that is constructed by and serves to maintain male dominance. Masculinity is not just that which pertains to men, since men can be seen, and consider themselves, to be insufficiently masculine. Indeed, this is precisely what gay men before the 1970s frequently considered themselves, and were considered by others, to be. Masculinity is not, then, a biological fact, something connected with particular hormones or genes. Masculine behaviour or appearance or artefacts, and design, signify 'manhood' as a political, not a biological, category. In this understanding masculinity cannot exist without its supposed opposite, femininity, which pertains to female subordination. Neither masculinity nor femininity make sense or can exist without the other as a reference point (Connell 1995).

Though writers on masculinity such as Robert Connell tend, these days, to use the term 'masculinity' with an 's' on it – i.e. masculinities – I deliberately do not do so. I recognize that the form taken by male dominant behaviour, masculinity, can vary considerably, and is influenced by class, race and many other factors. The use of the plural, however, suggests that not all varieties of masculinity are problematic, and that some might be saved. Since I define masculinity as the behaviour of male dominance, I am interested in eliminating it rather than saving any variety at all, and therefore do not use the term 'masculinities'. To the extent that gay men as a group seek to protect their practice of masculinity politically, they can be seen to be acting in direct contradiction to the interests of women, and to lesbians as a category of women. They cannot, after all, have their masculinity (in any form) to make them feel better, without the existence of a substantial class of subordinate people representing femininity, and these are presently women.

Martin Levine's critical writings on gay masculinity have been published posthumously by his literary editor, Michael Kimmel (Levine 1998). They provide a profound analysis of the problem. He explains that post-gay liberation gay men appropriated masculinity as a compensation for the feminine stereotypes that had been forced upon them in earlier periods.

> I argue that gay men enacted a hypermasculine sexuality as a way to challenge their stigmatization as failed men, as "sissies", and that many of the institutions that developed in the gay male world of the 1970s and early 1980s catered to and supported this hypermasculine sexual code – from clothing stores and sexual boutiques, to bars, bathhouses, and the ubiquitous gyms. (Levine 1998: 5)

An exaggerated masculinity became the dominant style in gay culture, and, as Levine points out, through the influence of gay designers and gay disco music helped to create the fashion for such exaggerated masculinity in fashionable heterosexual culture as well. In *Unpacking Queer Politics* I will analyse the practices of masculinity that shape areas of gay male sexual culture and the queer political agenda as it relates to sexual practice. I will look at the effect that relating to gay men in a mixed gay culture that celebrates and eroticizes masculinity as the highest good has upon lesbians.

I will examine the political demands of some gay activists, in groups such as Outrage in the UK and Sex Panic in the USA, for sexual freedom in the areas of public sex, pornography and sadomasochism, and argue that they are based upon a traditional patriarchal agenda. Such activists tend to say that they are challenging the public/private distinction in which sexual activity is usually confined to the private sphere. However, the campaigns to extend 'private' sex into the public realm are based upon the notion that sex must continue to be recognized as 'private' – i.e. protected from political criticism and worthy of respect as an exercise of individual freedom even if carried out in a public park. The lesbian feminist agenda is likely to womanifest in challenging the public/private distinction on which common understandings of politics are based. Lesbian feminists want a political democracy inside and outside the home, with no distinction that protects a private slavery of sexual exploitation and violation.

The lesbian feminist project of creating an equality in the private world of sex and relationships, based on the understanding that the personal is political, can be the basis of creating a public world that is healthy for women to live in. The lesbian feminists who live now according to these principles, those who are derided in queer media and fora as politically correct, sex-phobic fascists, should perhaps be understood as the vanguard of radical social change.

Gay Liberation and Lesbian Feminism

Today many young lesbians and gay men will call themselves 'queer' without a second thought. But this is a term which became fashionable to describe lesbians and gays only in the last decade, and many lesbians still find the term abhorrent. Queer politics and theory emerged at a particular point in the history of the development of lesbian and gay movements. Proponents may well see queer politics as the apogee of this development. Many lesbian feminist critics see queer politics as constituting a backlash against the interests of women and lesbians. To understand the queer politics of today, we need to see how the ideas and practices develop from, or are a reaction to, what has gone before. In this chapter I will look at gay liberation and lesbian feminism as a context for understanding queer politics.

The ideas and strategies of gay liberation came out of the same crucible that gave birth to the other 'new' social movements of the late 1960s and early 1970s. These new movements were feminism, youth liberation, black liberation, Paris 1968 and the student movement. Socialist and feminist ideas infused gay liberation from the outset. Gay liberation's birth is commonly dated to the June 1969 so-called Stonewall rebellion in Greenwich Village, when lesbians, gay men and drag queens for the first time fought back in fierce street battles against the routine harassment of police raids on gay clubs. In fact, it needs to be understood as arising from a gradually intensifying mood of frustration and resistance which had been growing in and outside the earlier lesbian and gay organizations of the 1960s. These earlier organizations had laid the groundwork which allowed gay liberation to develop so swiftly (D'Emilio 1998, 1st published 1983). Stonewall was a catalyst, and well suited to symbolize the mood of the times, but it could not have ignited a political movement if the ground had not been well prepared.

What have been called 'homophile' organizations were set up in the 1950s and 1960s and pre-dated gay liberation. These organizations have been characterized by historians as 'assimilationist', aimed at gaining integration for homosexuals and ending legal penalties. What was different about gay liberation is that assimilation was repudiated in favour of 'coming out', 'gay pride' and demanding the dramatic social changes that were considered necessary for the freedom of women and lesbians and gays. Gay liberation activists, fuelled by the confidence gained from the spirit of the age, in which so many social groups were protesting, theorizing, demanding radical change, claimed their gayness and performed dramatic and fun protests in public places.

Gay liberation was originally conceived as the Gay Liberation Front. The word 'Front' suggests the socialist foundations of gay liberation. GLF was modelled on the liberation struggles conducted by colonized peoples around the world against imperialism, as in Vietnam. Lisa Power, in her history of GLF in London, comments that 'GLF London attracted, amongst others, people with a background in resistance to the Vietnam war, black rights, women's liberation, the underground press, the White Panthers (a support group to the Black Panthers), the International Marxist Group, the Communist Party, a wide variety of other leftist groups including Maoists, the drugs culture, transsexuals and rent boys' (Power 1995: 16).

The socialist analysis was applied to the situation of lesbians and gay men. There was a critique on the left at this time of what was seen as the 'general distortion of all sexuality in this society' for the purpose of social control and 'to sell the surfeit of consumer goods the economic system grinds out'(GLF 1971, quoted in Power 1995: 53). Gay liberation theorists engaged in a swingeing critique of the capitalist forces, exemplified by the gay sex industry and owners of gay clubs, which created the exploitation of gay men. They argued: 'GLF hopes to provide a desperately-needed escape for people who are tired of the alienated and exploitative 'gay' world, furtive sex in public loos, and dangerous excursions to Hampstead Heath. We want to provide a better scene for gay people' (p. 53). Gay liberation activists rejected the medical model of homosexuality as sickness. They campaigned, successfully, to have homosexuality removed from the US list of mental illness diagnoses, the DSM 3. They proclaimed that 'gay is good'. They believed that homosexual oppression was the result of male dominance, and that women's liberation and gay liberation were inevitably connected, such that one could not be achieved without the other.

Homosexual oppression and the oppression of women were both seen to result from the imposition of what were called 'sex roles'. Political activists of the left in this period were profoundly social-constructionist in their approach. Thus both gay liberationists and feminists saw sex roles, which would probably now be called 'gender roles', as being politically constructed to ensure male dominance. Women were relegated to the female sex role of the private sphere, nurturing and being concerned with beautifying the body in order to be an appropriate sex object. Lesbians were persecuted because they challenged the female sex role of sexual passivity and the servicing of men. Gay men were persecuted because they challenged the male sex role, which, as well as requiring masculine behaviour, was founded upon heterosexuality and sexual intercourse with women.

In the context of a current queer politics, which celebrates those who play out precisely these roles in the form of butch/femme, transgenderism and sadomasochism as the transgressive vanguard of the revolution, it is useful to understand how fully a gay liberation strongly influenced by feminism rejected them. The oppression of gay men was seen to be a reflection of the oppression of women, so 'sex roles' were a problem for gay men too. One US gay liberationist expressed it thus:

> Sexism is also reflected in the roles homosexuals have copied from straight society. The labels might differ, but it is the same unequal situation, as long as roles are rigidly defined, as long as one person exercises power over another. For straights it is male-female, master/mistress. For gays it is butch/femme, aggressive-passive. And the extreme, in either case, is sadist-masochist. Human beings become objectified, are treated as property, as if one person could own another. (Diaman 1992: 263)

A UK gay liberation activist wrote: 'We have been forced into playing roles based upon straight society, butch and femme, nuclear "marriages" which continue within the relationship the same oppression that outside society forces onto its women' (Walter 1980: 59). Another wrote: 'Playing roles in a society which demands gender definitions, sexual role-playing, masculine versus feminine – what can we do, those whom society dismisses and condemns as half-men? Too often we react by over-playing' (p. 87).

In the years of gay liberation, no argument was made that role-playing was an 'authentic' and uniquely lesbian or gay experience, as has happened in the 1980s and 1990s (Davis and Kennedy 1991). There was no shame in accepting that gays were involved in mimicking straight society when they embarked upon role-playing. Gays were understood to be constructed by the rules of straight society too. Carl Wittman of US Gay Liberation states:

> We are children of straight society. We still think straight; that is part of our oppression. One of the worst of straight concepts is inequality ... male/female, on top/on bottom, spouse/not spouse, heterosexual/homosexual, boss/worker, white/black, and rich/poor. . . . For too long we mimicked these roles to protect ourselves – a survival mechanism. Now we are becoming free enough to shed the roles which we've picked up from the institutions which have imprisoned us. (Wittman 1992: 333)

A women's group that formed part of gay liberation in the USA, the Gay Revolutionary Party Women's Caucus, rejected firmly the idea of sex role-playing for lesbians, because it holds no advantages for them.

> Although none of us has ever been educated in the conduct of relations of roleless equality, lesbians can come closer to this achievement than others because none of the sexist role-playing training everyone receives helps make their relationships work. Role-playing gets them nowhere, because the "butch" gets none of the male sexual, social, or economic rewards while the "fem" does not have a man to bring home a man's wages or to protect her from other men's attacks. (Gay Revolutionary Party Women's Caucus 1992:180)

Such sentiments, from those who would have seen themselves at the time as the vanguard of gay politics, stand in stark contrast to the attitude towards lesbian role-playing that developed later in some areas of the lesbian community. In the late 1980s and 1990s

lesbian writers such as Joan Nestle (1987) built themselves considerable reputations by celebrating and romanticizing role-playing as
the most authentic form of lesbianism. Whereas in gay liberation
the answer to roles was to 'shed' them, in later decades they were
picked up, polished and redeployed for the purposes of sexual excitement (Munt 1998; Halberstam 1998a; Newman 1995).

Another common current between gay liberation and women's
liberation at this time was the challenge to marriage and the nuclear
family. Marriage was considered by both to be a contract of exploitation and male dominance, which necessitated precisely the 'sex
roles' which were seen to be so oppressive. So fundamental was
the opposition to marriage that it was emphasized by Jill Tweedie,
an influential *Guardian* opinion columnist, in a positive piece
about gay liberation: 'Gay Lib does not plead for the right of homosexuals to marry. Gay Lib questions marriage' (quoted in Power
1995: 64).

Two aspects of gay liberation theorizing distinguish it dramatically
from queer politics. One is the understanding that the oppression of
gay men stems from the oppression of women. Another is that many
forms of gay male behaviour, which today are lauded in queer politics, are the result of gay oppression, and cannot be ended without
ending the oppression of women. Forms of behaviour which historically were part of the behaviour of men who had sex with men, such
as cruising and effeminacy, were seen by GLF activists to be the result
of oppression, rather than inevitable and authentic forms of gay
behaviour.

The original political excitement of gay liberation lasted only
a few years in the UK and the USA. In the UK some men returned
to practices that they had criticized when gay liberation was at
its height, such as cruising (Shiers 1980). Now that an out gay
community existed as a market, new gay businesses became involved
in the exploitation of gay men in the same way that straight and
mafia businesses had done in earlier times: gay capitalism was
born. Gay masculinity became the fashion, whereas gay liberation
politics had eschewed masculinity as the behaviour of male dominance (Humphries 1985). A politics of gay equal rights activism
began to develop, which some gay liberationists saw as deradicaliz-
ing and undermining the movement for radical social change. Why,
then, was the radical challenge of gay liberation not sustained?

Why did gay liberation fail?

John D'Emilio, in the new preface to the reissue of the US collection of GLF writings, *Out of the Closets*, argues that gay liberation was superseded by a more mainstream gay rights activism in the later 1970s. This new gay rights movement no longer saw itself as one amongst other movements of liberation working for fundamental social change. The agenda was narrower, and bought into the liberal politics of equal rights.

> [A]s the 1970s wore on, the gay and lesbian movement began to travel along many different paths. One of these might be labeled a gay rights movement. Composed mostly of white, middle-class, gay men, though with some lesbians and people of color as well, this reform-orientated politics focused on gay issues only and largely abandoned the broad analysis of oppression that animated gay liberation. These activists, many of whom were quite militant in the tactics they espoused, sought entry into the system on terms of equality. (D'Emilio 1992: p. xxv)

In particular, D'Emilio argues, these equal rights activists lost the gay liberation understanding that the oppression of gays was the result of sexism, and that gay men therefore needed to fight sexism alongside women. 'Unlike the gay men in *Out of the Closets*, who saw sexism as the root of gay male oppression, now sexism is perceived as being about "them"' (p. xxvi). Gay rights activists, D'Emilio explains, also lost the gay liberation understanding that homosexuality, like heterosexuality, was socially constructed. Gay and lesbian identities, he says, came to be seen once again, as in the pre-Stonewall period, as 'fixed identities, determined early in life (if not at birth), but natural, good, and healthy rather than unnatural, bad, or sick' (p. xxvi).

But D'Emilio is critical of the breadth of social criticism engaged in by gay liberationists. He sees the radicalism of their agenda as being one of the reasons for their failure. He has taken on board the arguments made by sexual libertarians in the 1980s and 1990s that gay liberationists, like radical feminists who were similarly attacked, were, in his words, 'moralistic and condescending'. In their attacks on 'roles, anonymous sex, objectification, and bar culture, they ended up constructing a prescriptive sexual politics. . . . [T]hey teetered on the edge of becoming a new vice squad' (p. xxvii). It is interesting to see how close these accusations are to those flung at radical feminists in the so-called feminist sexuality debates of the 1980s (Vance 1984). In those 'debates' radical feminist criticism of pornography and prostitution was also attacked for being right wing and moralistic. Whilst in male gay communities and politics there was no fierce debate, and the gay liberation understandings simply wilted away, amongst lesbians and feminists the battle to vanquish the radical feminist critique was furious (see discussion of these 'debates' in Jeffreys 1990a).

D'Emilio says that the problem of gay liberationists was that they had a 'naivete about the dynamics of sexual desire; change was assumed to be easier than it was' (D'Emilio 1992: p. xxviii). He remains critical of the sexual liberalism that has replaced the gay liberation critique: 'Yet, in reacting against that, it often seems as if we have given up any possibility of thinking critically about sexuality. Our sexual politics often reduces to a campaign against prohibitions' (p. xxviii). But he appears too tired and too disillusioned to try to maintain the critique of the construction of sexuality that was so vital in earlier years. 'In a culture in which sexuality has come to define the truth about the self and in which sexual desire appears coterminous with who we are, perhaps it is too divisive, too volatile, to subject something so personal to political scrutiny' (p. xxviii). This resignation comes less easily to feminist campaigners, since it is women who suffer so directly from the exercise of a male sexuality constructed around objectification and aggression, in the form of rape, murder, sexual harassment, pornography and prostitution. D'Emilio's resignation is a luxury which those of us who continue to seek an end to male violence cannot afford.

Karla Jay and Allan Young, in their new introduction to the *Out of the Closets* collection, explain that they have abandoned their dreams of revolution as simply impractical, because they do not have enough popular appeal.

> Like our straight counterparts in the New Left, we were infatuated by the slogan "Revolution in our lifetime." But we were oblivious to the fact that such far-reaching goals had little meaning for the great masses of American people – even most gay and lesbian Americans – encumbered as they were with jobs, homes, children, and other responsibilities. As for the insistence on linking the personal and the political, it could be very rewarding, and served as cheap therapy for many, but its

extreme application made life rather difficult. (Jay and Young 1992: p. xxxvii)

They ask: 'So, what is the "real" gay liberation? Is it the assimilation of gay people into every stitch of the fabric of existing American life? Or is it the total revolutionary movement that motivated the writers of *Out of the Closets*?' (p. xliv).

One development that is likely to have hastened the abandonment of feminist insights by many gay activists is the withdrawal of lesbians in large numbers from gay liberation, in order to concentrate their energies on lesbian feminism. Lesbians had always been a minority in gay liberation, and in the UK quite a small minority. Their withdrawal in the USA, the UK and Australia was occasioned by the developing strength of feminism, which led the lesbians to concentrate on their interests as women, and to be sensitive to the sexism of their male colleagues. One issue which was a source of serious schism between men and women in gay liberation was sexual practice. Denise Thompson describes the lesbians' disenchantment in Australia thus: 'The model of "sexual freedom" espoused by gay liberation was and remained intransigently masculine – fucking for fucking's sake, erotic stimulation confined to the genitals and a few selected erogenous zones, anonymous sex at the beats (public pickup places), bars, clubs, and bath houses' (Thompson 1985: 70). Gregg Blatchford of Sydney Gay Liberation reflects on the casual misogyny in what he calls 'homosexual subculture' thus:

> [W]omen are often referred to by their sexual organs; 'ish' is a common term for a woman and 'cunty' is used as an adjective referring to something that possesses the qualities of a woman. The derogatory term 'fag hag' is used to describe a woman who enjoys the company of gay men. Besides these peculiarly gay male expressions, most references to women are similar to the way heterosexual men can be seen to respond to women: 'cow', 'old woman', 'slag', 'tart', 'cheap', 'scrubber'. (Quoted in Thompson 1985: 56)

Men in gay liberation had to make an effort to overcome this element of gay culture, and were not always successful.

The majority of lesbians involved in Gay Liberation in the UK walked out *en masse*. As Nettie Pollard, one of those who stayed, describes it: 'Four or five of us stayed and the rest, thirty or so, walked out' (Power 1995: 241). Lisa Power offers several explanations.

For her oral history of the London GLF she interviewed men and women who had been involved in early 1970s gay liberation. One man, Tim Clark, explained that the men were united by all the sexual activity that took place between them. 'And by and large they were excluded from the mass sex that the men were having, which acted as a bond' (p. 240). One lesbian interviewee supported the idea that the men and women divided over the men's determination to see their sexual practice as the very stuff of liberation: 'What caused trouble between the men and women was that so many of the men wanted to talk about cottaging [sex in public toilets] in the meetings' (Carla Toney, quoted in Power 1995: 242).

Another issue that angered the lesbians was the adoption by some men in gay liberation of drag. The understanding that sex roles were at the root of women's and gay oppression was sometimes expressed by gay men in ways that lesbian activists found troubling. In the UK, for instance, some gay liberation men chose to wear frocks on the underground, in the street, and in everyday life. They chose to engage in traditionally feminine practices, including knitting, during meetings. The lesbians present were unlikely to wear frocks, and some found this imitation of stereotypes of women offensive. As Power explains: 'Drag...increasingly fuelled the anger of many GLF women who saw it not as men breaking down their own inhibitions and machismo, but as a guying of traditional womanhood' (p. 242). One ex-GLF man gave Power a graphic description of what this 'guying' entailed. At one GLF gathering a drag queen 'had this white dress on with two splits up the side and he had no knickers on and he was showing it all.... The women had trousers on' (Harry Beck, quoted in Power 1995: 242). Mary McIntosh, the lesbian sociologist, who was also involved in GLF, explained: 'I remember one Ball where some men were wearing what felt like very mocking radical drag and others were doing a striptease. None of it had been thought through' (Mary McIntosh, quoted in Power 1995: 243). The GLF women were under pressure to accept pre-operative male-to-female transsexuals as women and allow them into the women's groups. This made the women's group 'like a mixed group', because 'there might be ten transsexuals and about twelve women', and 'Some of the women felt that these people had very male attitudes and were very patronizing to women and trying to steal women's oppression while not giving up their prick power' (Power 1995: 244).

But the gay men who were into drag considered that masculinity was the sex role in need of challenge, and that by their imitations of traditional women's clothing they were helping to destroy masculinity. They were doing what might now be called 'gender as performance' (Butler 1990) in a very direct and politically motivated way. What was absent from gay liberation was any 'performance' of masculinity by men or women as a good thing. Masculinity was generally understood to be problematic. This was to change in the late 1970s and early 1980s when gay masculinity in the form of sadomasochism and other manifestations, such as the group Village People, became fashionable once again.

The US lesbian Del Martin, when bidding farewell to gay liberation in favour of women's liberation, described herself as 'pregnant with rage' as she bitterly decried a 'brotherhood' whose preoccupation with bars, camp, pornography, drag and role playing had resulted in homosexuals becoming the 'laughing stock' of the public' (quoted in Heller 1997: 7). Two male stalwarts of UK GLF wrote a pamphlet in support of the women's walk-out and addressing a male gay liberation. They accused gay liberation of having degenerated into simply a gay activism in which 'gay males seek their full share of male privilege' by striving for social equality with heterosexual males whilst male supremacy remains in place. They seem to have a very good understanding of the women's concerns.

> In their eyes a gay male is simply a man who likes sex with men, and where they're at in their heads is very visible from a look at their literature, full of bulging cocks, motorbikes and muscles, exactly the symbols of male supremacy and the oppression of women, supporting the gender-role system that is the basis of their own oppression. (David Fernbach and Aubrey Walters, quoted in Power 1995: 24)

Considering the cult of masculinity that was to burgeon within male gay culture through leather clubs and sadomasochism over the next thirty years, their argument seems prescient.

Lesbian feminism

The Women's Liberation Movement which got underway in the UK and the USA in the late Sixties was full of lesbians (see Abbott and

Love 1972). But these lesbians were not immediately able to place their concerns on the movement agenda. Betty Friedan famously referred to lesbian politics in the National Organization of Women in the USA as the 'lavender herring' (Abbott and Love 1972). Lesbian feminism emerged as a result of two developments: lesbians within the WLM began to create a new, distinctively feminist lesbian politics, and lesbians in the GLF left to join up with their sisters. Since the 1950s in the UK and the USA there had been lesbian organizations which were determinedly separate from organizations of men, which identified their own goals separately from the domination of male interests and criticized the sexism of male gay groups (see D'Emilio 1998). Some of these earlier organizers, such as Phyllis Martin and Del Lyon of Daughters of Bilitis in the USA, became influential activists and theorists within the new movement.

Lesbian feminism starts from the understanding that the interests of lesbians and gay men are in many respects very different, because lesbians are members of the political class of women. Lesbian liberation thus requires the destruction of men's power over women. It is not possible here to describe the politics and practice of lesbian feminism in any detail. I cannot do justice to all the groups, activities and ideas. It is important, however, to describe those principles which inspired lesbian feminism from the beginning, and which distinguish it from subsequent forms of politics that lesbians have adopted, particularly in queer politics. The principles of lesbian feminism, which distinguish it quite clearly from the queer politics of today, are woman-loving; separatist organization, community and ideas; the idea that lesbianism is about choice and resistance; the idea that the personal is political; a rejection of hierarchy in the form of role-playing and sadomasochism; a critique of the sexuality of male supremacy which eroticizes inequality.

Woman-loving

The basis of lesbian feminism, as of the radical feminism of this period, was woman-loving. Lesbian feminists understood woman-loving to be fundamental to feminism. As Charlotte Bunch expressed it in 1972: 'We say that a lesbian is a woman whose sense of self and energies, including sexual energies, center around women – she is woman-identified. The woman-identified woman commits herself to other women for political, emotional, physical, and economic support. Women are important to her. She is important to herself' (Bunch 2000: 332). As feminist philosophers have pointed out, male supremacist philosophy and culture are hostile to women's love and friendship towards other women. Janice Raymond explains, 'In a woman-hating society, female friendship has been tabooed to the extent that there are women who hate their original Selves' (Raymond 1986: 6). The creation of woman-loving was a task necessary for the very survival of feminism. If women did not love themselves and each other, then they had no basis on which to identify and reject atrocities against women. For a feminist movement solidarity of the oppressed was a necessary basis for organizing. But woman-loving was always seen as constituting more than a woman's version of comradeship.

Raymond invented the term 'Gyn/affection' to describe the woman-loving that is the foundation of feminism. Gyn/affection 'connotes the passion that women feel for women, that is, the experience of profound attraction for the original vital Self and the movement toward other vital women' (p. 7). Feminist politics needed to be 'based on friendship . . . Thus, the basic meaning of Gyn/affection is that women affect, move, stir, and arouse each other to full power' (p. 9). For many feminists the obvious conclusion of woman-loving was lesbianism (Radicalesbians 1999). Raymond explains that though her concept of Gyn/affection is not limited to lesbianism, she does not understand why any woman-loving women would stop short of lesbianism.

> If Gyn/affection embraces the totality of a woman's existence with and for her Self and other women, if Gyn/affection means putting one's vital Self and other women first, and if Gyn/affection is movement toward other women, then many women would expect that women who are Gyn/affectionate and Gyn/affective would be Lesbians. . . . I do not understand why Gyn/affection does not translate into Lesbian love for many women. (Raymond 1986: 14).

The bonding of women that is woman-loving, or Gyn/affection, is very different from male bonding. Male bonding has been the glue of male dominance. It has been based upon recognition of the difference men see between themselves and women, and is a form of the behaviour, masculinity, that creates and maintains male power.

Mary Daly characterized bonding between woman-loving women as 'biophilic (lifeloving) bonding', to distinguish it from other forms of bonding in the male dominant 'sadosociety'. She emphasized the difference: 'bonding, as it applies to Hags/Harpies/Furies/Crones is as thoroughly Other from "male bonding" as Hags are the Other in relation to patriarchy. Male comradeship/bonding depends upon energy drained from women' (Daly 1979: 319). Marilyn Frye, the US lesbian philosopher, in her essay on the differences between gay male and lesbian politics sees male homosexuality as the apogee of the masculine bonding that forms the cement of male supremacy. The bonding of lesbian feminists, however, is heretical: 'If man-loving is the rule of phallocratic culture, as I think it is, and if, therefore, male homoeroticism is compulsory, then gay men should be numbered among the faithful, or the loyal and law-abiding citizens, and lesbian feminists are sinners and criminals, or, if perceived politically, insurgents and traitors.' (Frye 1983: 135–6).

Woman-loving does not survive well in male-dominated queer politics. In a mixed movement the resources, influence and just sheer numbers of men give them the power to create cultural norms. As a result, some lesbians became so disenchanted with their lesbianism, and even their femaleness, that there are presently hundreds, if not thousands, of lesbians in the UK and the USA who have 'transitioned' – i.e. adopted the identity not just of males but of gay males with the help of testosterone and mutilating operations (Devor 1999).

Lesbianism as choice and resistance

The lesbian of lesbian feminism is a different creature from the female homosexual or female invert of sexology or earlier assimilationist movements. She is very different, too, from the gay man of gay liberation. Whilst gay liberation recognized that sexual orientation was socially constructed, there was no suggestion that gayness might be subject to voluntary choice, and might be chosen as a form of resistance to the oppressive political system. The lesbian feminist sees her lesbianism as something that can be chosen, and as political resistance in action (Clarke 1999). Whereas gay liberation men may say 'I am proud', lesbian feminists have gone so far as to say 'I choose'. Raymond expresses it thus: 'women are not born Lesbians. Women become Lesbians out of choice' (Raymond 1986: 14). This does not mean that all those who chose to identify as lesbian feminists consciously chose their lesbianism. Many had been lesbians before lesbian feminism was first thought of. But they still adopted an understanding of their lesbianism as what Cheryl Clarke, in *This Bridge Called my Back*, the historic anthology by US 'women of colour', has called 'An Act of Resistance'. Clarke explains, 'No matter how a woman lives out her lesbianism...she has rebelled against becoming the slave master's concubine, viz. the male-dependent female, the female heterosexual. This rebellion is dangerous business in patriarchy' (Clarke 1999: 565).

Genital connection was not always seen as the foundation of a lesbian identity. Lillian Faderman, the US lesbian historian, explains that lesbian feminists of the 1970s resembled the 'romantic friends' of the nineteenth century whom she writes about, who emphasized love and companionship, and would not necessarily include genital connection in their relationships (Faderman 1984). Lesbian feminist identity regularly included such ingredients as putting women foremost in one's life and affections, and not being sexually involved with men. Though genital connection might not, for some, have formed the basis of their identity, an enthusiasm for passionate sexual relationships certainly marked the lesbian feminism of the period. Sex was not absent, but it did not have the significance that it has for 'queer' lesbians who excoriate lesbian feminists for being 'anti-sex'. Mary Daly, the US lesbian feminist philosopher whose writings provided an inspiration for the movement of the 1970s and 1980s and continue to do so, expresses the role of sex in relationships thus: 'For female-identified erotic love is not dichotomized from radical female friendship, but rather is one important expression/manifestation of friendship' (Daly 1979: 373).

Separatism

Lesbian feminism is distinguished from other varieties of lesbian politics by its emphasis on the need for some degree of separation from the politics, institutions and culture of men. Such separation is necessary because lesbian feminism, like its foremother, radical feminism, is based on the understanding that women live, as Mary Daly describes it, in the 'state of atrocity' (Daly 1979). The state of atrocity is the condition in which women have, for centuries, in different parts of the world, survived terrible violence and torture. These eras include witch-burning, for instance, the epidemic of domestic violence that is now destroying women's lives in both the rich and the poor worlds, and the sex industry and its current variant of a massive, vicious international industry of sex trafficking. As Daly puts it:

> Patriarchy is itself the prevailing religion of the entire planet, and its essential message is necrophilia. All of the so-called religions legitimating patriarchy are mere sects subsumed under its vast umbrella/ canopy. All – from buddhism and hinduism to islam, judaism, christianity, to secular derivatives such as freudianism, jungianism, marxism, and maoism – are infrastructures of the edifice of patriarchy. (Daly 1979: 39).

This condition in which women live is created out of, and defended by, a system of ideas represented by the world's religions, by psychoanalysis, by pornography, by sexology, by science and medicine and the social sciences. All these systems of thought are founded upon what Monique Wittig calls 'the straight mind' – i.e. framed by heterosexuality and its dynamics of dominance and submission (Wittig 1992). This 'straight mind' in the eyes of radical lesbian feminists is all-pervasive in the systems of thought of male supremacy.

The lesbian feminist critique of this whole system of male supremacist thought is far reaching in its vision and originality, its courage and creativity. When I speak of radical feminism and lesbian feminism in the same breath, that is because most often the leading thinkers of radical feminism have also been lesbians (Millett 1977; Daly 1979; Dworkin 1981), and lesbian feminism grew from a radical feminist foundation. The visionary thinking required to create the new world-view of lesbian feminism could not easily be developed from within a mixed gay liberation movement. In the mixed movement it was the traditional masculine ideas of Freudianism, for instance, that dominated discussion. The critical analysis and swingeing rejection of Freudianism as an anti-woman philosophy *par excellence*, formed a crucial building block in the creation of feminist theory. Freudianism was taken apart as early as 1946, by Viola Klein in *The Feminine Character*, and then, when feminism resurfaced in the late Sixties, was once again subjected to swingeing critiques in Kate

Millett's *Sexual Politics* and Eva Figes's *Patriarchal Attitudes* (Klein 1971; Millett 1977; Figes 1970).

The ideas of Foucault, also based upon the traditions of male supremacy, and thus on the erasure or degradation of women, became central to the gay men's movement in the late 1970s. Raymond shows how Foucault revered the Marquis de Sade, saying, 'A dead God and sodomy are the thresholds of the new metaphysical ellipse...Sade and Bataille' (quoted in Raymond 1986: 45). Sade's claim to fame, it has been pointed out by many feminist commentators (Dworkin 1981), was the brutalization of women in newly extreme ways.

The setting up of space to create the new world-view was one crucial reason for lesbian separatism. Lesbian separatism is the separation of lesbians from mixed gay organizing, and in some cases, in the USA in particular, from the women's liberation movement. Lesbians separated to form their own groups, bookstores, cafes and publishing companies. Most often the separate spaces that lesbians set up were for women in general, rather than specifically for lesbian women. It was the energy of lesbians that underpinned most separate women's spaces, including refuges from domestic violence.

There are two rather different ways in which lesbians separate. Some separate to create a lesbian culture, space and community in which they can live as separately as possible from the malestream world. That is the goal. This form of separatism can hold dangers for the feminism that such lesbians espouse. It can become a dissociation from the world, such that the context in which certain practices and ideas originated in male supremacy is forgotten, and anything done or thought by a lesbian can be supported. Janice Raymond explains:

> Even radical and voluntary dissociation from the world, originally undertaken as a necessary and daring feminist political stance, can produce a worm's-eye view of the world that exposes women to attack. A major consequence of dissociation is that women can become ignorant of conditions in the "real" world, conditions that may militate against their very survival. (Raymond 1986: 153)

Thus sadomasochism created by lesbians, or butch/femme role-playing, can seem to be practices invented by lesbians instead of having emerged from male dominance. Raymond explains that 'Although lesbian sadomasochism may arise in a context where women are dissociated politically from the wider world, at the same time it assimilates women very forcefully into a leftist and gay male world of sexuality' (p. 167).

Raymond recommends a different kind of separatism, in which the 'inside outsider' manages to live in the world men have made, whilst working to change it from a separate base in women's friendship and culture. 'The dissociation that I criticize is not that of women coming together separately to then affect the "real" world. Rather it is a dissociation that proclaims a withdrawal from that world' (p. 154). In this form of separatism, which revolutionary feminists in the UK in the 1970s called 'tactical separatism' rather than separatism as an end in itself, lesbian feminists are able to develop ideas and practices against a background of the reality of the lives of most women. They are aware of the state of emergency and work to end it; thus sadomasochism, for instance, must be evaluated as to its origins in male supremacist culture, what it means for the lives of women, and whether it is well suited to the collective survival of women. The basis of lesbian feminism has always been a separate lesbian feminist culture and institutions.

The personal is political

Lesbian feminists took from radical feminism the understanding that 'the personal is political' (Hanisch 1970). This phrase sums up the important revelation of the feminism of the late 1960s and the 1970s that equality in the public sphere with men was an insufficient, if not a nonsensical, aim. Some feminists simply said that women who wanted to be equal with men lacked ambition. Others analysed the limitations of the strategy in more detail, pointing out that it was the dynamics of personal heterosexual life which imprisoned women and limited their engagement in public life, and that the very notion of public life itself, including its forms and content, derived precisely from men's possession of a servicing 'angel in the house'. Bat-Ami Bar On explains that this principle of radical feminism emerged from the deprivatizing and politicizing of personal life that was begun by the New Left in the 1960s (Bar On 1994). Hierarchy had to be eliminated from personal life if the face of public

life was to change, and if the barriers between public and private
were to be broken down.

Thus lesbian feminists, like many gay liberationists before them,
rejected role-playing and any manifestation of inequality in lesbian
relationships. They saw lesbians who engaged in role-playing as imitating the noxious patterns of heterosexuality and standing as obstacles in the path of lesbian liberation (Abbott and Love 1972). The
lesbian feminist vision of the future did not consist of a public world
of official equal opportunity based upon a private world in which
inequality could be eroticized and milked for excitement. The public
and private were to be all of a piece, and to be shaped to represent
a new ethic.

Lesbian feminist theorists extended the understanding that the
personal is political into a critique, not just of some oppressive
aspects of heterosexuality, but of heterosexuality itself. They argued
that heterosexuality is a political institution rather than the result of
biology or individual preference. Adrienne Rich, for instance, says
that heterosexuality needs to be analysed as a political system which
is as influential as capitalism and the caste system (Rich 1993). In the
caste system of heterosexuality women are constrained to the role of
servicing men sexually and in other forms of labour. The labour is
extracted through women's subordinate position in the 'family' and
justified by romantic love or cultural expectations. The system is
enforced by what Rich calls the 'erasure of lesbian existence', male
violence, family pressures, economic constraints, the desire to 'fit in'
and to avoid ostracism and discrimination. Lesbian feminist analysis
of heterosexuality requires new language. Janice Raymond has sup-
plied some words for analysing the way in which heterosexuality as
a political institution works, such as 'heteroreality' and 'heterorela-
tions' (Raymond 1986). I have suggested that the term 'heterosexual'
be used to denote sexual practice which originates in male power and
female subordination and eroticizes power differentials, and that the
word 'homosexual' is more suited to desire which eroticizes sameness of power or equality (Jeffreys 1990b). Such language gives a new
value to the term 'homosexual' as opposed to the favoured sexuality
of male dominance which is 'heterosexual'. In the 1990s UK lesbian
feminists edited volumes which took the discussion forward by en-
couraging both lesbian and heterosexual feminists to analyse heterosexuality and their rejection or embrace of the institution and
practice (Wilkinson and Kitzinger 1993; Richardson 1996). Gay

male theorists have not engaged much with this issue. A deracinated version of the lesbian feminist critique has been carried into queer politics. But the queer version analyses heterosexuality as a problem for those who see themselves as 'queer' rather than an institution which oppresses women.

It was the lesbian feminist and radical feminist critique of sexuality and relationships, the idea that the personal is political and needs to change, that came to be challenged in the 1980s in what have since been called the 'feminist sexuality debates', or 'sex wars'. A new breed of lesbian pornographers and sadomasochists derided lesbian feminist understandings of 'the personal is political' and the importance of equality in sex and love as anti-sex (see my book *The Lesbian Heresy*, Jeffreys 1993).

Eroticizing equality

The creation of a sexuality of equality in opposition to the sexuality of male supremacy, which eroticizes men's dominance and women's subordination, is a vital principle of lesbian feminism. Radical feminists and radical lesbian feminists in the 1970s and 1980s argued that sexuality is both constructed through, and plays a fundamental role in maintaining, the oppression of women (Millett 1977; MacKinnon 1989). Sexuality is socially constructed for men out of their position of dominance, and for women out of their position of subordination. Thus it is the eroticized inequality of women which forms the excitement of sex under male supremacy (Jeffreys 1990a). As a result, radical feminist critics argue, the sexuality of men commonly takes the form of aggression, objectification, the cutting off of sex from emotion, and the centring of sex entirely around penile entry into the body of a woman. For women sexuality takes the form of pleasure in their subordinate position and the eroticizing of men's dominance. This system does not work efficiently. Thus, throughout the twentieth century, a whole army of sexologists and sex advice writers sought to encourage, train and blackmail women into having orgasms, or at least sexual enthusiasm, in penis-in-vagina sexual intercourse with men, preferably in the missionary position so that the man could remain 'on top'. The sexological enforcers have identified women's failure to obtain such pleasure as political resistance, or even a 'threat to civilisation' (Jeffreys 1997b).

The construction of sexuality around the eroticized subordination of women and dominance of men is problematic for other reasons too. This sexuality underpins male sexual violence in all its forms, and creates men's sexual prerogative of using women, who dissociate to survive, in the prostitution and pornography industries. Thus radical feminists and lesbian feminists have understood that sexuality must change. A sexuality of inequality, which makes women's oppression exciting, stands as a direct obstacle to any movement of women towards equality. It is hard to work for equality when realization of that goal would destroy the 'pleasure' of sex. Thus it is important to make equality exciting. Only a sexuality of equality is a goal consonant with women's freedom. In the 'sex wars' of the 1980s this feminist understanding of sex, as being shaped by male dominance and in need of reconstruction, became the object of fierce assault.

The lesbian 'sex wars' developed simultaneously with the feminist 'sex wars', which started as a backlash against the successes of the feminist campaign against pornography of the late 1970s and early 1980s. Some feminists and lesbians (Duggan and Hunter 1995; Vance 1984), mainly those from socialist feminist rather than radical feminist roots or those involved in mixed gender politics, campaigned in opposition to the anti-pornography politics developed by radical and lesbian feminists. At that time it looked as if radical feminist critiques of pornography and sexual violence were gaining some recognition in malestream society. It seemed that feminist understandings of pornography as violence against women, for instance, might lead to the introduction of legislation in some states in the USA in the form of the anti-pornography ordinance drawn up by Andrea Dworkin and Catharine MacKinnon (see Jeffreys 1990a; MacKinnon and Dworkin 1997). The UK group Women Against Violence Against Women was having some success in the early 1980s in getting the then Greater London Council to remove sexually violent advertisements from underground trains. There was a moment around 1980–1982 when it really did seem that feminist anti-pornography campaigns had some chance of being successful. In reaction, some women in the USA (Feminist Anti-Censorship Task Force, or FACT) and in the UK (Feminists Against Censorship, or FAC) began campaigning and writing in defence of pornography, either on a free speech basis or because they positively approved of pornography and wanted it to be more available to women.

The furore of the arguments that took place around the very important question of whether it was necessary to challenge pornography have been called by those who took the position of defending the rights of pornography makers and consumers 'the sexuality debates' or 'sex wars'. The wars or debates constituted a politically crucial watershed in the history of this wave of feminism. The 'debates' halted real progress towards creating a sexuality of equality, and set in train a backward march in which the sexual and gender practices that feminist theorists and activists had challenged as hostile to women's interests came to be promoted as 'freedom', or even 'transgressive', and politically revolutionary in themselves. The power difference between men and women was eroticized in sadomasochism, for instance, rather than dismantled.

The 'lesbian sex wars' focused on the issue of 'lesbian' pornography and 'lesbian' sadomasochism (SM). Kimberley O'Sullivan, who was on the pro-porn and pro-SM side, says that the 'sex wars' were entirely restricted to the lesbian community in Australia, and did not percolate out into mainstream feminism (O'Sullivan 1997). Lesbian feminists argued that when lesbians engaged in the practices of porn and SM, they imported the dominance/ submission values of male supremacist sexuality into lesbian culture (Linden et al. 1982; Saxe 1994). These practices replicated the woman-hating of malestream culture even when the perpetrators and pornographers were lesbians. Lesbians, it was pointed out, are raised in male supremacist culture. Some are trained to be sexual in child sexual abuse and in prostitution/pornography. Whereas lesbian feminists choose explicitly to reject this training, some lesbians embrace and celebrate it. The sex wars were fuelled by what I have called a 'lesbian sexual revolution' (Jeffreys 1993). A sex industry was created by and for lesbians, selling lesbian pornography, sex toys and dildos, in the early 1980s. The sexual values of this industry came from prostitution and men's pornography, and so did many of its personnel. The lesbian who started the main porn magazine for lesbians in the USA, *On Our Backs*, for instance, was a stripper (O'Sullivan 1997). It was fuelled also by the fact that some lesbians who took pleasure in pornography and sadomasochism were determined to protect this pleasure from lesbian feminist criticism. Lesbians who criticized the sexuality of dominance and submission did not conceal the fact that their sexual responses, too, were affected by the culture of the sado-society, but they sought to change this (Jeffreys 1990b). Those who defended the

sexuality of inequality did not want to change. Protecting this sexuality required the reprivatization of sexuality. In order to make sexual
response and practice off limits for political analysis, they had to be
separated out from the political, and made private once again.

Gayle Rubin, the US lesbian sadomasochist, provided an important
theoretical foundation for the reprivatization of sex. She engaged in
a bold and remarkably successful ploy to insulate sexual practice from
feminist discussion. In a 1984 piece entitled 'Thinking sex' she argues
that sexuality and gender need to be separated theoretically (Rubin
1984). Thus 'gender' is that which may properly be analysed through
a feminist lens, whilst 'sexuality' is not suited to feminist analysis and
should be seen as a separate form of oppression, to be analysed by
sexual libertarians and sadomasochists like herself. Her ploy conveniently removes sadomasochism and other practices of hierarchical sex
such as child sexual abuse from feminist critique, and has made her
essay extremely celebrated within the new queer studies. It is constantly reproduced, even in feminist anthologies, despite the fact that
it can be seen as an attempt to limit feminist analysis and shut out
troublesome women from looking at mainly male gay practices.

Her tactical strike has been seen as problematic by the doyenne of
queer theory herself, Judith Butler, who points out that Rubin's
'liberation' of sexuality from feminism 'dovetails with mainstream
conservatism and with male dominance in its many and various
forms' (Butler 1994: 20). Lesbian feminists have noted the centrality
of her work to the reprivatizing of sex. The feminist philosopher Bat-
Ami Bar On describes Rubin as having engaged in a 'flight from
feminism', and says that she 'contributes to the construction of
a feminism for which the personal is not political' (Bar On 1994:
60). Rubin's work provided the theoretical foundation for the considerable opposition that developed to lesbian feminist understandings of the need to analyse politically and transform sexuality that
developed in the 1980s, the 'lesbian sex wars'. The sex industry
provided the commercial motive.

All the principles of lesbian feminism came under attack in the
1980s and 1990s. Separate lesbian organizing, culture and existence
were attacked as some lesbians in the 1990s developed a newly close
relationship with gay men in queer politics. Woman-loving was
regarded with suspicion as masculinity became the highest value in
a mixed queer culture. Sexuality was the crucial point of difference in
the lesbian sex wars. It is also, I will argue in this volume, the most

important point of difference between lesbian feminism and queer politics. Though much could be written about the queer agenda in other respects, it is the queer agenda for sexuality that will be examined here in detail. Those lesbians who sought to depoliticize sexuality, to oppose feminist criticism of eroticized dominance and submission in sadomasochism, in the dynamics of pornography and prostitution, identified with the new queer politics. For them, attacking lesbian feminism as boring and unsexy was something of a rite of passage into the new politics (Walters 1996).

Queer Theory and Politics and the Lesbian Feminist Critique

Queer politics emerged in a very different political climate. In the late 1980s and early 1990s neoliberalism was at its unchallenged height. The 1990s was the time of TINA, 'There Is No Alternative', the famous phrase of Margaret Thatcher. This was a time when deregulated rogue capitalism was allowed to appropriate the resources of the world and destroy the conditions of workers from the USA to Australia. It was a time when the feminist and anti-racist policies that had been adopted by education authorities and universities in the UK and the USA were being denounced as 'political correctness'. The term 'politically correct' was a term of abuse used automatically and unthinkingly by many, whenever challenges were raised to practices which entrenched the rights and interests of rich white men. This was not an auspicious time for the creation of a radical politics, and indeed queer politics incorporated the contemporary biliousness towards 'political correctness', and demonstrated the ways in which gay politics had capitulated to the economic imperatives of the time.

Where practices that gay liberationists had analysed as resulting from oppression were commodified by business interests, as in bathhouses and transsexual surgery, they were celebrated in the new queer politics instead of criticized. A powerful new gay economic sector was now making serious profits from a gay sex industry of pornography and prostitution. Its interests were defended and given theoretical legitimacy within queer politics. Queer politics was not anti-capitalist so long as the capitalism was gay, or the profits were coming from practices seen as 'transgressive'. This was a very different time. This chapter will examine the origins, ideas and practices of queer politics and the ways in which they are distinguished from those of gay liberation and lesbian feminism. It will analyse the components of the queer coalition and assess their revolutionary potential for lesbian politics.

American lesbian political scientist Shane Phelan lists four sources for the development of queer politics. The first of these was the fact that 'the feminist sex wars exhausted many lesbians and led them to seek new locations' (Phelan 1994: 151). The second is the demand of bisexuals for inclusion in gay and lesbian communities. The third is the impact of AIDS in creating a basis for alliances between lesbians and gay men based upon the sympathy of lesbians for the plight of their gay brothers. Lastly, she says, post-structuralist ideas created the foundation for the development of queer theory in the academy.

There is a surprising level of agreement amongst both proponents and detractors that queer politics emerged in some fashion from the so-called feminist 'sex wars'. The lesbians who fled a radical lesbian feminist analysis of sexuality entered into a queer politics which was founded upon a traditional masculine notion of sexual freedom. This traditional view is represented historically by those gentlemen, such as the Marquis de Sade, whose power and privilege included the right to access women and children at will, both inside and outside marriage (Kappeler 1990). Men's 'sexual freedom' was sanctified in the two supposed sexual revolutions of the twentieth century, which institutionalized women's sexual servicing of men within both marriage and prostitution. Men's sexual rights, renamed as the release of repression and claimed to be biologically necessary by the science of sexology, were enshrined in a new regime of sexual liberalism (Jeffreys 1997b). Gay men's version of men's 'sexual freedom' is celebrated by queer theorists such as Michael Warner as the end goal of queer politics (Warner 1999).

The bias of queer politics towards the celebration of a specifically male gay sexual freedom agenda is clear in the selection by the important progenitor of queer theory, Douglas Crimp, of Guy Hocquenghem's *Homosexual Desire* (1978) as what 'may well be the first example of what we now call queer theory', though written two decades before queer theory was thought of (quoted in

Jagose 1998: 5). Hocquenghem's book, originally published in 1972, contains nothing about lesbians or women. It is, in fact, a very good example of a fundamental problem with generic words such as 'gay', 'homosexual' and 'queer'. They mean men unless women are explicitly included. The book is a paean of praise to public sex between gay men in cruising grounds, referred to as 'the plugging in of organs', something which women would find hard to do.

The lesbians who fought radical lesbian feminists in the sex wars adopted the gay male sexual freedom agenda. Some even tried to do public sex, but this did not catch on (see Smyth 1992). Instead of placing women first, and seeking values from the separate culture that women and lesbians had created, the 'sex radicals', as Phelan calls them, 'found themselves more often in alliance with nonlesbian "sexual minorities" than with lesbian feminists', so that '"Queer" has eventually become the umbrella that...covers all of Rubin's dancing partners' (Phelan 1994: 152). Rubin's dancing partners include sadomasochists and paedophiles. She renames paedophilia 'cross-generational sex' to show her positive approach to that male practice. It is appropriate that Phelan identifies the 'sex wars' as the first source of queer politics, since the repudiation of radical lesbian feminism does seem to have been fundamental. Queer criticisms of lesbian feminism are based upon the attacks launched during the lesbian 'sex wars' – i.e. lesbians are anti-sex. The US theorist of sadomasochism Pat (now Patrick) Califia describes those in the lesbian and gay movement who were critical of the practice as 'arch-conformists with their cardboard cunts and angora wienies' (Califia 1994: 157). Suzanna Danuta Walters, in her incisive critique of queer politics in *Signs*, offers a pretty accurate description of the way in which queer politics has represented lesbian feminists – i.e. as boring, old-fashioned, ugly prudes.

> [O]nce upon a time there was this group of really boring ugly women who never had sex, walked a lot in the woods, read bad poetry about goddesses, wore flannel shirts, and hated men (even their gay brothers). They called themselves lesbians. Then, thankfully, along came these guys named Foucault, Derrida, and Lacan dressed in girls' clothes riding some very large white horses. They told these silly women that they were politically correct, rigid, frigid, sex-hating prudes who just did not GET IT – it was all a game anyway, all about words and images, all about mimicry and imitation, all a cacophany of signs leading back

> to nowhere. To have a politics around gender was silly, they were told, because gender was just a performance. (Walters 1996: 844)

In this queer politics vision it was the post-structuralist boys who came to the rescue and showed how meaningless and unnecessary this lesbian feminism was. Queer politics, then, was created in contradistinction to lesbian feminism. The dreadfulness of lesbian feminism was its founding myth.

The second source cited by Phelan is the demand by bisexuals for inclusion in lesbian and gay politics. Certainly the inclusivity of queer politics is a main reason touted by its proponents for the usefulness of the category 'queer', whilst it is also a main reason for criticism by its detractors. The word 'queer' was adopted, its proponents explain, because it was inclusive and easy to say. Gabriel Rotello says that it overcomes the need to keep repeating lists by covering the variety of those in the 'community' under one umbrella word: 'When you're trying to describe the community, and you have to list gays, lesbians, bisexuals, drag queens, transsexuals (post-op and pre-), it gets unwieldy. Queer says it all' (Rotello, quoted in Duggan 1995: 166). Escoffier and Berube say that a new generation has adopted the word 'queer' because the other words 'lesbian, gay and bisexual' are 'awkward, narrow and perhaps compromised words', and because the word expresses the 'confrontational' nature of the new politics (quoted in Duggan 1995: 171). 'Queer' covers, they say, those 'who have been made to feel perverse, queer, odd, outcast, different, and deviant', and who want to 'affirm sameness by defining a common identity on the fringes'.

Those who were most outraged by the new term were lesbian feminists, who observed that though the term was supposed to be inclusive, it appeared to specifically exclude lesbians and lesbian feminists. The experience of lesbians has been that generic words for male and female homosexuality quickly come to mean only men. Whole books have been written by gay male writers about 'homosexual history' or 'homosexual desire' in which lesbians are not mentioned (Rowse 1977; Hocquenghem 1978). The words 'homosexual' and 'gay' did not start out meaning only men, but came to do so as a result of a simple material political reality, the greater social and economic power of men, the power which has allowed men to define what culture is and to make women invisible. For lesbians, having a name specific to women who love women has been crucial to asserting the existence and difference of lesbians, and to the assertion of a lesbian pride based not on being an inferior variety of gay men, but wild and rebellious women who refuse subordinate status. In fact, lesbian feminists struggled hard for twenty years to get the word they had chosen to express their specific and different history, culture, practice and politics onto the political map. By the late 1980s the word 'lesbian' was starting to appear in the titles of conferences on 'Lesbian and Gay History' or 'Lesbian and Gay Literature' and in book titles. The word 'lesbian' was even, quite reasonably considering the historical erasure of lesbian existence, put first. The adoption of the word 'queer' changed all that. The struggle to get the word 'lesbian' included was scarcely won when the tables were turned and lesbians were buried again under 'queer'. Lesbians were told by queer activists that they were 'included' in queer along with many others such as transsexuals and sadomasochists whose interests were, arguably, in complete contradiction to the interests of women's liberation.

Some descriptions of the queer coalition include only lesbians, gays, bisexuals and transgenders. Even this pared-down version of the inclusiveness of queer poses a problem. Both bisexuality and transsexualism are forms of behaviour which have been criticized by lesbian feminists as being contrary to lesbian interests rather than consonant with them. Though bisexuals occupy an equal space in the most common understandings of the queer LGBT coalition with lesbians, gays and transgenders, it is by no means obvious that the interests and goals of bisexual women and men are consonant with those of lesbians and gays. Certainly within bisexual anthologies there is considerable hostility expressed towards the lesbian feminist project. Any lesbians or gay men who question the consonance of political interests between themselves and bisexuals are likely to be accused of being 'monosexists' – i.e. interested only in the opposite sex and not both – or 'gender fascists' – ditto (see Jeffreys 1999). A whole new language has been developed within bisexual politics to attack those who voice any critique of the inclusion of the 'B' in LGBT.

Lesbian feminist analysis does not understand transsexualism as being a progressive phenomenon. Janice Raymond (1994) has argued convincingly that transsexual surgery is about social control. The medical industry that has grown up to profit from transsexualism pushes those who do not feel comfortable with politically constructed categories of gender and sexuality to mutilate their bodies to fit in. I have argued that transsexual surgery needs to be understood as a harmful cultural practice and a violation of human rights (Jeffreys 1997b). The more inclusive the queer coalition becomes, the more difficult it is for lesbian feminists to accept it as being in any way progressive. One formulation from an early 'Queer Power' leaflet distributed in London is as follows: 'Queer means to fuck with gender. There are straight queers, bi-queers, tranny queers, lez queers, fag queers, SM queers, fisting queers in every single street in this apathetic country of ours' (quoted in Smyth 1992: 17). Since lesbian feminists have defined their politics precisely in opposition to the heterosexual imperative, 'straight queers' are not seen to have similar concerns at all. Similarly, 'SM queers' are a problematic inclusion, since sadomasochism is a practice that eroticizes the dominance and submission that are seen to result from male-dominant heterosexuality. The constituencies to be included in 'queer' came to represent precisely those forms of behaviour that, according to lesbian feminist analysis, resulted from male supremacy and the subordination of women, and helped to keep that subordination going. A coalition politics based upon the acceptance of anyone with an unusual sexuality or practice of self-mutilation could not be more different from that of lesbian feminism, a politics based upon woman-loving which seeks to topple the structures of male power, including a sexuality of violence and aggression.

Implicit in the word 'queer' is the politics of outsiderhood, and this is another way in which queer politics is antithetical to lesbian feminism. There are gay male theorists too who argue that the practice of taking a term of contempt which specifically connotes marginality and exclusion, and seeking to make it a politically positive term, is misguided. Stephen O. Murray, for instance, says in his critique of queer theory: 'First, I balk at the term "queer," which I do not think can be defanged' (Murray 1997). Whereas queer politics celebrates the minority status of homosexuality, lesbian feminism does not see lesbians as representing a transhistorical minority of one in ten or one in twenty at all. The experience of the 1970s, in which hundreds of thousands of women in the Western world chose to re-create themselves as lesbians, is living proof of the falsity of such an understanding. Lesbian feminists have maintained that 'any woman can be a lesbian', since the lesbian represents political rebellion against male supremacy, and is the very model for free womanhood.

Phelan's third source of queer politics is US AIDS activism. Gay male activists became increasingly angry at the way their interests were ignored by the US government, particularly in the area of releasing drugs aimed at ameliorating AIDS conditions. This, according to Simon Watney, founder of the queer politics group Outrage in the UK, was the impetus for queer activism (Watney 1992). This was a newly angry, creative activism aimed at being 'in your face' and making a fuss. The originality of the activist practices of queer politics has been questioned by feminist critics. They have pointed out that similarly outrageous practices have long been central to feminism and lesbian feminism, from the Miss World protests to the invasion of the House of Lords undertaken by lesbians involved in challenging Clause 28 of the Local Government Act in 1987, which outlawed the 'promotion of homosexuality'. This newly invigorated activism gained a theoretical foundation, as Phelan notes, from the post-structuralist theory taking the universities by storm in this period.

Queer theory

The varieties of post-structuralist thought which inspired queer theory were the ideas of Michel Foucault and a re-energized Freudianism. The work of Foucault was a popular source of queer theory because he was gay, a sadomasochist, wrote about sexuality and homosexuality, and, conveniently, managed to exclude women from his concerns. Surprisingly, Freudianism became popular despite the fact that previous generations of gay and lesbian activists had rejected Freud, and psychoanalysis in general, for being hostile to the interests of homosexuals.

From post-structuralism queer theory takes the celebration of lack of theoretical certainty about identity, or anything else, and the celebration of 'difference' for its own sake. Joshua Gamson expresses this as follows: 'The ultimate challenge of queerness, however, is not just the questioning of the content of collective identities, but the *questioning of the unity, stability, viability and political utility of sexual identities – even as they are used and assumed*' (Gamson 1996: 404). The postmodernist determination to refuse the certainty of identity was employed by some queer theorists to sound the death-knell of lesbianism itself. Thus Colleen Lamos, in the collection *The Lesbian Postmodern*, writes: 'the postmodern lesbian is not another lesbian but the end of lesbianism as we know it – as a distinct, minority sexual orientation' (Lamos 1994: 99). Her definition of the queer lesbian is surprisingly definite, however, and reveals strikingly different preoccupations from those of lesbian feminism. Lamos describes queer lesbian culture as being derived from the sex industry and gay men: 'The commercialization and aestheticisation of lesbian sexuality, manifest in the proliferation of sex toys, pornography, butch/femme sexual styles, s/m sexual practices, and phone sex – many of which have been adopted from gay men – attest to a queer lesbian culture that blurs distinctions between masculine and feminine and between gay and straight sexuality' (p. 94). Thus it seems to be only lesbian feminist identity which must be deconstructed.

Lesbian feminist identity is a social construction, I suggest, as is lesbian identity; but this does not mean that it needs to be abandoned. The lesbian is a product of a particular historical moment. In the creation of heterosexuality as a political institution, lesbianism was squeezed out. Lesbians are both the independent women who refuse heterosexuality and the frightening other who can be used to drive women into the heterosexual fold. Lesbianism needs to exist now to provide a refuge for those women who rebel, and as the basis of a movement for social change. The deconstruction of identity in queer theory has been criticized for making political action difficult, since people determinedly unsure of who and what they are do not make a powerful revolutionary force. But in the future, when women's oppression no longer exists, and heterosexuality as a political institution no longer plays a crucial political role, the possibilities open to women are likely to be different.

Queer theory has created its own canon of theorists, and they include some very significant women. Judith Butler has been credited with much of queer theory's determined celebration of challenging the essentialism seen to underpin the hatred of homosexuals, through 'performing' gender (Butler 1990). Annamarie Jagose explains that 'queer describes those gestures or analytical models which dramatise incoherencies in the allegedly stable relations between chromosomal sex, gender and sexual desire' (Jagose 1998: 3). By '[d]emonstrating the impossibility of any "natural" sexuality', queer theory 'calls into question even such apparently unproblematic terms as "man" and "woman"' (ibid.). What is puzzling about the great respect in which Butler is held is that what she has to say is so unoriginal. Resistance to essentialist understandings of gender has been fundamental to feminism since the late 1960s. But this resistance has usually been expressed in more straightforward language and in a more liberatory form, as in the need to eliminate gender rather than play with it. Butler's determination to hang on to gender, rather than simply abandon it, can be explained in terms of her own practice. She explains in an interview in a transgender anthology, *Reclaiming Genders*, that she 'situated' herself 'in relationship to butchness' in her early twenties, and has had 'an active and complicated relationship with both butch–femme discourse and S/M discourse probably for almost 20 years' (More 1999: 286). She 'negotiates' her identity in terms of these 'discourses'. Adherence to the feminist project of getting rid of gender would affect her chosen life-style.

Lesbian feminists tend, not unreasonably, to be unsympathetic to the inclusion within the ranks of the most significant 'queer' theorists of a heterosexual woman who writes only about gay men, Eve Kosofsky Sedgwick. Sedgwick is recognized as one of the most important progenitors and practitioners of queer theory (Jagose 1998: 5). Sedgwick's heterosexuality, of which she has made no secret, is attested to in her recent autobiographical fragment, which takes the form of a description of the therapy she entered after treatment for breast cancer, *A Dialogue on Love* (1999).

She says, 'queer stuff is so central in my life' (Sedgwick 1999: 9), but what could that mean for a heterosexual woman? Sedgwick makes her old-fashioned heterosexual practice very plain. She married at nineteen, and remains with that husband, engaging in missionary position sex. Her sexual life is 'vanilla sex, on a weekly basis, in the missionary position, in daylight, immediately after a shower, with one person of the so-called opposite sex, to whom I've been legally married for almost a quarter of a century' (p. 44). Her fantasy life is sadomasochistic, she says, about 'Violence and pain. Humiliation. Torture. Rape,' and about spanking in particular. She explains that she was afraid of her father, who was violent towards his children and spanked her. But she says that she does not act out any of her fantasy scenarios.

Her husband, Hal, works in another city, and is only home at weekends. She lives with a gay man whom she is 'in love with' and with whom she has a 'very passionate' bond, 'very physical, though we don't have sex; and I guess the emotional weather of my day will most often be determined by Michael's emotional weather' (p. 24). Her love for Michael means 'I'm very addicted to Michael's emotional sunshine. I often think I'd do anything to obtain or keep it'

(p. 25). Her emotional subordination to this gay man resembles the requirements of traditional heterosexuality for wives towards their husbands.

Her work, such as *Between Men* (1985) is all about male–male relationships and anal sex. Though she may not be involved in sex with gay men, it is gay men that she loves and devotes her life's work to. As she explains it:

> What I'm proudest of, I guess, is having a life where work and love are impossible to tell apart. Most of my academic work is about gay men, so it might seem strange to you that I would say that – not being a man, not even, I don't think, being gay. But it's still true. The work is about sex and love and desire . . . . Well, I should say that one true thing about me is that my love is *with* gay men. (p. 23)

She is not modest about her achievements in relation to queer culture and community. She describes herself as being 'an essential, central member of a queer family', and is kind enough to explain queer people to themselves and others by 'doing a lot of the work of articulating, making new, making compelling to others, queer ideology' (p. 55).

The book contains only one comment on Sedgwick's relationship to women. One of the sections which are in capital letters and seem to represent the views of the therapist describes Sedgwick's difficulties in relating to women.

> E SAYS THAT IN RELATIONSHIPS WITH WOMEN SHE FEELS SHE DISSOLVES, STOPS BEING HERSELF (IS SHE STILL EVEN A WOMAN?), IS AFRAID OF NOT BEING, OF NOT HAVING A SELF, OF BEING INADEQUATE, NEGLIGIBLE. WITH "PEOPLE WHO ARE NOT WOMEN" SHE FEELS SPECIAL, VERY POWERFUL AND PLENTIFUL. WITH WOMEN SHE FEELS NO SPECIAL POWER. (p. 125)

For lesbian feminists, a theory created by a heterosexual woman who considers herself to be in love with gay men is not appealing. Suzanna Danuta Walters comments that Sedgwick has described her identity as that of a 'gay man', and 'this does not even have the naive honesty of the fag-hag who simply grooves on the panache of gay men. Sedgwick, the postmodern intellectual subject, must not only identify or sympathize or politically ally, she must be' (Walters 1996: 847).

The main problem with queer theory, its masculine bias, is unlikely to be challenged by a woman who has devoted herself theoretically to celebrating gay men to the point that she considers herself to have become one. Sedgwick's rejection of her own womanhood and difficulty in identifying with women are the very opposite of the woman-loving that forms the basis of lesbian feminist philosophy and practice.

Gender and queer theory and practice

The Foucauldian notion of 'transgression' is central to queer theory. Within queer theory the idea of revolutionary activism that might challenge the material power differences between the sexes, of which gender is simply the expression, has been replaced by the idea, derived from Judith Butler's work, that 'transgression' on the level of dress and performance is revolutionary and will bring down the 'gender' system. Jeffrey Weeks, for instance, is enthusiastic about the importance of transgression: 'The moment of transgression, in which the whole social order is symbolically challenged, is actually necessary, it seems, to achieve citizenship. This is the attraction of queer theory and queer politics: they provide a theoretical justification for transgression, and practices of sexual dissidence and subversion which challenge the symbolic order' (Weeks 2000: 70). Transgression is a comfortable kind of night-clubbing activism. It consists of carrying out sexual practices seen to be outlawed under conventional mores, such as sadomasochism and public sex, or wearing the clothing conventionally attributed to one sex class whilst being a member of the other. Transgression does not require changing laws, going on demonstrations, or writing letters. It can be achieved by doing something that some gay men and lesbians may always have enjoyed, whilst relabelling it politically transformative in and of itself. Thus night-clubbing, if in rubber or gender-inappropriate clothing, can come to be seen as political action.

The sociologist Stephen O. Murray, in his incisive critique of queer theory, is particularly critical of queer notions that playing with gender is revolutionary, and the idea that 'whatever subalterns do must be "resistance" – in particular that "playing with" or "playing at" gender erodes gendered social organization of domination. Variant performances and discursive practices do not change societies'

(Murray 1997). He suggests that there should be less celebration of 'transgression' and more consideration of how the behaviours being celebrated may emerge from the internalized self-hatred of 'subalterns'.

Transgression has a long history amongst upper-class males. In eighteenth-century England gentlemen frolicked in the performance of their versions of sadomasochism in the Hellfire Club. Some morals may have been outraged, but the social structure of hetero-patriarchal England did not quiver. Transgression is a pleasure of the powerful, who can imagine themselves deliciously naughty. It depends upon the maintenance of conventional morality. There would be nothing to outrage, and the delicious naughtiness would vanish, if serious social change took place. The transgressors and the moralists depend mutually upon each other, locked in a binary rela-tionship which defeats rather than enables change. Also, transgres-sion depends upon the existence of subordinate others upon whom the sexual transgression can be acted out, mostly prostituted women and boys (Kappeler 1990). It is not a strategy available to the house-wife, the prostituted woman, or the abused child. They are the objects of transgression, rather than its subjects.

The idea that conventional gender differences can be transgressed by performance leads Judith Butler and other queer theorists to celebrate and include within the ranks of queer activists gay men who wear drag, transvestites, transsexuals, butch/femme role-players and all those who don the characteristics or clothing usually assigned to the sex class other than that in which they were brought up. These ideas have led to the notion that there should be a recognition of the existence of many 'genders'. The many genders might include, in this understanding, a butch lesbian or a femme lesbian, a drag queen or a masculine gay SM top, as well as a feminine heterosexual woman or a masculine heterosexual man, plus other combinations. This approach to gender detaches it from its material base in the oppres-sion of women. The problem becomes simply one of the scarcity of gender opportunities.

Radical/lesbian feminist approaches to gender could not be more different. Rather than seeing the political task as the creation of more and equal opportunities to act out masculinity and femininity in various varieties, radical/lesbian feminists seek to abolish what has been called 'gender', altogether. I am no fan of the word 'gender', and would prefer to abolish it in favour of expressions which refer directly to the political foundation of male domination. Thus I prefer to describe masculinity as 'male-dominant behaviour' and femininity as 'female-subordinate behaviour'. No multiplicity of genders can emerge from this perspective. Christine Delphy, the French radical feminist theorist, expresses this point of view most clearly (Delphy 1993). She explains that it is quite wrong to see the problem with gender as being that of rigid ascription of certain qualities and behaviours which could be solved by androgyny, in which the behaviours of masculinity and femininity can be mixed together. The two genders of the present, she says, are in fact the behaviours of male dominance and women's submission. With the end of male dominance, these behaviours would have no substance. They would become unimaginable, and human beings would need to imagine new ways of relating which did not include the behaviours that arose from a superseded political system.

The understanding of gender as dominant and subordinate forms of behaviour puts paid to the idea that there can be many 'genders'. There can only be ways of expressing dominance and submission by other than the usual actors. The genders remain two. The queer approach which celebrates the 'performance' of gender and its diversity necessarily maintains the two genders in circulation. Rather than eliminating dominant and submissive behaviours, it reproduces them. Thus those queer theorists and activists who seek to perform gender can be seen to be gender loyalists with a stake in the maintenance of the gender system of male supremacy. All those embraced within queer politics whose inclusion rests on the performance of male dominance and female submission by unusual actors, drag, butch/femme role-playing, transvestism or transsexualism are engaging in behaviours that are strictly time-limited. Their behaviours of choice, to which they give huge attention, financial investment and parts of their bodies, are not imaginable in a world beyond male dominance. Rather than being somehow revolutionary, they are historical anachronisms. These people are also engaging in behaviour which is in opposition to the feminist project of the elimination of gender, thereby helping to maintain the currency of gender. Thus they are incompatible bedfellows for lesbian feminists altogether.

It is interesting to consider why transsexuals/transgenders are included so determinedly within 'queer' politics as if they somehow fit naturally with lesbians and gays. The inclusion seems to hark back to an early understanding of homosexuality as constituting 'gender inversion'. Nineteenth- and twentieth-century scientists of sex, such as Henry Havelock Ellis, thought that homosexual men had the brains of women in the bodies of men and that homosexual women had the brains of men, in the bodies of women (Ellis 1913; Jeffreys 1997b). However they explained this, and chromosomes were not yet understood, it is clear that they saw same-sex love as impossible unless one partner was somehow, despite appearances, essentially of the opposite sex. This idea of homosexuality as gender inversion was overthrown by gay liberationists and lesbian feminists alike, who maintained that same-sex partners could love each other in ways that had nothing to do with the political constructions of masculinity and femininity.

Lesbian feminist analysis of transsexualism has been trenchant. Janice Raymond's *Transsexual Empire* (1994) remains the clearest and most cogent explanation of transsexual diagnosis and surgery as a form of social control. She explains that psychologists and surgeons eliminate any critique of the gender system by slotting those who do not adequately fulfil the requirements of one sex class into the other through surgery and medication. Rather than being in any sense 'transgressive', Raymond shows that transsexual surgery is a most conservative practice aimed at maintaining male dominance and women's subordination by shoring up the idea that there are two natural genders into which everyone must fit. At the time at which it was written (the late 1970s), lesbian feminists expected the perform- ance of transsexual surgery to end as the gender system was over- thrown by feminist activism. Once notions of natural masculinity and femininity were surpassed, then transsexualism would have no mean- ing. But transsexual surgery did not die out.

The birth of queer theory reinscribed the notion of gender inver- sion in understandings of homosexuality, through the association of lesbian and gay politics with transsexualism in the queer coalition of LGBT. This is particularly surprising, since transsexualism has historically been a mechanism for eliminating homosexuality. Gay men and lesbians who have been unable to cope with the idea of being homosexual have been cut and medicated into the 'opposite' sex so that they can be seen to be engaged in a grim and mutilated heterosexuality instead of homosexuality (see Thompson 1995; Rees 1996). Whereas sexologists up to the mid-twentieth century were only able to place homosexuals in a 'transsexual' category, the devel- opment of surgical and chemical methods in later decades enabled homosexuals to be physically transformed. Though not all of those being surgically reassigned present as clearly homosexual before the surgery, most, and the overwhelming majority of the women involved, do (Lothstein 1983; Devor 1999). Why would those escaping homosexuality through surgery be seen as inevitably aligned with precisely the category they go to such lengths to avoid, lesbians and gay men?

But even the savage mutilations of transsexual surgery are justified by queer theory. A good example of the queer/postmodern justification of transsexualism is an article in the academic queer journal *GLQ* by Susan Stryker. He identifies transsexualism with queer politics thus: 'I want to suggest in this essay that *transgender* can in fact be read as a heterodox interpretation of *queer*' (Stryker 1998: 149). He waxes lyrical about a 'generation of scholarship' he sees emerging, which can account for 'the wild profusion of gendered subject positions, spawned by the ruptures of "woman" and "man" like an archipelago of identities rising from the sea: FTM, MTF, eonist, invert, androgyne, butch, femme, nellie, queen, third sex, hermaphrodite, tomboy, sissy, drag king, female impersonator, she-male, he-she, boy-dyke, girlfag, transsexual, transvestite, transgender, cross-dresser' (p. 148).

He uses post-structuralist theory to justify the radical and transgressive nature of transsexualism. Thus he sees 'transgender phenomena' as emerging from, and bearing witness to, 'the epistemological rift between gender signifiers and their signifieds'. They 'disrupt and denaturalize' what he calls 'Western modernity's "normal" reality', particularly the idea that gender needs to be unified with a particular body type. 'Transgender phenomena' have achieved 'critical importance (and critical chic) to the extent that they provide a site for grappling with the problematic relation between the principles of performativity and a materiality that, while inescapable, defies stable representation, particularly as experienced by embodied subjects' (p. 147). When interpreted, this collection of postmodern/queer buzz words means that transsexuals are radical because they put surgically constructed genitalia on to bodies that would not normally have them, and cause some people to be confused about what is male and what is female. It is important to emerge from this obfuscation and grand language to consider the implications of inscribing into the heart of queer politics a practice aimed at the elimination of homosexuality.

Gay liberation and feminism changed the conceptual map of the vast majority of those who identify as lesbian or gay, to the extent that they are most unlikely to consider their homosexuality to be related to any problem with gender. We do not see ourselves as failed real men or real women. But transsexualism plays an increasingly important role in the elimination of homosexuality. This is particularly clear in the psychological label 'gender identity disorder'. After lesbian and gay activists achieved the removal of homosexuality as a form of mental disorder from the US Diagnostic and Statistical Manual in 1973, it was replaced, in 1980, by the addition of something called 'gender identity disorder' (GID). GID is applied to children who display what conservative America considers inappropriate behaviour, boys playing with dolls or girls learning to mend cars. The DSM 4 specifies that a child's subjective 'discomfort', qualifying him or her for a GID diagnosis, may be inferred from 'aversion toward rough-and-tumble play and rejection of male stereotypical toys, games, and activities' in boys, and by 'marked aversion toward normative feminine clothing' in girls (Minter 1999: 10). Children are taken to gender identity clinics, which are a nice little earner for the social control profession of therapy, where they suffer aversion treatment or other methods to change their behaviour to something more appropriate to their sex class. The vast majority of them still grow up to be homosexual, and many others to be bisexual whether treated for GID or not (ibid.). It is clear from the writings of the psychologists who administer the GID category that it is homosexuality they are concerned about and seek to prevent. As Lawrence Mass puts it, 'American psychiatry is . . . engaged in a long, subtle process of reconceptualizing homosexuality as a mental illness with another name – the ''gender identity disorder of childhood'' ' (quoted in Minter 1999: 12).

In the last decade the number of men, women, girls and boys identifying as transgender and seeking, or being assigned, surgery and hormone treatment seems to have increased. One reason may be the greater currency of the idea of transsexualism with which young lesbians and gay men who are unable to accept homosexuality, or have reasons to hate and reject their bodies, can identify. The media carry stories of transsexualism much more frequently. The Australian sociologist Frank Lewins interviewed 50 MTF transsexuals and found that 50 per cent 'realised' they were transsexual only when they saw an article in the media on this topic

(Lewins 1995). Internet resources now offer the idea of transsexualism. Sophia Pazos, in an article on social services with transgendered youth, says 'The Internet has opened the closet door for transgendered persons' (Pazos 1999: 71).

A crucial component of the present promotion and expansion of transsexualism is the idea that there is such a thing as a 'real' transgender person – i.e. not homosexual or just a butch lesbian or a femme gay man. The practitioners who recommend women and men for surgery, and the surgeons themselves, like to think that they are dealing with a defined category which can be clearly recognized. But this is not the case. They are in fact creating, through their diagnostic tools, the very category which they can then claim to have found. Transsexualism is essentialized in the very 'helping' professions who help in its construction. The collection *Social Services with Transgendered Youth* should sound alarm bells for those lesbian and gay activists who would like to help young lesbians and gay men to retain their own bodies and be proud to love the same sex. The collection seeks to help social workers to recognize an already existing category of 'transgenders'. The editor of the collection, Gerald P. Mallon, states that 'transgendered children are part of every culture, race, religion, and experience' (Mallon 1999: 62). This does not explain, of course, why the phenomenon is increasing in relation to the amount of publicity it is given.

The social workers are recommended to engage in 'acceptance and positive affirmation' of transgendered children (Burgess 1999: 45). They should not show any disapproval or seek to redirect them towards homosexuality, for instance. Mallon tells us that whilst 'it is important that transgendered children are not mislabeled as gay or lesbian, although they frequently self-label as such prior to coming to a full understanding of their transgendered nature, it is also important that gay and lesbian children are not mislabeled as transgendered' (Mallon 1999: 60). In fact, no such easy distinction can be made. This is particularly true in respect of young people from ethnic minority cultures in which homosexuality is totally despised and transgenderism is seen as more acceptable. In the case of fifteen-year-old 'Faheed', the family was East Asian and Muslim, and 'The patient was well aware that homosexuality was absolutely forbidden by his religion, and his parents had told him the penalty for being caught could be death' (Swann and Herbert 1999: 26). Many accounts by transgender persons of their motivations make it quite plain that they are desperate to avoid seeing themselves as homosexual, desperate enough to subject themselves to extremely mutilating surgery.

Unless we accept that there is such a thing as a real and essential transsexualism, a notion which should be antithetical to queer theory's supposed anti-essentialism, then the inclusion of this category within queer politics does seem extraordinary. It defies the proud pro-lesbian and gay politics that are required in a liberation movement by celebrating the castration of those who love the same sex. The inclusion of transsexuals also supports the notion that gender is essential, and the most retrograde notions of gender at that.

The postmodern and queer approaches to gender have led to the development of a form of 'gender' politics which is in clear opposition to, and serves to replace and render invisible, feminism. A US organization called GenderPAC, formed in 1999, represents these new anti-feminist gender politics very well. GenderPAC, though run by and for transsexuals and transgenders, has devised a broad mission statement. When reading this, it is useful to look for where women might be expected to fit in. Since 'gender' is a term so widely adopted by feminist theorists and activists, it might be assumed that its use here had some relevance to the interests of women, but this does not seem to be the case.

> GenderPAC is the national advocacy organization working to ensure every American's right to their gender free from stereotypes, discrimination and violence, regardless of how they look, act or dress or how others perceive their sex or sexual orientation. We are especially concerned with the way discrimination based on gender intersects with other kinds of discrimination, including those of race, class, ethnicity and age. GenderPAC believes that gender ought to be protected as a basic civil right, and we look forward to the day when it is universally respected and recognized as such. (GenderPAC 2001)

Women are not mentioned in GenderPAC material. Gender does not mean women here, but transgenders, most of whom are men, and homosexuality. Women are not even mentioned in the list of categories which GenderPAC would like to see as connected with 'gender'. These are race, class, ethnicity and age, not women. Women, especially if they are trying to dismantle the house of gender, could be seen as quite a problem for this politics. The political aim of GenderPAC is to enshrine 'gender' (the politically constructed behaviours of dominance and submission which result from male domination) within US law as something which deserves protection. This is an aim in complete contradiction to the aims of feminism. Even a liberal feminism which sees the problem of gender as consisting only in its rigidity, rather than its very existence, might have a difficulty with what is being protected here. Any criticism or confrontation with someone's or an organization's notion of what constitutes gender could be seen as discriminatory if GenderPAC were to be successful in its aims. I have been called transphobic and genderphobic for pointing out, in conferences, that gender needs to be abolished, not swapped. According to most feminist analyses of any political stripe, gender difference is seen as the very foundation of male dominance. Seeking to eliminate it could become much more difficult if the project of protecting gender achieves any success.

Lesbian critique of queer theory

In the last few years, queer theory and its implications for political action have been subjected to critiques from some gay sociologists who have not been prepared to abandon their materialist analyses for the delights of post-structuralism, as well as from lesbian feminists. These critics have argued that queer theory is the child of a certain anti-liberation historical moment, and is therefore individual-ist and anti-materialist as well as sexist. In his book *Queer Theory and Social Action*, Max Kirsch argues that queer theory makes action for social change impossible. Queer theory, he says, 'emerged within an institutional context where radical social critiques have become passé' (Kirsch 2000: 30). He sees queer theory, with its 'highlighting of the impossibility of identity and the relativity of experience', as emerging from and supporting a particular stage of capitalism which requires the construction of self-contained individuals, in order to reach 'the economic goal of creating profit through production and its by-product, consuming' (p. 17). He says that queer theory 'decon-structs collective community, encourages political apathy as it rela-tivizes all sexuality and gender' (p. 8). Queer theory, he explains, emerged from a particularly conservative period in the academy. Whilst race, sex, gender and class have become 'buzzwords in the university setting', they are played with in theory rather than being used to 'take on the foundations of the larger socio-political structure' (p. 31).

The sociologist Stephen O. Murray, in a piece entitled 'Five reasons I don't take "queer theory" seriously', attacks queer theory for ineffectual intellectual pretension: ' "Queer theory" romanticizes ineffectual playing at "transgressiveness" as a substitute for the hard work of changing the real world' (Murray 1997). He calls the 'fascination with idiosyncratic readings of texts' forms of 'juvenile acting out' and 'infantile post-leftist adventurism'. He considers the return to Freudianism, under the new form of 'Lacanian rhetoric', a real puzzle which requires analysis from the point of view of the sociology of knowledge and concludes: 'If and when queer theorists produce a theory that seems to explain or predict something other than textual representations, I will be attentive. Until such a time, aware as I am of the quietist anti-empiricist zeitgeist, I am content to be considered a pre-postmodern, skeptical, empiricist and comparative social scientist'.

The sociologist Steven Epstein accuses queer theory of hubris in falsely claiming to have invented social constructionism, and in determinedly failing to recognize its origins in sociological theory of earlier decades. Some recent students of sexuality working outside sociology, he explains, assume the concept of social construction 'to have sprung, like Athena, fully formed from the head of Michel Foucault' (Epstein 1996: 146). 'By tracing their lineages back no further than Sedgwick and Foucault', he explains, practitioners of queer theory risk 'reinventing the wheel' (p. 157). He also criticizes queer theorists for producing a rarefied, abstract theory from their focus on 'discourses and texts', in which 'crucial questions about social structure, political organization, and historical context' are left out (p. 157). Clearly, some male gay sociologists, who have roots in socialism and are seriously interested in social change, have been as impervious to the allure of queer theory as have radical and lesbian feminists.

Radical feminist theorists have also refused to succumb to the institutional obsession with post-structuralism, which dominates much academic feminist theory. Post-structuralist feminist theorists such as Chris Weedon (1987) and Linda Nicholson (1990) represent the postmodern ideas which they derive from the work of male French intellectuals as somehow a branch of feminism. It is a feminism, too, that in effect trumps all the feminist theory that has gone before, by showing how essentialist and retrogressive that old-style feminism has been. Somer Brodribb, and contributors to the radical feminist anthology *Radically Speaking*, have taken post-structuralist theory to task in detail for its misogyny, obscurity and uselessness for analysing male violence (Brodribb 1992; Bell and Klein 1996). Radical feminist scholars find Chris Weedon's assertions that radical feminists have not liked or done theory and her list of the great theorists from whom feminists can develop theory – all male, mostly French and mainly gay – very puzzling. Such confident discounting of any independent thought by women raises the interesting issue of what should count as theory at all. Clearly, in Weedon's view, Mary Daly, Andrea Dworkin and Catharine MacKinnon, who have all contributed most significantly to lesbian feminist theory, are not theorists. This may be because they are not men, or do not refer respectfully to the masculine canon, but only criticize, or because their ideas are unassimilable to the masculine schema which she recognizes as legitimate. As the radical feminist *Redstockings Manifesto* pointed out in 1969, the task of radical feminist theory is to overthrow the rules and regulations, the prejudices of the masters, and to create theory from women's experience. 'We regard our personal experience, and our feelings about that experience, as the basis for an analysis of our common situation. We cannot rely on existing ideologies as they are all products of male supremacist culture' (Redstockings 2000: 224). It is not easy for radical and lesbian feminist theorists to accept that the ideas of men who have not only been raised under male dominance but show that they hold all patriarchal prejudices intact are really useful for those seeking to overturn male power.

By the late 1990s, a good number of lesbian feminists were joining in a concerted critique of queer theory and politics, particularly in one notable collection *Cross Purposes* (Heller 1997). It may have taken that long for the noxious effects of such an exclusively masculine political agenda to become clear. Lesbian feminist critics have called into question the very obscurity of queer theory, pointing out that a revolutionary political theory needs to be intelligible to the activists it serves. Lesbian feminism sought to be entirely comprehensible, because it came from, and was aimed at inspiring, a political movement. In the *Cross Purposes* anthology Lillian Faderman, an important theorist of lesbian history, explains the obscurity of queer theory in terms of it being aimed at a quite different audience, those with power in the academy. She accuses it of being composed of hermetic, sleep-inducing jargon and sentence structure: 'The language queer scholars deploy sometimes seems transparently aimed at what lesbian-feminists once called the "big boys" at the academy. Lesbian-feminist writing, in contrast, had as primary values clarity and accessibility, since its purpose was to speak directly to the community and in so doing to effect change'. (Faderman 1997: 225). Queer theory, she says, 'appears resolutely elitist' (p. 226).

Many of the writers in the *Cross Purposes* anthology lament the losses suffered by lesbian feminism in the 1990s, which they attribute to the readiness of some lesbians to become integrated into a masculine queer politics. More and more resources crucial to a viable lesbian community were closed down – bookstores, cafés, galleries and presses. Sue-Ellen Case bemoans the effect on the lesbian community of the defection of lesbians to queer politics: 'Right after those queer dykes slammed the door on the way out of lesbian feminism, the dowdy old women-centred places began to close down: most feminist and lesbian theaters, bookstores, and bars have disappeared' (Case 1997: 210). The 'queer dykes', she says, were responsible, through their 'privileging of gay male culture' and their 'disdain and mis-remembering of lesbian feminism', for the dwindling away of lesbian cultural resources – socially, economically and theoretically (p. 211).

Faderman mourns the loss of such resources too, calling this the loss of lesbian space. The creation of women's and lesbian space, both geographically and in terms of ideas, was of fundamental importance to the development of feminism from the 1960s onwards. Faderman confesses to finding it 'mystifying ... that female queers have not seen an analogous need to claim their own space but rather have let themselves be disappeared in what is essentially male queer space' (Faderman 1997: 226). Queer females, she explains, 'now seem to have given up entirely a conceptual space for themselves as lesbians in adopting the term and the concept "queer"'.

Faderman considers queer politics to be just as problematic for women as any other male dominated politics, to the extent that 'female queers cannot make a happy home with the male of the queer species', and she states categorically that 'males, queer and straight, ultimately overshadow and overpower females, queer and straight. All space becomes male space unless females maintain a concerted effort to mark a space for themselves' (p. 227). Faderman describes the position of the lesbians in queer politics as resembling that of the lesbians who served in mixed organizations before lesbian feminism was invented: 'queer females are an auxiliary to the *real* queers, just as homophile women were an auxiliary to the *real* homosexuals in the homophile movement of the 1950s, before lesbians consciously created their own political spaces' (p. 227).

Faderman expresses bitter disappointment and puzzlement at the repudiation of feminism by women within queer politics. She explains that many of those who, like herself, were lesbians before 1960s feminism was born felt 'exuberance and relief because it articulated our deepest feelings' (p. 221). Feminism also 'provided a space for lesbians to dream of an Amazon nation and a place to invent a women's culture' (p. 222). Feminism offered such valuable gifts, she says, that lesbians like her were 'shocked and even furious when we saw emerging a new generation that seemed to take for granted what feminism made possible and, with no little hostility to feminism, sought after what seemed like strange gods – queer alliances' (p. 222).

The incompatibility between queer politics and lesbian feminism is particularly clear, according to Sue-Ellen Case, in the move towards a gay consumer market rather than a community. The values of lesbian feminism are totally unsuited to this new queer market, because lesbian feminist enterprises were ideologically committed to preventing hierarchy. Thus they operated collectively, and were not about individuals getting rich. The bookstores and other gay businesses that continue in the wake of lesbian feminist collectivism function very differently. She comments that 'What was once a lesbian or gay community is now becoming a market sector' (Case 1997: 212). The once activist Queer Nation, she explains, has formed the 'Queer Shopping Network of New York', and in 'some circles... "queer" has been commoditised so that it is constituted by such things as body piercings, leather and spike haircuts' (p. 213). Queer academics, she says, have complemented this development by creating a philosophy that celebrates shopping: 'Many "queer" academics write this affluent, commodity fetishism.... They invent queer discourse out of an addiction to the allure of the mass market.... Class privilege and the celebration of capitalism are compounded with the queer sex industry' (p. 213). Thus Queer Nation 'does seem to unfurl that same old banner of the individual that liberal democracy keeps hanging out to dry' (p. 217).

Bonnie Zimmerman, an important creator and defender of lesbian studies and lesbian literature, considers that it is feminism which 'gives the richest and most complex set of meanings to lesbian experience' (Zimmerman 1997: 166), whereas queer theory 'can actually be argued to obliterate lesbianism as a specific identity, subject position, or signifier'. She points out that although queer theory is 'currently fashionable', it is unlikely to 'permit a distinct lesbian experience, identity, or critical practice' (p. 166).

It is ironic that Teresa de Lauretis, whom many commentators credit with being the progenitor of the expression 'queer theory', should be one of those decrying the direction that queer theory and politics have taken in the *Cross Purposes* anthology. She criticizes queer theory for disappearing lesbians within the generic term 'queer', and for requiring those lesbians who get taken up by queer theory to repudiate femininity and the female body to the extent of even becoming male.

> In sum, it seems that a new imaginary has developed out of the progressive repudiation of femininity and, now, also the repudiation of the female body: the discourse on sexuality has moved from the impossibility of a feminine identity theorized by feminists since the late 1970s, to the alleged "subversion" of gender identity in queer/ lesbian studies, to the literal becoming-male of lesbian PoMo. (De Lauretis 1997: 47).

Queer theory has been criticized for providing a theoretical justification for a series of specifically male practices that have been significant forms of male gay expression but were the object of critique in gay liberation and feminist theory. Butler's ideas about the transgressive potential of 'performing' gender, for instance, have been used to support the notion that drag, transvestism, transsexualism, camp, role-playing and sadomasochism are quintessentially queer political practices (Jeffreys 1994). Sue Wilkinson and Celia Kitzinger make this point forcefully: 'The queer critique not only ignores, but sometimes reverses, key feminist critiques, particularly radical feminist critiques: of sadomasochism; of gay male culture; of transsexuality/ transvestism; of bisexuality; and of heterosexuality' (Wilkinson and Kitzinger 1996: 380).

As the chorus of rebellion against the hegemony of queer ideas and practices grows, a new lesbian and gay politics must emerge to take its place. Such a new politics would have to return to the feminist project of eliminating gender, in complete contradiction to the politics of GenderPAC, in which the project of protecting 'gender' has emerged seamlessly from queer theory and politics. The gender protection racket is an important reason to reject queer politics, but there are many other reasons. Queer politics is founded upon the repudiation of the ideas and practices of lesbian feminism, particularly the idea that the personal is political and that sexual and emotional relationships should be conducted on the basis of equality. It is a politics which, by its very name, excludes lesbians from asserting their difference from gay men in political position and demands. It is, as male gay sociologists as well as lesbian feminists have pointed out, trivial in its obsessions and practices, and antithetical to any politics of real social change. In the rest of this volume I shall examine aspects of the queer agenda that pose particular dangers to women and lesbians, and show that lesbian feminism, rather than being a suitable object for derision, is in fact the crucial foundation for woman-friendly social transformation.

Public Sex and the Creation of a Queer Sex Agenda

'Public sex' is the performance by men of multi-partner sex acts in supposedly public space, traditionally toilets and parks. Lesbians are not, any more than any other women, demanding the right to act out sexually in public. This is a quintessentially male demand. Public sex has been the object of very considerable criticism by notable gay male journalists and some AIDS activists in the 1990s (Signorile 1998a; Rotello 1997). In response, many of the most famous names in queer theory came forward to defend the right to 'public sex' (Rofes 1998a; Warner 1999). The case for 'public sex' is forcefully put in the collection *Policing Public Sex*, by Dangerous Bedfellows (1996). The editors explain that they consider public sex to be the fundamental queer politics issue of the time: 'For queers especially, the late '90s are not so much about identity coming out as about sex going public' (Dangerous Bedfellows 1996: 15). Public sex is currently a very contentious issue within gay politics, but the campaign to promote it has very worrying implications for women and lesbians too. Women are prevented by the threat and reality of male violence from entering public space on equal terms with male citizens. The queer politics demand for social recognition of 'public sex' has the potential to further limit women's freedom to walk in parks, on beaches and on towpaths.

In pre-Stonewall days the activity of 'cruising' for sex in public places, called 'cottaging' in the UK and using 'beats' in Australia, was a traditional practice for men who wanted sex with men (Carbery 1992). It has been explained as an adaptation to the oppression of homosexuality – thus men who wanted sex with men had to seek it furtively and with strangers, for fear of publicity. This is not an adequate explanation. Since this form of sexual practice never played any part in lesbian history, despite lesbians also suffering oppression, a feminist explanation that takes into account the socially constructed differences between male and female sexuality is necessary. During the early years of gay liberation there was some critique of this practice (Walter 1980), but this fell into desuetude in the 1970s as entrepreneurs set up venues to exploit the excitements of 'public sex' without the risk of police harassment. Sex clubs, bathhouses, bookstores and bars with backrooms promoted the sex of 'cruising' as the liberated sex of the new era, and the burgeoning gay porn industry, whose stock-in-trade was 'public sex', served as propaganda to this end.

As this change took place, some influential gay theorists underwent a convenient revelation. They 'realized' that the 'public sex' that was explained by gay liberationists as the product of oppression was actually a revolutionary activity, the very model of liberated sexuality. *Homosexual Desire* (1978, first published 1972), for instance, by the French theorist of homosexuality, Guy Hocquenghem, is not just a paean of praise to public sex, but argues that this practice is gay men's revolutionary contribution to improving the world for everyone. It is important to point out that although the book might appear from its title to include female as well as male homosexual desire, it does not do so. For Hocquenghem, women are not significant enough to merit a mention. He argues that the important function of the gay movement is 'abolition of the difference between public and private' (p. 131). It is the revolutionary role of the male homosexual to overturn the shame that heterosexual society has attached to sex, through the performance of sex in public: 'The special characteristic of the homosexual intervention is to make what is private – sexuality's shameful little secret – intervene in public, in social organisation' (p. 122). He writes a celebratory description of male gay promiscuity in public. He rejects criticism of what he calls 'homosexual "scattering" – the fact that homosexuals have a multitude of love affairs, each of which may last only a moment'. Such behaviour did not, he argued, show 'the fundamental instability of the homosexual condition', but was something to be proud of.

> But instead of translating this scattering of love-energy as the inability to find a centre, we could see it as a system in action, the system in

which polyvocal desire is plugged in on a non-exclusive basis.... The homosexual condition is experienced as unhappy because its mechanical scattering is translated as absence and substitution. We could say that on the contrary homosexual love is immensely superior, precisely because everything is possible at any moment: organs look for each other and plug in, unaware of the law of exclusive disjunction. Homosexual encounters do not take place in the seclusion of a domestic setting but outside, in the open air, in forests and on beaches. (p. 117)

It is clear from this description that Hocquenghem was thinking only of men. Lesbians have no organs to plug in. The utopia that he envisages anthropomorphizes the penis, so that it becomes an organ with a mind of its own. The men he speaks of are slaves to their overactive plugs seeking sockets. Hocquenghem is proud of this form of sexual activity, because he sees it as 'natural', the way sex would be if people were not forced to be moral. 'If the homosexual pick-up machine... were to take off the Oedipal cloak of morality under which it is forced to hide, we would see that its mechanical scattering corresponds to the mode of existence of desire itself' (p. 117). Homosexual promiscuity turns out to be the very model of sexual freedom for humankind.

There were other gay theorists too who proposed gay male public sex as the archetypal practice of the supposed sexual revolution of the 1970s. John Rechy, for instance, called 'promiscuous homosexuals' the 'shock troops of the revolution'. As he explained: 'The streets are the battleground, the revolution is the sexhunt, a radical statement is made each time a man has sex with another on a street' (Rechy 1981: 299). Andrew Hodges and David Hutter from UK gay liberation express similar ideas in their 1974 article 'With downcast gays', which purports to be about the self-oppression that is embraced by gay men in response to gay-hating in the culture and in their families (Hodges and Hutter 1999). It turns out that the best way to fight self-oppression is to act out sexually in public. Self-oppression consisted very largely of gay men thinking that they should be like heterosexuals and seek not to be promiscuous. They argue that 'Puritanism lies at the heart of the distrust of promiscuity'. The result is that 'Gay sex, unencumbered as it is with conception and contraception, could be as free and available as sunshine and air' if it were not for pressures to mimic 'the outward forms of family life', in order to gain social respect (p. 554).

When the AIDS epidemic revealed its ferocity in the early 1980s, some concerned gay activists linked it to gay male promiscuity and commercial sex venues such as the bathhouses. Randy Shilts made this argument in *And the Band Played On*, and received merciless vilification for this insight (Shilts 1987; Crimp 1997). Larry Kramer, who had written a powerful critique of public sex in his novel *Faggots* (1978), before the epidemic hit, continued to criticize and to be attacked for doing so. But these voices were silenced. The dogma that won out in AIDS activism, as Gabriel Rotello (1997) points out, was that AIDS accidentally targeted gay men and had nothing to do with their sexual practices.

What gave rise to a challenge to this orthodoxy was a fresh wave of AIDS diagnoses in the 1990s, which showed that safe-sex promotions of condom use had been no solution. As infection rates rose, and as huge proportions of the urban gay populations in the USA continued to be infected, disturbing trends became clear, showing that some men cared not at all about whether they became infected or even sought out infection. Several influential gay activists and journalists took a stand. These men – Ian Young, Gabriel Rotello, Michelangelo Signorile, Walt Odets and Larry Kramer – spoke out because they recognized a state of emergency, and were desperate to keep gay men in the USA alive. In response to their work, and in response to the attack launched by Mayor Giuliani in New York on Times Square sex shops in the mid-1990s, including those with backrooms for gay men's 'public sex', a clamorous opposition developed. A group, Sex Panic, was set up by men such as Eric Rofes, Michael Warner, Douglas Crimp and other prominent queer theorists. The critics of gay sexual culture were labelled 'fascists', precisely as feminists who opposed pornography had been in the previous decade. Gay male sex debates were now well and truly launched.

In the period of the so-called feminist sexuality debates of the early 1980s there was no 'debate' amongst gay men. The gay male theorists who wrote about sexuality tended to take sides most determinedly with those female 'sex radicals' who attacked lesbian feminism. Jeffrey Weeks, for instance, lauds the US proponents and practitioners of sadomasochism Gayle Rubin and Pat Califia in his book *Sexuality and its Discontents*, whilst castigating the 'moral feminism' that opposes pornography, paedophilia, SM and public sex (Weeks 1985). Libertarian lesbians were a useful stick with which to beat lesbian feminists. Gay men could relax and exclude feminist critiques of their sexual practices, secure in the knowledge that sensible lesbians – i.e. sadomasochists – would imitate and promote the practices that the men loved and defend them from feminism. In the gay male sex debates, the same libertarian lesbians – such as Amber Hollibaugh, Gayle Rubin and Pat Califia – are returning the favour. They are supporting the queer promoters of public sex against their gay male critics.

The gay male critique of public sex

The gay male critics I shall consider here – Ian Young, Gabriel Rotello and Michelangelo Signorile, though to some small extent aware of feminist critiques of male sexuality and the fact that lesbians behave very differently – barely make reference to the insights of feminism in their attempt to understand gay male sexual culture. They do, however, provide compelling analyses of the ways in which the dominant gay sexual culture endangers the lives and happiness of gay men. Ian Young, in *The Stonewall Experiment* (1995), seeks to explain how the early promise of gay liberation declined into a sexual culture dangerous to gay men's interests and conducive to the AIDS epidemic. He sees gay liberation as having failed because the oppression of gay men over centuries has caused such damage that they were in no state to transform the world, and were overwhelmed by the seductions of an exploitative culture. Nineteen-seventies gay liberationists, he says, faced 'a struggle not only against obvious social antagonists but also against a powerful, invisible adversary: our own self-identification with the myth of the homosexual, the unconscious image we held of ourselves as leprous outcasts and willing sacrificial victims' (Young 1995: 35). He argues that most gays after Stonewall still 'bought into the myth of the homosexual as merely a walking sex crime, wounded and ultimately self-destroying' (p. 58). Gay men fled the discrimination and harassment they suffered from family, school and neighbourhood, and ended up in what Young calls the concentration camps or ghettos that are the gay areas of cities like San Francisco.

These 'refugees' did not have 'the social skills essential for emotional equilibrium', because 'The emotional, physical and sexual abuse many of them had been subjected to would have protracted and severe psychological effects' (p. 63). With no other resources or means of emotional support, they fell victim to the Mafia-controlled porn magazines, bars and sex clubs which promoted a damaging lifestyle organized around impersonal sex, drugs and alcohol. 'Mob-controlled "gay" magazines... served as advertising flyers for the ultimate consumer product – a permanent sex holiday' (p. 64). He describes the development of the commercial sex industry for gay men in the 1970s as the repackaging of 'centuries of sexual repression and distortion' as simply 'Pleasure or Freedom' (p. 77). Gay men, he says, had no rules or guide-lines 'for men to relate affectionately and erotically with one another' (p. 77). He explains the replacement of gay liberation meeting places by SM venues in the late 1970s as gay men eagerly internalizing the 'popular American myth of the doomed outlaw' (p. 96).

Young argues that the harmful sexual culture, derived from the unprocessed damage of gay oppression, caused severe health problems in gay men in the 1970s which compromised their immune systems and thus allowed the AIDS epidemic to develop. In support of this, he quotes Michael Callen, who was already HIV-positive when he wrote *How to Have Sex in an Epidemic*, in an attempt to keep other men safe. Callen describes his promiscuity and the effects this had on his health thus:

> I calculated that since becoming sexually active in 1973, I had racked up more than three thousand different sex partners in bathhouses, back rooms, meat racks, and tearooms. As a consequence, I had also had the following sexually-transmitted diseases, many more than once: hepatitis A, hepatitis B, hepatitis non-A/non-B, herpes simplex types 1 and 11, venereal warts, amoebiasis, including giardia lamblia and entamoeba histolytica, shigella flexneri and salmonella, syphilis, gonorrhea, nonspecific urethritis, chlamydia, cytomegalovirus (CMV), and Epstein–Barr virus (EBV), mononucleosis, and eventually cryptosporidiosis and, therefore, AIDS. (Young 1995: 178)

Young's explanation of the disaster is feminism-free. Thus he does not recognize that the masculinity of those who suffered has anything to do with events. It is the oppression of homosexuality, 'America' and the 'Mafia' who are to blame. His book is useful for an understanding of the ways in which post-Stonewall gay men failed to acknowledge the damage they had suffered from oppression and thus incorporated the harm into the heart of a supposedly new, liberated life-style. But the failure to acknowledge the role of manhood limits the usefulness of his analysis.

Gabriel Rotello's *Sexual Ecology* (1997) was also created out of a sense of emergency. Rotello writes to explain why AIDS infection rates were rising in the 1990s after falls in the late 1980s, and to suggest a solution. Rotello's thesis is that AIDS, like other epidemics, develops in core groups whose behaviour and circumstances are conducive to infection. Urban gay men are the core group for AIDS, and the behaviour is that of sexual promiscuity and sexual risk-taking. He explains that AIDS follows the pattern of other epidemics, in that, after a peak when all available for infection have been infected, there is a fall in the infection rate. Then the rate rises again when a new group available for infection presents itself and engages in the same behaviours – i.e. a new generation of young gay men still sexually promiscuous and engaging in multi-partner sex in commercial sex clubs. Rotello acknowledges that most AIDS commentators claim that the rising infection rate is the result of a failure of the 'condom code', but he does not agree. He argues that the harm minimization of the condom code was never likely to counter AIDS effectively as long as behaviour remained unchanged. The condom code, he says, justified and enabled the continuance of sexual promiscuity. It may even have increased the occurrence of the most infective behaviour, anal intercourse, because advertising suggesting that men should use condoms 'every time' they had sex implied that anal intercourse was all there was to 'sex'.

His book is devoted to countering the dominant understanding amongst AIDS educators and activists that the sexual promiscuity of gay men had nothing to do with AIDS. As long as promiscuity and 'sexual freedom' were defended as the be-all and end-all of gay life, he points out, AIDS activists argued that there were no 'risk groups, just risky behaviors' (Rotello 1997: 48). He quotes British gay socio-historian Jeffrey Weeks expounding this orthodoxy: 'It was an historic accident that HIV disease first manifested itself in the gay populations of the east and west coasts of the United States' (p. 89). This opinion, he explains, 'has been almost universal among gay and AIDS activists even to this day'. On the contrary, Rotello asserts, 'there is little "accidental" about the sexual ecology described above', and he sets out what he considers to be the cause: 'Multiple concurrent partners, versatile anal sex, core group behavior centered in commercial sex establishments, widespread recreational drug abuse, repeated waves of STDs and constant intake of antibiotics, sexual tourism and travel' (p. 89).

He argues that urban gay men placed themselves at risk of AIDs through the sexual behaviour developed in response to gay liberation in the 1970s. They adopted new practices that ensured the transmission of many infections, such as analingus or rimming, and anal intercourse, which he considers to have been historically much less significant than oral sex as a signature gay practice. They racked up huge numbers of partners through the newly available bathhouses and bars with backrooms which allowed commercial public sex. As a result of the repeated infections with STDs (sexually transmitted diseases) from such practices, there was a general decline in the immunity of these groups of men through antibiotic and other drug use to combat them. Recreational drug use further compromised immunity. Commercial sex venues offered historically unprecedented numbers of available partners for multi-partner sex. The first several hundred gay men with AIDS had an average of 1,100 lifetime partners (p. 62).

The result of these new circumstances was an 'unstable sexual ecology' such that by the end of the Seventies gay men accounted for 80 per cent of the 70,000 cases of syphilis treated by San Francisco's public health clinics each year. Massive rises occurred in gonorrhea rates too. By the early 1980s, syphilis and gonorrhea occurred several hundred times more often among gay men than among comparable straight men. By 1980, 20 per cent of all gay men in the USA were infected with *Entamoeba histolytica* from the new practice of oral-anal sex. In 1976, Rotello tells us, a new disease syndrome was identified, called 'gay bowel syndrome', which included, as well as the above, other parasites: giardiasis and shigellosis, condyloma acuminata; anal syphilis or gonorrhea; bleeding haemorrhoids; anal fissures, abscesses and ulcers; hepatitis; and pruritis ani. By 1981, San Francisco health officials estimated that 73 per cent of all gay men in the city were infected with hepatitis B, and most other known sexually transmittable diseases increased at extraordinary rates, including CMV and Epstein–Barr virus, which was found in up to 98–100 per cent of subjects in one study (p. 76).

Rotello explains that any criticism of this version of 'sexual freedom' is completely outlawed in AIDS politics. Any 'detailed examination of these mechanisms' in relation to AIDS prevention is impossible, and indeed, 'Their very discussion is considered offensive, homophobic, self-loathing' (p. 89). The AIDS prevention movement, he says, is made up of sexual libertarians whose 'primary allegiance' is 'the principle of almost absolute sexual liberty' (p. 152). The sexual freedom politics is backed up by the 'powerful forces fighting to turn the maximum profit from gay sex': the bar and bathhouse owners and porn producers (p. 152).

Rotello makes the important point that gay men's ideas about sexual freedom are not specifically gay, but are 'shared to some extent by all men in our culture'.

> One is a belief that sex ought to be without consequence and responsibility. Another is a sense of entitlement about sex. Still another is the notion that males, straight or gay, are at the mercy of biological forces beyond their control, forces that impel us to seek as many partners as possible and that overwhelm whatever feeble cultural roadblocks we place in their way. We are, in this conception, the victims of our hormones. (p. 203)

Rotello, however, does not offer an analysis of this damaging form of sexual behaviour in terms of masculinity, whereas Michelangelo Signorile does.

Signorile's *Life Outside* is a swingeing critique of a gay sexual culture which he describes as a 'cult of masculinity'. Many gay men in the USA, he says, are 'living a life of *enforced cult homosexuality*, with parties, drugs, and gyms ruling their lives' (Signorile 1998a: 27). One of the 'most detrimental effects' of this cult of masculinity is ' "Body oppression" – or "body fascism," ' which 'devalues so many men in the eyes of both themselves and their peers' (p. 27). This 'body fascism' 'deems an individual completely worthless *as a person*, based solely on his exterior' (p. 28). The successful exponent of this cult is 'the circuit clone with his huge muscles, close-cropped hair, and shaved and waxed body' (p. 37). The circuit is the round of massive dance parties, including Sydney's Mardi Gras that gay men travel to internationally. For Signorile, dominant gay culture was a problem not just because it led to AIDS, but because it achieved the opposite of happiness for any men too sensitive or not physically perfect enough to reap the benefits – i.e. most gay men.

He agrees with other critics such as Young, Levine and Rotello that it was commercial interests that transformed the previously furtive sexual behaviour of pre-Stonewall gay men into a nice little earner through the creation of public sex venues, 'They represented the introduction of capitalism and the American marketplace to the sexual activity gay men had known for decades. The cult of masculinity needed this commercialism to take root and grow' (p. 52). These commercial institutions promoted a 'rebel lifestyle' (p. 58). There was a momentary halt to the 'religion' of public sex when AIDS deaths started 'piling up', but gay leaders told gay men that 'they could continue in the behaviors and lifestyle they'd been used to in the past but to simply "use a condom every time"' (p. 62). Signorile says that 'sexual liberation' was confused with 'gay liberation', and may have 'allowed a kind of sexual fascism to come in, where if you don't want to do it in esoteric ways with lots of people you are less queer than the happily married queens down the block with the white picket fence' (p. 274). The sexual libertarians may be out of step with gay public opinion, he suggests, since an *Advocate* sex survey found that '71% preferred long-term monogamous relationships' (p. 214).

Signorile recognizes that the problem arises from masculinity, but does not analyse masculinity in any searching way. His suggested way forward is to deprogram gay men from the cult of masculinity. The role models he suggests that gay men emulate are 'the American women, heterosexual as well as lesbian, who began making dramatic and still-occurring changes in their lives' (p. 307). If women could do it, he argues, why could not gay men? He urges gay men to 'involve lesbians in our lives and learn a lot from how they construct their relationships and their families and how they deal with such issues as homophobia' (p. 320). But his mention of women and lesbians, though heartening, is perfunctory. The furore that erupted in response to his critique was extraordinary in its ferocity.

The defence of public sex

Queer theorists like Michael Warner and Douglas Crimp and AIDS prevention activists such as Eric Rofes led the attack. They created a group for this purpose called Sex Panic, and set out to bolster the gay sexual freedom agenda. Eric Rofes explains, using Allan Berube's definition, what a sex panic is: 'a moral crusade that leads to crackdowns on sexual outsiders' (Rofes 1997). The 'public sex' that Sex Panic was set up to defend is rather different from the traditional, pre-Stonewall version. It is less focused upon the great outdoors, and more firmly commercial. It seems that the commercialization of gay male sexuality has been taken up by these queer theorists as comprising the very essence of what was once 'public sex'. Instead of taking place in public toilets for free, it now takes place in commercial venues that make a profit for the sex industry; but it is still, apparently, revolutionary. John Rechy's sexual outlaws were unlikely to be noticed by the majority of the citizenry as they fought for the sexual revolution under bridges or on beaches at night (Rechy 1981). The hordes of bodies in sex clubs would certainly not be able to confront the sensibilities of the masses, as they were efficiently tidied away out of sight.

The 'public sex' of the 1990s turns out to include a combination of three elements. One is men cruising for sex with other men in public places such as toilets and parks. Another consists of commercial venues set up to make a profit from men's public sex, such as the backrooms or bars or bookstores which have cubicles for sex, and bathhouses or sex clubs which are often modelled to represent toilets or other public cruising grounds. The third element is commercial sex in which men access the bodies of other men for money, in pornography and prostitution. Overwhelmingly, the definitions offered by public sex advocates focus on commercial sex in some form. Public sex generally means sexual exploitation for profit, either of gay men themselves, who pay for space in which to engage in sex with each other, or of men and boys who are paid for sexual use.

The romantic vision of the way things used to be in toilets and parks is still of importance to the queer theorist Douglas Crimp. He explains the damaging effect of the AIDS epidemic on public sex thus: 'what many of us have lost is a culture of sexual possibility: back rooms, tea rooms, movie houses, and baths; the trucks, the piers, the ramble, the dunes. Sex was everywhere for us, and everything we wanted to venture' (quoted in Munoz 1996: 355). But for others, public sex is only of the commercial kind. Wayne Hoffman, in the Dangerous Bedfellows collection, describes what he sees as the 'public sexual culture' that 'exploded' for gay men after Stonewall. It is 'gay pornography' and 'commercial sex establishments' (Hoffman 1996: 339). This commercial sex, called by Hoffman a 'public culture of queer sexuality', is politically important, because 'public displays of sexuality', even if they are only for other gay men in sex clubs or in pornography, 'challenge the enforcement of gay invisibility in public spheres. They also build communal spaces where sexual behavior, identity, techniques, and etiquette can be shared and refined' (p. 350). Lesbians managed to create identity without any of these sexual means in the 1970s. Meetings and conferences, living rooms, restaurants, theatres, novels and educational courses were sufficient. But gay men, it seems, needed sex clubs.

Carl Stychin, an exponent of queer legal theory, argues that public sex is transgressive: 'Queer Nation's appropriation of public space as a realm of openly sexual expression transgresses the boundaries of public and private' (Stychin 1995: 152). The revolutionary nature of public sex is that what oppression had relegated to the private, homosexual sex, is being performed in public in the form of 'a new queering of public space' (p. 153). The effect is that 'the issue of what is public and what is private space itself is interrogated' (p. 153). Stychin is enthusiastic about all that the newly concerned gay critics question. He waxes lyrical about 'the current re-emergence of a gay male culture of sexual adventurism and experimentation'.

> There now appears to be a renaissance of a gay male *sexual* culture, emphasising safe sex practices, eroticism and experimentation.... Sex clubs, sadomasochism, saunas, phone sex, and 'jerk off' parties all exemplify a carnivalesque reassertion of a gay male eroticism that transgresses the cultural equation of homosexuality with disease and death. (p. 152)

The fact that lesbians showed little interest in most of these practices did not cause the enthusiasts to be any less keen. Lesbians are simply not assimilable to these revolutionary queer tactics. The resistance of lesbians to the allure of commercial public sex is spelt out in the Bedfellows collection. Jocelyn Taylor, one of the two black lesbians who set up the Clit Club, a lesbian club based on a gay male model, including a backroom for sex, is interviewed. She states categorically that 'women did not play in the backroom at the Clit Club' (Thomas 1996: 62). The backroom 'didn't take off', she says. Women might have sex in the bathroom or behind the bar, but 'they just weren't doing it in what I would call a performative arena' (p. 62).

Thus gay male exponents of public sex were not able to find lesbians who would demand the right to public sex for themselves.

To make the demand seem less biased towards men's interests, they enlisted female advocates of the heterosexual sex industry. Three of the female writers in the Bedfellows anthology, for instance, are women associated with the sex industry. Priscilla Alexander (1996) is a long-time worker in pro-prostitution organizations such as COYOTE. Eva Pendleton (1996) is a 'professional sexual deviant'. Carol Leigh describes herself as 'a public woman as prostitutes have sometimes been called' (Leigh 1996: 252). Indeed, the only women likely to be using public spaces for sex are 'public' women who are bought for sex by men – sometimes called, as in the British legal system, 'common prostitutes', or women held in common by men. Public sex as a recreational activity is not a practice of women or lesbians. The women who support queer male demands here, it needs to be said, do not represent the vast majority of prostituted women, who, research shows, wish to leave prostitution (Perkins and Bennett 1985). 'Public women', far from recreationally using public space, are those who are used and abused. Similarly, the men and boys used in pornography and prostitution are the objects of other men's recreational activity.

The male bias of the campaign for public sex is clear in the example of queer utopia offered in the Bedfellows collection. For instance, Jose Esteban Munoz, who teaches performance studies, treats us to his queer utopian vision, and it turns out to be toilet sex. He says that queer politics needs a real dose of utopianism, and he looks at moments in a few gay cultural works that 'imagine utopia through "*queer utopian memory*"' (Munoz 1996: 357). One example is a work of poetry about anal-oral sex and hard fucking in a public toilet, described as 'a picture of utopian transport and reconfiguration of the social, a reimaging of our actual conditions of possibility' (p. 360). At the end of the section on the public sex poem he says grandly, 'Queer worldmaking, then, hinges on the possibly [sic] to map a world where one is allowed to cast pictures of utopia and to include such pictures in any map of the social' (p. 362). What does he mean by all this grand language? The next example is the photography by Tony Just of 'public men's rest rooms in NY City' which were closed after AIDS because of their use as public sex venues. There follows a couple of pages of photos of urinals, toilet seats and taps. It is hard to imagine lesbians, or any women, finding utopia in a public toilet. The gulf separating women from this variety of queer politics is extremely wide.

Barebacking

When Sex Panic was formed, it seems that the founders did not anticipate the seriousness of the controversy in which they were to become embroiled. Their original concern was Mayor Giuliani of New York's campaign to clear up the streets and regulate sex businesses. Caleb Crain, in his coverage of the group's origins, suggests that their founding concern was a myth, as there was no evidence that sex clubs were being closed down (Crain 1997). But very soon the issue became not just sex club regulation, but condomless anal sex, or 'barebacking'.

The barebacking controversy took off with the speech of Tony Valenzuela, an HIV-positive porn star and prostituted man, at the NGLTF conference in San Diego in 1997. In Signorile's words, Valenzuela 'criticized "safe sex absolutism," extolled the joys of "bareback" – or condomless – sex, and discussed his becoming HIV positive. "The message few people are paying attention to is that sex is a powerful desire and behavior, one that throughout time people have risked their lives for," he explained. "The level of erotic charge and intimacy I feel when a man comes inside me is transformational"' (Signorile 1998b). Valenzuela went on to declare in *The Advocate* later that year that 'he'd gone bareback with 50 people last year, implying that he was a top in at least some of those sexual encounters and did not always know his partners' serostatus' (1998b). Signorile explains that though some Sex Panic members were privately upset by Valenzuela's remarks, they felt they could not criticize his sexual practice lest they be seen as moralistic.

M. Scott Mallinger, in an article in *Gay Today* in 1998, showed to what extremes the barebacking phenomenon had already gone on the Internet. On an Xtreme Sex website for HIV-positives the excitement of deliberately risking HIV is described.

> The site eroticizes HIV and unprotected sex among HIV-positive men. It would seemingly encourage both HIV-positive and HIV-negative men to engage in unprotected sex with positive men. The site refers to HIV/AIDS as "the gift" and to "Pozcum" as the "Fuck of Death". In a bizarre twist, a small number of HIV-negative people on the site would seem to seek HIV infection. One personal introduction reads, "I've tested negative six times. Guess I haven't found the right virulent strain . . . yet." (Mallinger 1998: 6)

The motivation for seeking infection is described on this site as 'very much like some people feel about being beaten or pissed in or on, or any of those kinds of things' – i.e. it is a form of masochistic self-mutilation (p. 7). The promotion of barebacking on the Internet is but one example of the ways in which Internet technology has facilitated and helped in the construction of a 'public' gay male sexuality in the last decade. The anonymity and alienation of the Internet have greatly encouraged forms of objectifying sexual practice such as pornography, cruising and all aspects of the sex industry.

A recent academic collection, William Leap's *Public Sex* (1999), makes the practice of public sex respectable through the attention of anthropologists and sociologists. One thing that is remarkable about the collection is the way in which all the social and ethical issues that public sex raises are glossed over or ignored even when, as in these writings, they are most evident. In one piece, for instance, Clatts, a medical anthropologist who develops public health programmes, writes of the degree of risk of HIV transmission in public sex activities around the Stonewall Bar in Greenwich Village (Clatts 1999). The bar's clientele are city businessmen and prostituted young men and boys. They negotiate sex, and repair to the foyer of an apartment building inhabited mainly by elderly people who are not expected to venture out in the small hours. In the scene he describes here, both prostitution sex and non-commercial sex are taking place:

> The individual who has inhaled the poppers turns his back, bends over and, reaching behind him, he inserts the other man's penis into his rectum.... One of the onlookers approaches the man who is bent over, trying to position his groin near the man's face, soliciting oral sex. The attempt is coarse and is abruptly rebuffed. The other onlooker begins to masturbate but does not intrude. After several moments, one of the men groans, pulls his penis out of the other's rectum, makes several more groaning sounds suggesting climax, and slips off the condom – throwing it on the floor.... Soon after, one of the other onlookers finishes masturbating and leaves as well. Leaving the building and returning to the streets, I see that both James and Tim are back hustling on the corner. (Clatts 1999: 149)

Clatts simply comments that the activities described are no riskier for disease transmission than if they had been conducted in someone's home. They are, however, considerably more problematic from the standpoint of what used to be called 'public nuisance' or social responsibility. The foyer has been confiscated from the residents, who would be horrified to have to traverse it on such a night. The man using a young prostitute is extremely abusive. The non-commercial sex actors drop used condoms on the floor for the elderly residents to negotiate in the morning. The men involved could choose their homes or a commercial venue for their activities, but deliberately choose the entry to an apartment block for their 'public sex'.

Gay masculinity and sexual practice

The public sex activities that so many queer academics and activists are treating as either 'natural' or even 'revolutionary' can be explained as arising from male dominance. It is in gay male sexual practice, that, according to Martin Levine (1998), Christopher Kendall (1997, 1999) and other gay male critics that a distillation of gay masculinity is to be found. Martin Levine explains that gay male sexuality represents an unreconstructed version of traditional adolescent male sexuality. He considers that gay men are socialized to be masculine just as heterosexual men are. Men, he says, 'become men through an elaborate process of socialization, negotiations between the individual and his environment', and gay men share in this (Levine 1998: 8). The masculinity of gay men is shaped by the experience of homosexual oppression. Levine described the clone as 'first and foremost, a man, whose sexual experiences were shaped by masculine socialization and the stigmatization of homosexuality' (p. 11). An important component of masculinity, he says, is risk-taking (p. 13). Gay males learn, like all other boys, that 'masculinity is a means of achieving status in the eyes of other males' (p. 15). That masculinity is demonstrated most noticeably in relation to sexuality: 'Sex becomes, for all boys, regardless of future sexual orientation, organized as detached from emotion, privatized, phallocentric, and objectified' (p. 18).

Whereas heterosexual men are encouraged to moderate their adolescent sexuality by girls who 'teach boys the techniques required for sociosexual relations' and urge them to 'redefine sex as an activity expressing emotional intimacy' (p. 19), gay men miss this tutelage. They thus remain 'fully committed to the masculine sexual scripts of early adolescence, more fully wedded to non-relational, nonprocreative, and fully recreational notions of sexuality than are het-erosexual boys' (p. 20). In sexual practice, aggressive masculinity is enacted most energetically. Levine illustrates this with the language he heard in a bathhouse during a sexual encounter: 'That big fucking cock is going to be plowing your ass, ramming and ramming your manhole.... Suck that man's dick. Yeah. Suck it, cocksucker. Also Take it, fucker. Take it like a man. Yeah' (p. 78). Truly masculine sex has to be 'Hot sex. Heavy sex. Rough sex' (p. 79). So the clone both 'took it like a man' and he also 'gave' it like a man. 'It was in their sexual conduct – both the cruise and the contact itself – that gay men demonstrated most convincingly that they were "real men" after all' (p. 79).

Walt Odets, in his book *In The Shadow of the Epidemic* (1995), which analyses the effect of the HIV epidemic on the emotions and practices of gay men, both positive and negative, also sees masculinity as the source of the sexual difficulties that cause so many men to seek public sex. He is incisively critical of gay male sexual practice in bathhouses, for instance, in which 'sexuality is relatively unintegrated into feelings or relationships'. This form of sexuality is exemplified in the use of 'glory holes', through which a man could 'insert your penis into an adjoining room and have it sucked by you-never-had-to-know-who. This is sex with a mouth – or, for the receptive partner, a penis – rather than with a person' (Odets 1995: 128). He explains such practice in terms of learnt masculinity, since 'Men, homosexual or not, are acculturated to neither experience nor express feelings' (p. 126), but also in terms of the difficulties of growing up in a gay-hating culture which induces self-hate, so that, 'For a young man growing up homosexual, many feelings are homosexual feelings', and he 'feels danger in allowing any feelings' (p. 126). Thus the damaging effects of homosexual oppression cause an exaggeration in gay men of the affectless, objectifying sexuality that characterizes masculinity in general.

Levine explains the AIDS epidemic in terms of masculinity, as Signorile does, but his critique is more strongly influenced by feminist insights. Levine's partner died of AIDS at age thirty-five in 1986, and Levine himself was to die of the disease. He had good reason to want to understand the social origins of the disease in the gay community. He explains in a 1989 piece written with Michael Kimmel that though no one was talking about AIDS as a men's disease, there was a relationship between AIDS and masculine risk-taking behaviour.

This cultural construction of masculinity indicates that men organize their conceptions of themselves as masculine by their willingness to take risks, their ability to experience pain or discomfort and not submit to it, their drive to accumulate constantly (money, power, sex partners, experiences), and their resolute avoidance of any behavior that might be construed as feminine. Results are higher rates of stress-related illnesses and venereal diseases. (Levine and Kimmell 1998: 145)

'Real men', he says, ' "score" by having lots of sex with many partners, and they are adventurous and take risks' (p. 146). Safer sex messages of risk reduction could not work, because they were 'in direct contradiction with the norms of masculinity. The norms of masculinity propel men to take risks, score, and focus sexual pleasure on the penis.' AIDS precautions were seen as rejecting the pleasuring of the penis, and behaviours that were recommended, such as 'Abstinence, safer sex, and safer drug use', were seen as compromising 'manhood'. The big problem for AIDS prevention was that 'The behaviors required for the confirmation of masculinity and those required to reduce risk are antithetical' (p. 147). Presaging the development of the barebacking/gift-giving phenomenon in which HIV-positive men were deliberately infecting younger men with their consent, he states: 'To demonstrate manliness, seropositive men may actually give the virus to someone else' (p. 148).

The main aspect of male sexuality which made gay sex so unsafe was risk-taking. As Levine puts it, 'gay male sex is, above all, male sex, and male sex, above all, is risky business' (Levine 1998: 152). Where such a risky sexual script is in operation, ' "safe sex" is an oxymoron' (p. 153). He also points out that one reason given for unsafe sexual practice amongst gay men was force and rape (p. 207).

Uncontrollable urges? Gay male sexuality and social responsibility

Radical feminist theorists have analysed the construction of male sexuality as resulting from ruling class status and the availability of a subordinate class of women on whom to act out (MacKinnon 1989; Jeffreys 1997a). This form of sexuality is extremely dangerous to the interests of women, inasmuch as it leads to the rape and murder of women. This has not been a popular point of view amongst gay activists or sexual libertarian lesbians and feminists who have attacked those feminists who demand that men change, as 'anti-sex' or 'essentialist'. The radical feminist critique has now been powerfully taken up by many of those concerned to contain the global AIDS epidemic. The Panos Institute publication, *AIDS and Men: Taking Risks or Taking Responsibility?* (Foreman 1999), argues that AIDS is an epidemic which has a political cause in the form of masculine risk-taking and irresponsible behaviour originating in the inequality between men and women. AIDS, according to this analysis, can be seen as a disease of male supremacy.

The Panos Institute collection contains introductory chapters explaining why and how AIDS can be seen as an epidemic for which men are responsible. It is, argues Martin Foreman, men's behaviour which propels the spread of the epidemic. As he explains:

> [W]ithout men there would be no AIDS epidemic. Men are involved in almost every case of sexual transmission; perhaps one in every 10 cases is the result of transmission solely between men. Four out of every five drug injectors are men. With more sexual and drug-taking partners than women, men have more opportunity to transmit HIV. More often than not, it is men who determine whether sex takes place and whether a condom is used. In general, women are more liable to contract HIV without passing it on, men are more liable both to contract and transmit the virus to others. (Foreman 1999: p. vi)

But the explanation offered for men's irresponsible, promiscuous and risk-taking behaviour is not a biological one. Men's behaviour is the result of the attitudes and expectations of masculinity that train them into a destructive pattern of behaviour. 'Most men grow up believing, implicitly or explicitly, that their identity as men, and therefore as individuals, is defined by their sexual prowess.... As long as men ... are influenced by such concepts of masculinity, HIV will continue to spread' (p. x).

Men's behaviour is different from women's, Foreman argues, because of their different social and political situations, rather than because of biology. Women do not have the social and economic power to control their own lives, including when or whether to have sex, to insist upon condom use, or even to question their male partners' behaviour with other women. But some men and adolescent boys are also vulnerable, because 'Those who are younger, poorer or physically or psychologically weaker are liable to contract HIV from other men through sex or shared drug-injecting equipment . . . . Transvestites and transsexuals and pre-adolescent children may also be compelled by force or circumstances into situations where they contract HIV from men' (p. x).

This is an analysis based upon a recognition of power difference and an understanding of male dominance and female subordination. It is an analysis which is fundamentally challenging to much contemporary gay male theory, particularly the position of Sex Panic and much of queer theory which determinedly eschews morality and value. The position of Michael Warner, a founder of queer theory and Sex Panic, who defines 'the appeal of queer sex' as lying for many 'in its ability to violate the responsibilizing frames of good, right-thinking people', seems more like the norm for men in many cultures rather than 'transgressively' queer (quoted in Crain 1997: 30).

The masculine sexuality which is exemplified in public sex, barebacking and promiscuity fits very well the description of normative male sexuality developed in the Panos collection. It does seem likely, then, that those activities proposed by some queer academics as essential to queerness are just those typical of unreconstructed male sexuality of the kind that requires reconstruction for the sake of women and the ending of AIDS. Even the practice of engaging with numerous sexual partners, considered by theorists such as Hocquenghem to be crucial to the revolutionary potential of gayness, when seen in a global context, can seem simply representative of the behaviour of the dominant class of men. Foreman comments, for instance, that 'Polygyny is authorised by religion and law in Islamic countries and sanctioned by social attitudes in parts of the Caribbean or Africa' (p. 18). The behaviours so representative of queer transgression, when seen in a global context, look extremely like those male behaviours which, deriving from men's dominance, wreak havoc upon women's happiness and material and physical health. It is ironic that whilst the Panos Institute collection is asking, 'why do a minority of men consistently endanger themselves and others, and how can we persuade those men to change their behaviour?', queer theorists of the Sex Panic variety attack as 'fascists' precisely the gay men who are asking those questions.

Gay AIDS in the USA is not a disease of wealthy white men who are insulated from the rest of the world. As the Panos Institute points out, 'Worldwide, 10 percent or more cases of HIV infection may be the result of sex between men, and the actual total may be much higher' (Foreman 1999: 110). Many of these men will also have sex with women, particularly in countries in which an exclusive gay identity is less common than in the West. Outside the queer, academic community of men in the USA, the disease is causing immeasurably more devastation than that experienced by gay Americans. For instance, in Uganda alone, 2 million people in a population of 20 million are believed to have died from the disease; 1.7 million children have lost one or both parents to the epidemic; and more than 900,000 adults and children in 1999 were living with the virus (p. 103). Amongst black gay Americans the impact of AIDS is very much more severe than amongst white gay men. A Centre for Disease Control study in 2001 found that among African-American gay and bisexual men aged twenty-three to twenty-nine 14.7 per cent were newly infected, compared with 2.5 per cent of white and 3.5 per cent of Latino men. Of all the men surveyed, 7 per cent of the white men were infected, 14 per cent of the Latino men, and 32 per cent of the African-American men (Osborne 2001).

The model of sexuality which underlies the queer promotion of 'public sex' is one which is profoundly problematic for women, children, and vulnerable and marginalized men and boys internationally. If the interests of constituencies other than privileged white American gay men are to be taken seriously, then this kind of sexuality needs to be transformed, rather than protected. There are other practical implications of public sex for women's interests which should be a matter of concern. The defence of a 'public sex' defined as forms of the sex industry is a considerable problem for feminists who understand prostitution to be a form of violence and wish to end the sexual exploitation of women and boys (Jeffreys 1997a). Also, whilst women campaign through Reclaim the Night marches for the right to walk in public space unmolested and unafraid at night, or even at other times of day, the demands of any group of men to sequester areas of public space for their own use is a real problem. From women's perspective, the take-over of areas of parks or beaches for men's sexual purposes is a transgression of the rights of women. It is a confiscation of that space from women, who do not yet have the right to walk in it, let alone perform acts that would interfere with any other group's freedom of access.

Gay Male Pornography

Pornography, as we have seen, is a major aspect of the definition of public sex offered by queer theorists and Sex Panic members. Pornography has achieved iconic status in queer theory, and its defence is central to the agenda of queer politics. Well-known queer art critics, legal theorists and queer theorists state that pornography is crucial to gay men's survival, to their identities, and to their ability to do sex. For feminists who understand pornography to be the 'propaganda of womanhatred' (Barry 1979) and wish to eradicate it, gay men's defence of their own form of pornography is a significant obstacle. Gay men constitute an influential lobby group. By arguing, as many do (Burger 1995; Stychin 1995), that gay porn is necessary for gay men's survival, they protect pornography, in direct contradiction to feminist concerns that it is an active threat to the survival of women.

In the 1980s a lesbian sex industry developed in which lesbian porn was made for lesbians, to go alongside the popular 'lesbian' porn that has always been a staple of straight male porn (see my *The Lesbian Heresy*, 1993). Lesbians have not made such grandiose claims for pornography, which suggests that its political function for lesbians is a little different. But both lesbian and gay porn supporters have reviled anti-pornography feminists and the men who support that analysis. Scott Tucker, for instance, accuses radical feminists of 'Bambi-Among-the-Buttercups-Utopianism' for their opposition to pornography (Tucker 1991: 265). Gay pornography is clearly an immensely important issue to create such a powerful response. This chapter will look at the gay defences of pornography and the critique from pro-feminist gay men such as John Stoltenberg (1991) and Christopher Kendall (1997).

The feminist critique

Feminist critiques of pornography have been misleadingly represented as being simply old-fashioned, puritanical or 'anti-sex' by those who support the porn industry. In fact, as the feminist legal theorist Catharine MacKinnon points out, traditional masculine objections to pornography, as in obscenity law, are about morals 'from a male point of view, meaning the standpoint of male dominance'. The feminist critique, on the other hand, 'is a politics, specifically politics from women's point of view, meaning the standpoint of the subordination of women to men'; it sees the sex of pornography as 'Sex forced on real women so that it can be sold at a profit to be forced on other real women' (MacKinnon 1987: 147). MacKinnon and Andrea Dworkin drew up an ordinance which would have given women the right, had it not been defeated on the grounds of free 'men's' speech, to challenge the damage they suffered in and through pornography in civil law. The ordinance defines pornography as 'the graphic sexually explicit subordination of women' (p. 262). Pornography as propaganda, according to feminist analysis, represents women as objects who love to be abused, and teaches men practices of degradation and abuse to carry out upon women (Everywoman 1988).

The harm to the women abused in the production of pornography is a fundamental concern of those feminists who seek to eradicate pornography. The moving documentary by Swedish feminist filmmaker Alexa Wolf, *Shocking Truth* (2000), sets out to show how child sexual abuse seasons women and boys for sexual exploitation in pornography and the harm that is done to them in its production. *Shocking Truth* includes clips of pornography from a pseudo-documentary shown on Swedish TV in which women are portrayed being sexually abused and are then interviewed on the set immediately afterwards. The women are shown being passed naked, except for high heels, from one man to another in pack rape situations in which penises are thrust violently into all their orifices at once or several men all thrust their hands in and out of a woman's vagina. When the women are interviewed, one with semen running out of her mouth, their eyes are blank from the trauma, and their faces expressionless. The woman who is the focus of the documentary suffered savage sexual assault in her teens and was abused in pornography for two years, from age eighteen. She explains that on one occasion, when she was bleeding, she asked to be taken to hospital, only to be told not to make a fuss. She was wrapped in a nappy to soak up the blood so that the penetration could continue. The pornographers would tell her to 'smile' and 'giggle' for the camera.

Despite the power of the feminist critique, there has been fierce opposition from some women, such as those who formed FACT (Feminist Anti-Censorship Taskforce) in the USA and FAC (Feminists Against Censorship) in the UK (see Burstyn 1985). Such women, who set out to defend the pornography industry, find powerful allies in the malestream porn-loving media. The defence by gay men of their own porn, and often of straight porn too, has been almost universal, however. Few gay theorists have taken the unpopular course of criticizing the effect of porn on the men and boys used in it and on all gay men. For all the strength and cogency of feminist arguments against pornography, they are rejected out of hand by the porn apologists I shall examine here.

Arguments for gay porn

The most extensive apologia for gay pornography is Burger's *One-Handed Histories*. The book was originally an M.A. thesis in Performance Studies from New York University. Burger explains that gay pornography developed in the early 1970s as gay men expressed the 'right' that had previously belonged to heterosexual men to own and view pornography. The claiming of pornography for gay men was part of a desire for the same privileges that heterosexual men possessed by virtue of their dominant status. He says that gay pornography is 'a warehouse of our cultural heritage and memory, as well as an important site for the production and modification of this heritage and memory' (Burger 1995: p. x). He sees gay pornography as 'an attempt by gays to rewrite themselves into American history' (p. 4). In his view, it performs the vital function for gay men of legitimating their homosexuality. It is also important, he says, because by 'documenting the sexual and erotic trends and practices of gay men, pornography serves as a form of historiography' (p. 21). Pornography both 'reflects' gay sexual practices, and 'construct[s] new erotic trends' (p. 22). In particular, gay pornography serves an important function for men who are just coming out, in teaching them what they can do sexually. It functions, he says, as sex education (p. 24).

Other queer commentators are equally effusive about the usefulness of pornography. Christopher Hogan argues that pornography has become 'the safest forum in which gay men can examine their culture.... Within the gay community men who avoid overt political or cultural discussions are engaged in these issues through pornography' (Hogan 1996: 244). Charles Isherwood, in his biography of a dead gay male pornography star, Joey Stefano, concurs on the importance of pornography. He says that gay men lack role models. Thus porn stars are 'the only gay movie stars' and get attention and respect in gay culture (Isherwood 1996: 84). In a world in which gay men have no positive images, he argues, they have to find them in pornography. He says that pornography is the only place where gay male sexuality is represented.

The queer legal theorist Carl Stychin proposes that the law should specially protect gay pornography from censorship because of the important political role it performs for the sexual minority of male homosexuals: 'In legal terms, gay pornography becomes protected speech, but based upon its role in securing the political rights of a subject forged from a marginalised political experience' (Stychin 1995: 62–3). Gay pornography is a 'point of resistance in an oppositional discourse to male dominance', because it 'makes visible what has been made invisible by male heterosexual culture' (p. 63). Stychin chides anti-pornography feminists for not realizing that gay pornography is different from heterosexual men's pornography. They have failed to see 'the usefulness of the subversive acts of gay men operating at the fringes of the dominant sexual discourse'. Pornography has become, for Stychin, the motor force of gay liberation itself: 'Pornography may be a means of achieving both resistance to the dominant culture and, potentially, gay liberation' (p. 75).

Another influential defender of gay pornography is the late John Preston, who was a major writer of sadomasochist pornography. Before entering the porn stage of his career, he was the editor of *The Advocate*, a magazine central to conservative gay culture in the USA. He says that he and other gay men 'learned the parameters of our sexual life' from pornography (Preston 1993: 34). It was where they developed their 'fantasies, both sexual and emotional'. It is interesting that gay pornography and sadomasochism are defended as countercultural and transgressive by proponents such as Carl Stychin, yet are also clearly part of the agenda of men as straightforwardly conservative as Preston. Through this issue, both the left and right wings of queer politics are united. Preston explains that gay leather clubs are 'for all practical purposes . . . composed of the same men in racial, class, and economic terms as Rotary and Lions' in the straight world' (p. 134). If you go to a meeting of such a gay leather organization, he says, you will see from 'its nationalistic bent, patriotic fervor, and reliance on ritual, with the singing of common songs and the pomp and circumstance of its hierarchy . . . that the need being fulfilled is strikingly similar to what is going on at any other men's civic benevolent society' (p. 134). In the way that Preston writes about SM, as an initiation of gay boys into manhood, like the military for straight men, there is a yearning for the masculine privileges of straight, middle America.

Preston, like many other gay male defenders of pornography, felt impelled by the early 1980s to confront feminists over their opposition. For gay men who attributed their gay pride and identity to gay porn, it was a severe shock when an organization as significant to feminism as the National Organization for Women passed a resolution at its 1980 conference condemning 'pederasty, pornography, sadomasochism, and public sex as matters of "exploitation, violence, or invasion of privacy," and not issues of "sexual/affectional preference/orientation"' (Tucker 1997: 11). Scott Tucker tells us that this sent 'shock waves through much of the gay community'. Gay men responded by getting lesbian and bisexual women, often with vested interests in the newly developing lesbian sex industry, to support them against the anti-pornography feminists. They sought to split the opposition, so that they could maintain their porn and their privileges. But the counter-resolution, put up by Janet Bellwether and Susie Bright, about freedom of sexual expression was voted down. Scott Tucker takes comfort in the fact that some feminists chose, in the feminist sexuality debates, to defend pornography. He congratulates Ellen Willis and Ann Snitow for challenging anti-pornography feminists (p. 85). He accuses the anti-pornography activists and theorists Andrea Dworkin and John Stoltenberg of proposing a 'utopia of detumescence' (p. 92).

Preston became virulently hostile to feminists in his writings. He attributes to feminism the 'emasculation' of gay men. 'We have', he says, 'in many ways been emasculated, first by the general society and then by a movement that is so focused on either gender equality or on certain narrow definitions of feminism that any acting out of masculine roles is forbidden' (Preston 1993: 133). He was clearly deeply hostile to the feminist imperative of seeking to deconstruct aggressive masculinity. Preston's professions of hustling and writing SM pornography, his pleasures of being a top in SM, and, it would seem, his very identity rely on aggressive masculinity. His remark about emasculation is preceded by a description of a particular sexual delight of his. 'One of my preferences... is to take a nice young man who is wearing Jockey shorts and put him over my knee and spank him, hard. (It doesn't count unless he cries)' (p. 132).

The virulence of his antipathy to anti-pornography feminists is clearest in his most famous, most quoted non-fiction piece entitled 'Goodbye to Sally Gearhart', from 1982. He accuses feminists of 'bullying' gay men about their sexual expression in forms such as sadomasochism, promiscuous sex and 'intergenerational' sex (i.e. sex with under-age boys). He says that feminists are against gay men because 'homosexuality is, after all, the most complete expression of male sexuality possible' (p. 180). Thus 'gay men feel betrayed by women' (p. 181) and must resist, because 'It also should be very clear to gay men that we cannot afford to give up the victory which is the celebration of that maleness' (p. 180). Preston says that although feminists say that gay men have the privilege of being men, that is not true, because 'Gay men have almost no sense of power. We have all too vivid perceptions, in fact, of our own powerlessness' (p. 181). It is the feminists, apparently, the emasculators, who have the power. Though women have had a difficult struggle, they have 'constructed a power base' for women that does not exist for gay men (p. 184). They get academic appointments, whilst gay men do not, and can get into politics in ways that gay men cannot. Lesbians have 'positions of influence and leadership', whereas 'Gay men have no comparable situation in their lives' (p. 184). This is a particularly blunt, ignorant misogyny.

The message is that these powerful, privileged women should lay off poor, vulnerable gay men and their few resources. Feminists who protest at pornography stores are 'cruel'. Gay men need these places, because they use the backrooms for sex. Feminists who oppose pornography stores 'make unfair assaults on a delicate and even poignant space for men whom we see less and less as enemies and more and more as victims. Their assailants are bullies, difficult to differentiate from the adolescents who beat up strays on the beach' (p. 188). Feminists who oppose pornography, then, are just like any other gay-bashers.

Women in general, not just feminists, are accused of a 'misconception' in seeing aggressive gay male sexuality which celebrates masculinity as related to straight male sexual violence. Gay male sexuality, Preston, says, is quite distinct. The sexuality that gay men are 'attempting to develop', doubtless with the tutelage of his sadomasochist pornography, is 'a force attempting to make men equals, a process dependent upon consent, a celebration of the male body which is not dependent upon the denigration of the female body' (p. 191). A representative quote from one of Preston's stories shows how this creation of equality works: 'He grabbed my hair and roughly speared my mouth. I choked; he only pressed down harder.... He slapped my face with his free hand. It stung. He did it again, and a hot pain spread over the right side of my head. Again. More pain. "Fucking whore!" he shouted at me. Another slap. "Fucking whore!"' (Preston 1984: 15).

Sometimes the young man created into a slave in the story gets to become a master in his turn. It works rather like fagging in boys' public schools in the UK, where a younger boy has to service an older one and then gets serviced in his turn. This is equal turns at being the oppressor. It is the inculcation of respect for hierarchy, rather than equality, and often the 'bottoms' do not get a turn. 'Gay male lust', he says, is 'the manifestation of a primary form of gay liberation', and if women find it 'repulsive', that is their problem to deal with. Feminists cannot accept gay male pornography, he suggests, because 'it is the affirmation of the male's love for other men. It is the purest elevation of male beauty and male sensuality' (p. 193). Feminists are guilty, in Preston's view, of homophobia for not being able to accept gay male pornography. He describes feminist criticism as an 'insistence on seeing filth in the fact of homosexuality', which would force the 'gay everyman to return to a time when he saw himself as filthy, perverse, and undesirable' (p. 195). Thus the gay 'leadership' must reject the 'increasingly irrelevant feminist ideology', and make 'a covenant with its population' (p. 195).

The irredeemably anti-woman nature of gay pornography is illustrated in the aggressive masculinity of the work of the man credited with being inspirational by many gay pornographers, Tom of Finland.

Preston claims that the inspiration for his own pornographic career came from Tom of Finland: 'Tom of Finland's drawings promised me that ... the future was going to be fun' (Preston 1993: 193). Tom of Finland has been recognized by so many gay male writers as foundational to their notion of gay male identity, as well as to the values and practices of gay male porn and sexuality, that it is useful and instructive to analyse his contribution to gay male sexual culture.

The inspiration for gay male pornography: the work of Tom of Finland

Tom of Finland's work is treated by many gay commentators as the very bible of gay male belief about sexuality and identity. As his artistic biographer, Micha Ramakers, puts it, he became 'the best-known and most widely appreciated producer of gay erotica of the second half of the twentieth century. He provided immeasurable pleasure to several generations of gay men and, furthermore, offered what had seemed unattainable for many of them: tools for an affirmative identity' (Ramakers 2000: p. ix). Ramakers explains that legendary gay artists such as Andy Warhol, David Hockney and Robert Mapplethorpe 'made no secret of their admiration, and the latter collected and promoted the Finnish pornographer's work' (p. x). 'For many gay men', he says, 'Tom of Finland's work has played an important role in the creation of an identity' (p. xi).

Tom of Finland started life as a graphic artist in Finland. By the 1950s his work, showing men with exaggerated musculature, was published in the American physique magazines that served as gay male pornography in the period. From the beginning, his drawings are cartoons in which men with hugely muscled chests and hips so narrow that it is a wonder they are still standing are also possessed of penises as wide as their forearms and as long as their thighs. The penises penetrate other men's orifices or bulge down their trousers. By the 1960s he was specializing in sadomasochist pornography. The sadists were clearly Nazi soldiers in the early pictures; but, as Ramakers explains, he was persuaded by some outrage at this clear worship of fascism in the gay community, to mute the Nazi symbols. By the 1970s, the characters in his SM porn were likely to wear black leather uniforms and caps that were stylized Nazi uniforms. Swastikas were uncommon, although they, along with spread-eagles and SS insignia, still appear (pp. 126, 164). Masculinity is the distinguishing feature of his characters. They wear other uniforms of 'real men' suited to an American gay culture: those of prison guards, cowboys, bikers, construction workers – all the Village People array of types. The faces of the characters are indistinguishable. Ramakers points out that they all look exactly alike in facial features. What is important about them is not who they are, but the size of the penises they bear. Ramakers describes the content of Tom's cartoons thus:

> [H]is representations of sexual acts belong to a male tradition that emphasizes genitals, their size, and rough sex. The most common sexual acts found in his work are butt-fucking, cocksucking, and tit play. Simultaneously, sadomasochistic scenes and displays of submission and dominance occupy prominent places throughout the body of work. It seems fair, therefore, to term this a hypermasculine vision of the world. (p. 106)

Though the men being roughly penetrated by one or two enormous penises or whipped are shown to be smiling, so that the aggression can be said to be consensual, in some pictures they are obviously in pain (image on p. 164).

Tom of Finland's work came to be seen as vital to gay men's liberation when the 'butch shift' took place in the late 1970s. Prior to gay liberation, male homosexuality was understood to be restricted to queens, pansies or sissies, men who adopted feminine ways and were failed men. Their sexual objects were not found among their own ranks. Masculinity, not femininity, was erotic, and what was desirable was the straightness of 'real' men, not the damaged masculinity of faggots. Thus the queens desired and had sex with those seen to be straight and butch, even though they were clearly not straight, otherwise they would hardly be having sex with gay men. Choosing supposedly straight men was an expression of self-hatred. For men taught to despise themselves for not living up to manhood, homosexuality was not worthy; only straightness and real masculinity counted.

Post gay liberation, men who adopted the identity 'gay' began to seek sexual objects amongst their own kind. A newly available gay community provided potential partners. The only problem was that these partners might not represent the adored masculinity. Thus there was a cultural shift in which gay men adopted straight masculine models. They could then fancy each other. They could also feel a new self-confidence born of emulating the dominant sex class of men, rather than being downgraded into the class of women. This shift was certainly not without its critics. For many gay liberation activists, it symbolized the destruction of the gay liberation ideal which, like feminism, had been the destruction of gender hierarchy, not its celebration (Levine 1998). Tom of Finland was the perfect icon for those who participated in the shift to masculinity. Ramakers notes that in the late 1970s and 1980s young gay professionals 'rejected the idea that gay men would be less masculine than their straight counterparts.... Tom of Finland's work was perceived as emancipatory, as it is totally devoted to a world of supermen' (Ramakers 2000: 11). The most significant shift in post-war gay identities in the West has undoubtedly been this great trek towards masculinity.

> In a world dominated by homophobia, he held up a "mirror" to gay men in which they could see themselves as they were not: as *real* men, living in Tomland, where gay desires and acts were not considered a sad perversion, but ruled. Ultimately, Tom of Finland produced propaganda – homophile hyperrealism? – for a utopia controlled by a lustful brotherhood of Überfaggots. (p. 38)

An art gallery owner quoted in Ramakers's book estimates that 'Sixty percent of gay men construct their fantasies around the kind of scenes he makes' (p. 12). Another critic said in response to an exhibition of his cartoons in 1986, 'An exquisite X-rated draftsman called Tom of Finland produces serial drawings presenting homosexual sadomasochism and rape as healthy fun and *tres, tres* macho' (p. 13). The German publisher of his work, Benedikt Taschen, expressed its importance by saying that it 'gave gays a positive image for the first time' (p. 23). By 1998, Tom's drawings were acquired for permanent collections by four museums in Finland and the USA.

Tom's popularity showed the extent to which men adopting a homosexual identity felt they had suffered from being kept out of the palace of masculinity by virtue of their attraction to men. His work offered them the dream that they could be both real men and gay. They could look macho, even while being penetrated. There were no pansies in Tom's cartoons. As Tom said, 'I started drawing fantasies of free and happy gay men. Soon I began to exaggerate their maleness on purpose to point out that all gays don't necessarily need to be just "those damn queers," that they could be as handsome, strong, and masculine as any other men' (p. 65).

The sheer exuberant male entitlement of the cartoons is particularly clear in one in which a man is fucking a globe. Ramakers describes the image thus: 'Tom's world revolves around the phallus, a statement that may be taken literally, as is evident in a 1975 drawing of a man floating freely in the cosmos.... He is holding the earth in his arms, and his penis has penetrated the globe. Fucking the world' (p. 99). Tom of Finland can be seen to be giving back to gay men the male power and dominance that had previously been denied them. Unfortunately, the power of the penis, and male dominance in general, can be gained only at the expense of women. Without women's subordination, penises might just be bits of anatomy. The phallic cult that gay porn provides for gay men is in contradiction to the liberation of women, because the liberation of women would remove all the fun.

It is difficult to imagine an analogy to Tom of Finland-style pornography for lesbians. The lesbian pornography that began to be produced with the development of a sex industry for lesbians in the 1980s does not have a symbol of femaleness forming the very basis of authority and realness. Female genitalia are visible, as in straight men's pornography, but masculinity once again is what is erotic. Pornography does not deliver to lesbians a way into the superior class of manhood. Lesbians are women, and remain so unless they too seek to acquire masculinity. Pro-pornography lesbians say that they learnt to appreciate pornography by looking at gay male porn and subsequently incorporated 'gay male sexual iconography into their fantasies, sex play and cultural representations' (Smyth 1992). The highest value absorbed through such incorporation is that masculinity is to be worshipped. In the 1980s this was reflected in a revaluing of lesbian 'butchness', and in the 1990s in the evolution of 'transmen', many of whom sought to become 'gay men' after surgery, despite, in most cases, the absence of any form of phalloplasty. There may be no men in pornography produced for lesbians, but masculinity is there in the form of masculine attitudes and sexual practices, the importance of dildos, sadomasochism and the same array of masculine uniforms eroticized in gay porn. The pursuit of the penis and the masculine privilege derived from male dominance is a sad and hopeless quest for lesbians. Even surgery cannot supply such a holy grail, since transsexual operations cannot construct a functional phallus.

It is interesting to note that gay men are not as fascinated by lesbian porn as some lesbians purport to be by the gay male variety.

Overwhelmed by the 'ick factor', some gay men are quite horrified by lesbian porn. Roberto Bedoya writes about having watched a Barbara Hammer lesbian porn movie: 'I honestly felt repulsion through the whole movie' (Bedoya et al. 1998: 246).

The critique of gay male pornography

A number of gay male commentators have criticized the masculinity of gay male porn and the wider cult of masculinity in gay culture in recent decades as being antithetical to support for women's liberation (Stoltenberg 1991; Kendall 1997). They have pointed out that gay men cannot have their masculinity if women are to be free from oppression. These critiques have not been heeded by gay men who support pornography, most likely because their gay audiences have not known why they should bother about women. They have been concerned only for themselves. For this reason, critics of the values and practices of gay porn have sought to frame their arguments in ways that appeal to gay men's sense of self-preservation. Thus John Stoltenberg of Men Against Pornography explains that pornography arises from the homophobia that is responsible for the oppression of gay men. That homophobia is a product of male supremacy. Thus cultural homophobia is a 'by-product of cultural misogyny' (Stoltenberg 1991: 250). Thus 'the faggot is stigmatized because he is perceived to participate in the degraded status of the female' (p. 250). Stoltenberg uses the concept of 'internalised homophobia' to mean too that 'as a gay man you ... dread the degraded status of anything feminine about yourself' (p. 251). The result of this hatred of the feminine in themselves is that gay men are attracted to the exaggerated masculinity portrayed in gay pornography. They can identify with, or imagine themselves incorporating through being sexually used by, or ingesting the semen of, a 'real' man.

The term 'homophobia' is politically problematic. As the lesbian feminist psychologist Celia Kitzinger has pointed out, 'homophobia' is an unsuitable term to describe lesbian and gay oppression. It was invented by psychology, and is a psychological diagnosis. Phobia means an irrational fear or dread. This concept, Kitzinger, explains, reinforces the power of psychology to label people as 'sick' or healthy, and 'depoliticizes lesbian and gay oppression by suggesting that it comes from the personal inadequacy of particular individuals suffering from a diagnosable phobia' (Kitzinger 1997: 162). Though I agree with this criticism, it is hard to avoid using a term which is so generally and uncritically used by gay writers when commenting upon their work.

Chris Kendall is a gay critic of pornography who has used similar arguments to express the harm that porn does to gay men. He points out that 'adherence to power in the form of hypermasculinity simply reinforces those models of behaviour that are the source of hetero-sexual male privilege and the homophobic rejection of any public expression which challenges it' (Kendall 1999: 158). He explains that homophobia works by silencing and oppressing all those men who do not uphold the unequal gender system of hetero-patriarchal male dominance. Hatred of gay men stems from male dominance, because gay men are seen as disloyal to the system, and particularly disloyal to the support of masculinity, men's claim to dominance and the prac-tice by which they maintain it. Commitment to hypermasculinity thus colludes with the very reason why gay men are oppressed in the first place, rather than helping to end it. By failing to reject gay pornography and its values, he says, 'gay men commit to a male, heterosexist power structure that is central to their own oppression and the oppression of all women' (p. 161).

Apologists for gay porn argue that the inequality in the materials is not harmful because it is not women who are subordinated in it (Stychin 1995). Kendall answers that it is the inequality that is the problem, not the morphology of the bodies involved: 'There is always a top and there is always a bottom, carefully articulated so as to differentiate between those with and those without power. What proponents of gay porn are really advocating is that gay men partici-pate in a rather bizarre form of mutuality based on reciprocal abuse' (Kendall 1999: 163). Pointing out that he does not personally 'want to control or be controlled. I neither want to dehumanize or be dehumanized. I neither want to overpower or be overpowered', he says that he wants 'real equality, something not offered in gay male pornography' (p. 164). Kendall questions the argument made by many gay apologists for porn: that it is necessary to gay identity and survival. He asks what it says about gayness 'that our chosen identity must be realized at the hands of a masculine, ostensibly straight male' (p. 164). It is, he argues, about gay self-hatred, rather than proud self-assertion. He says that though, in theory, gay men have the choice to be either top or bottom, it is the top who is 'very much the focus and idealized masculine norm'. Thus he has the 'liberty to refer to those beneath him as "girlie," "whores," "bitches," "sluts" – read "female" socially defined' (p. 165). This reduction of the male homosexual to lowly feminine status is the dominant way in which heterosexual masculinity is supported, and boys perceived to be 'different' are harassed and abused in the school systems of the Western world (Plummer 1999). Gay porn uses the very mechanisms of oppression that damage boys world-wide and lead to the high rates of suicide in gay-identifying youth (Remafedi 1994) as the erotic core of its appeal. For Kendall, this is deeply problematic, and so it should be for all who care about the healthy survival of boys who challenge the hierarchy of gender.

Kendall argues persuasively that gay porn educates gay men in values and behaviours that are dangerous to their interests. 'Gay porn', he says, 'creates, packages and resells a sexuality that epitomizes inequality: exploitation and degradation of others; assertiveness linked with aggression; physical power linked with intimidation; and non-consensual behavior advanced, and sexually promoted, as liberating' (Kendall 1997: 33). He considers that pornography that makes abuse exciting, and shows gay men as the appropriate objects of abuse, plays a part in creating the attitudes that lead to rape and battering by men of each other. The queer theorists who celebrate commercial sexual violence carried out in pornography or sadomasochism never mention the everyday violence suffered by gay men who are abused by their male partners. Kendall very sensibly asks gay men to reflect upon what it means for gay men's present and future that they find 'validation in submission linked with degradation' (p. 43): 'Why must sexual pleasure be found in the form of punishment and physical battery? One might have hoped that gay men had had quite enough abuse for one lifetime. Are we now to believe that our sexual identities depend on and require abuse?' (p. 43). Another reason why pornography is damaging to gay men, according to Kendall, is that it damages their self-esteem by making those who do not measure up to its values and 'who never belonged anywhere else not belong in gay community also' (p. 49). Signorile makes a similar argument about pornography in *Life Outside* (1998a), where he criticizes the creation of gay hypermasculinity for the negative effects it has had on gay men's self-esteem and sexual health. He explains that the gay porn industry played a central part in the construction of a masculine gay identity, so that: '*Indeed, by the late 1980s and into the 1990s the ideal was no longer something that occurred in nature. It was a completely manufactured man, an artificially created version of masculinity.* The masculine body type that was now most revered could perhaps only be attained by surgery, drug use, and computer enhancement of images' (p. 69). But Signorile is critical only of some of the content of pornography, not of pornography itself.

Racism and gay male sexual culture

Pornography is an arena in which the exclusion of ethnic minority gay men is enacted and enforced, and where ideas of desirability are created which include only certain kinds of masculine, white men. Ethnic minority gay men are excluded or marginalized in many areas of gay culture and politics. Tony Ayres, an Asian gay man from Australia, is one of a growing number of gay men and lesbians who are writing about the ways in which they have been excluded from, or racially victimized within the gay community (Ayres 1999). He explains that in the early 1980s 'being Chinese in a gay bar was one of the worst things you could be' (p. 89). Some white men would shout at him, 'Go back to your own country', or gay personal classifieds would state, 'No Fats, Femmes or Asians', or men in public sex arenas would hiss, 'I'm not into Asians' (p. 89). Some wanted to relate sexually to him as an exotic sexual stereotype of Asianness. Others just ignored him completely, so that he got the 'demoralising feeling that I am, in the eyes of the majority of the gay male population, as undesirable as a woman' (p. 90), and what could be worse than that? In research on the exclusion of consideration of gay Asians in policy on HIV/AIDS, Carl Gopalkrishnan notes that the 'gay community' in Australia is becoming more, and not less, masculine and Anglocentric, and excludes 'anybody who doesn't support a strong masculinity image reminiscent of Berlin in the 1930s and so powerfully embodied by Finnish artist/photographer Tom of Finland' (Gopalkrishnan 2000: 12). Since gay pornography plays such an influential part in constructing the model of what is desirable, Richard Fung suggests that the answer is to get more Asians into porn.

Asian men, Fung explains, are stereotyped as desexualized in US film generally, in contrast with black Americans, who are represented as voracious and as being simply penises (Fung 1999). In gay porn they are conspicuous by their absence. Where they do appear, they represent the racist sexual stereotypes that excite the white male consumers – i.e. they are passive and are shown being penetrated by white men, and often in situations of servitude or punishment. Fung notes that the experience of being a gay Asian man in white American culture is one of alienation and often overt racism from sexual partners, so that 'For me sex is a source of pleasure, but also a site of humiliation and pain' (Fung 1999: 523). Fung's article is not critical of porn in general, only of the racism within it. He considers that a less demeaning representation of Asian men in pornography might help to reduce racism in gay culture, because 'Porn can be an active agent in representing and reproducing a sex-race status quo' (p. 524). So Fung accepts the importance and inevitability of porn in gay culture, and just asks that Asian men be included. This tactic is similar to that of those lesbians who have chosen to create 'lesbian' porn. Through such a tactic, oppressed minorities become side-tracked into seeking equality in institutions that are actually created precisely from their exclusion. Inclusion, rather than social change, becomes the goal. Unfortunately, the inclusion of Asian men or other marginalized constituencies into pornography, supposing that this could be achieved in the face of a racist sex market, would simply create new categories of victims.

Chris Kendall draws attention to another aspect of the damage done by pornography. This is the harm done by gay male porn to the men who are the sexual objects used in its production. The defences of gay porn as vital to gay identity, history, etc. do not consider these men and boys, except in occasionally treating the idea of being a porn model as exciting and productive of higher social status and desirability. It is hard to get information on what happens to gay male porn models, and what damage may be done to their bodies and lives. This may be because gay male researchers have seen no reason to do research in an area which is supposed to be fine and good. It is possible to glean some information from the numerous biographies of gay porn stars which are published for their fans. Gay porn stars are icons, and thus books about them are worth writing. The porn stars represent the masculinity to which gay porn consumers aspire. Any consideration of the damage suffered by these icons, such as the fact that they die young from suicide or AIDS, would dampen the excitement.

The men in pornography

The biographies are written to celebrate the careers of the icons, so they are not concerned with documenting the damage that porn may have done to the lives of these men. There are clues in the texts, however. The porn stars of the three biographies and the one auto-biography that I shall consider here are all dead. Stefano, who was HIV-positive, committed suicide, and the other three – Cal Culver, Scott O'Hara and Al Parker – all died of HIV/AIDS-related conditions. How these latter three came by the disease that killed them cannot be ascertained, since they were all highly sexually active as prostituted men, as recreational sex actors, and as the living objects of penetration in porn movies in which the sex was most often unsafe. Their sex industry experience and their deaths may therefore be related. The damage done to his self-esteem by the sexual abuse of porn movie production seems most likely to have been a factor in the suicide of Stefano.

Stefano was a bottom. As a bottom, he experienced considerable abuse in pornography, and he became HIV-positive. He ended up taking a drug overdose at age twenty-six after a previous suicide attempt. He was held in contempt 'by the very people who were paying for his services' in prostitution, and despite his pornography stardom. He was unable to leave the industry, because he was un-educated and untrained. He was constantly pressured into having things done to him on film which were dangerous to his health and his sense of personhood. One of these was unprotected sex, but other kinds of physical abuse were inflicted. 'I try so hard, and I do too much sometimes! I've done things on stage that I never do myself. I've been fisted, taken two dildos up my ass, and I would never do that in my personal life' (Isherwood 1996: 103). His appeal declined, and he found it hard to make money. He was forced to continue in prostitution and stripping, because porn did not pay well, involving one-off fees of US$500–1500. Having been fisted on film, he lost status. 'Afterward all I heard from every queen in town was how I got fisted in New York and how I was this big slut' (p. 116).

Scott O'Hara became famous for practising auto-fellation. He had a five-year career in gay porn videos after winning the title 'Biggest Dick in San Francisco'. He was famed for his promiscuity and enthu-siasm for public sex. But in the last months of his life he said, 'I'm

tired of being Scott O'Hara .... I hate to rewrite history, but
I wonder how much I actually enjoyed [sex]. I think I liked the idea
of sex more than the actual act.' He added: 'I've become practically a
Puritan' (O'Hara 1999: p. xii).

Though famous for a 'big dick', his sexual preference lay in being
subordinated, and he considered himself 'more of a bottom by
nature' (p. 184). Both at home and in public, he cleaved to practices
that degraded and humiliated him. He had a particular interest in
being urinated on, and wanted that to be done in a way that was
careless of his person and his home. He wished that sexual partners
would urinate over him and his bedding without concern.

> But I would love to have a bed that's covered with stains, that conveys
> silently to any visiting trick the assurance that it's okay to let loose
> here, others have done it before you. I want to lie down on my
> stomach, and then feel his hot stream hitting my back, my ass, my
> hair; I want him to leave me soaking in it. Having done that, I suppose
> he could do most anything he wanted, next: Fuck me, beat me, spit on
> me, recite his poems, or just walk out. (p. 116)

When his 'personal sexual abilities began to wane' (p. 181), he
developed quite a radical critique of the gay male sex culture that
had made of him an icon: 'The gay male community is mostly based
on/revolves around sex' (p. 182). When he first had difficulties
getting the required erections, he found he had 'an emotional impo-
tence' too, which meant he didn't know 'how to relate to someone in
an intimate way without fucking' (p. 187). He had to learn this, and
in his last years wanted nothing so much as to be cuddled. He realized
that his fabled promiscuity had often been about being 'more than a
little bit desperate to be liked' (p. 191).

The transformation of his attitude to sex was stimulated by hearing
Signorile speak about his book *Life Outside*. He 'realized that [Sign-
orile] was putting down on paper – and putting out there for thousands to read – lots of the same thoughts that I'd been thinking, but
hiding' (p. 193). He considered that after he came out as gay, he
'swallowed the party line ... and made myself over into a sex machine' (p. 193). As a 'sex professional', his body had to be in a
constant state of arousal. He writes of a lover in his last years making
him 'feel like a blow-up doll', and how he came to hate the kind of
sex this man demanded: 'The roll on, get off, roll off kind' (p. 198).
O'Hara's story lends itself to being read as one of sexual abuse and

the harm it does to the victim's sense of self and health, but O'Hara's fans are unlikely to read it that way, because that would be detumescent.

There are similarities in the story of Cal Culver, another porn star dead from AIDS-related conditions. In the foreword to his biography, Jerry Douglas writes 'that Cal was as sexually driven as any individual I've ever known' (Edmonson 1998: p. viii). As with O'Hara, his teenage youthful promiscuity, in which he serviced men in subordinate roles, stemmed from a desire to please: 'It was a surefire way for Cal to gain approval. It was so easy to make a person happy' (p. 15). In his cruising activities, he played the role of 'bottom' too. A man used to seeing him cruising said he was surprised to see him as a model: 'It was such a shock when I was used to seeing him on his hands and knees, taking it up both ends' (p. 32).

He went into prostitution when sacked from a teaching job and unable to pay his rent. Like most porn models, he remained in prostitution as his main job throughout his short life. He became very famous for an early 1970s film entitled *Boys in the Sand*, in which he played a character called Casey Donovan. His biographer waxes lyrical about the film, saying that it 'almost single-handedly managed to legitimize gay hard-core.... On the day that *Boys* premiered, gay chic was born' (p. 2). The film achieved cult status, with even such important gay figures as Yves Saint Laurent saying how much they enjoyed it.

In the film a 'rubber-boot' man simulates anal intercourse with Cal. Cal's biographer describes the ensuing discussion thus: 'Would you like me if you couldn't fuck me?' Casey asks plaintively. '"You talk too much," the rubber-boot man replies gruffly' (p. 58). Cal became a star because he looked masculine, like a blonde, boy-next-door, outdoors type. The film featured fistfucking which was just becoming accepted as a regular, even archetypal male gay practice, as a result of the popularity of the burgeoning cult of sadomasochism. Edmonson describes the scene thus: 'For one brief scene lasting mere seconds, he fists Cal. The expression on Cal's face – eyes wide, teeth bared – reveals the animal behind the classically handsome face' (p. 77). It seems more likely that he was in pain, but that is an inadmissible idea in a male gay culture committed to seeing porn modelling as an illustrious occupation. Part of the tragedy of this story is that Culver always expected to be able to break into non-porn movies. But this was not possible, because porn stardom relegates an actor, whatever their apparent cult status, to the ranks of the disreputable.

Edmonson is very enthusiastic about Cal Culver's contribution to the gay community. 'And he had a terrific impact on the gay community. He did a great amount to dispel the shame that gays had always been forced to feel about their sexuality and their bodies' (p. 136). Cal's own view of himself as a prostitute was as 'an uncredentialed sex therapist, doing his best to make men more comfortable with their sexuality' (p. 177). Unfortunately, he was destroyed in the course of helping other men feel more comfortable and less ashamed. A long-time co-star reported that Cal 'refused all safe-sex practices in his films and in life' (p. 219). The price was much too great. He suffered violence outside prostitution and pornography too. He was involved for several years in a battering relationship with a gay male movie star, Tom Tryon, who rejected him when the degradation visited upon Cal in the movies became too embarrassing.

A description of a typical scene in one of Cal's films, *Heatstroke* 1982, gives an idea of what he had to suffer in order to, as his biographer put it, enable other gay men to feel less ashamed: 'he services all and sundry, black and white, both orally and anally, with enthusiastic elan .... And by the time the scene ends, he is literally drenched with jism, his lean body glistening, his eyes hooded, sated by the sheer excess of it all' (p. 195). Once again the biographer's account may not give an accurate representation. When it is women being abused in such 'orgy' scenes, satiation by excess has nothing to do with it.

By the end of his career Cal Culver was destroyed, like the women in *Shocking Truth*. What was being done to him is quite clearly traumatic abuse. Even his biographer, so determined to paint a rosy picture of his idol, seems shocked by this description offered by a friend of Culver's of a scene from a late 1986 movie called *Fucked Up*.

"Fucked Up was the saddest thing I had ever seen .... It was a horrible film. When I saw it I just couldn't believe it. Cal was so far gone, and he was being so used and abused. The whole thing was beyond abandoned. He was holding what appeared to be a big mayonnaise jar full of poppers or ethyl chloride – I'm sure there were other drugs in him at the time as well – sitting in the corner of a room. These faceless people arrive and push toys and fists up into him. He's drooling, and it is absolutely terrifying. I couldn't believe it when I saw it." (p. 223)

Edmonson's conclusion to this tale of terrible abuse unto death is relentlessly positive. 'Cal Culver was the first real gay porn star. He helped gays create a new, liberated, positive image of themselves. He tested limits, pushed boundaries. His legacy is that he captured a golden moment in gay history and fixed it in our collective consciousness' (p. 230).

There are some interesting insights into the experience of being used in the production of male gay porn in Matt Adams's book *Hustlers, Escorts, Porn Stars* (1999). The book purports to be an 'insiders' guide' to the male prostitution 'market' which Adams claims to have observed extensively for over twenty years. He does not say whether he has been a prostitute or a client, but the book is mainly for clients and tells them where to find prostitutes. Despite the positive tone of the book, which is after all aimed at creating more clients for the gay prostitution industry, there is some recognition of what porn stars face. Adams notes that men entering the industry need to be careful and seek advice, because 'A model with a bad experience in the adult film industry may have psychological effects from their experience for many years' (Adams 1999: 117). He explains that a porn career is likely to be very short and not remunerative. At present, he says, 'models' are likely to get offers for only two or three films, instead of the twelve they could previously have expected, and will earn only US$400–500 for each, instead of the previous $1000. Those who become involved are likely to be prostitutes seeking to increase their earnings through the publicity and prestige. Adams says that the studios will provide incidentals for the models, such as enemas for use before fisting and 'drugs to enhance or allow for performance on set' (p. 131). Injuries on set are an increasing problem, because

> Many studios are filming riskier forms of sexual behavior including fisting, sadomasochism, and other forms of non-vanilla sex. Many of these activities involve some form of physical risk. Unfortunately, as studios venture into these new areas, the studios do not always hire models trained in the sexual activity to be performed on set. In one instance a model had their colon ruptured by a model with had [sic] no prior experience fisting. (p. 134)

Scott O'Hara tells of how he had to give an enema to another man on camera with a garden hose and cold water (O'Hara 1997). Even

O'Hara, who had developed a deftness for reinterpreting abuse as 'pleasure', considered this abusive.

There is another form of violence that is connected with pornography, apart from that which takes place on set, and that is the early sexual abuse which seasons the victims of pornography to accept the violation. Feminist researchers have explored the ways in which sexual abuse seasons women and girls for the violation of prostitution and pornography (Herman 1994; Russell 1995). There is a need for research into the connections between childhood sexual abuse and young men's entry into the sex industry. One famously 'masculine' gay porn icon, Al Parker, who, like the other porn stars considered here, died young, suffered a terrifying sexual assault at knifepoint at the age of fifteen as his initiation into gay sexuality (Edmonson 2000). When his attacker performed oral sex, he had his first 'orgasm with another person', and after escaping his attacker, 'I jerked off four times that night thinking about it' (pp. 12–13). His biographer connects this experience with 'the kinky chain of sexuality that Drew later celebrated in his X-rated screen classics' (p. 13). The implication is that Parker was trained, through sexual response in a situation of violent assault, to eroticize violation. A small-scale study by Barbara Gibson of boys in street prostitution in London strongly suggests a link between childhood sexual abuse and prostitution for boys (Gibson 1996). Self-mutilation is required of porn stars too. Like women in prostitution and pornography, the men in gay porn are required to engage in the self-mutilation of cosmetic surgery to look young and prolong their careers: 'The most common forms of plastic surgery are liposuction, chest implants, hair transplants, and facial surgery' (Adams 1999: 152).

Gay porn and political change

It is likely that there is a link between gay porn and straight porn, because practices developed in the gay male sex industry, such as anal sex and fistfucking, have become commonplace in straight porn, and thus are becoming established practices in heterosexual sex. In a piece for the *Guardian Weekend* on the increasingly violent nature of Gonzo pornography, Martin Amis quotes a pornographer explaining that 'assholes are reality. And pussies are bullshit.' In Gonzo porn,

Amis says, 'A double anal is not to be confused with a DP (double penetration: anal and vaginal)...And there have been triple anals too' (Amis 2001). The female star of a Max Hardcore movie explains: 'One of Max's favourite tricks is to stretch a girl's asshole with a speculum, then piss into her open gape and make her suck out his own piss with a hose' (Amis 2001). These practices are reminiscent of those which we have seen gay porn stars having to endure in this chapter. This is not surprising, considering that significant male-stream porn distributors such as Larry Flynt of *Hustler* also distribute gay porn (Stoltenberg 1991: 257). The queer defence of pornography has significant implications for all women, since gay porn cannot be defended separately from straight men's porn. Indeed, as Stoltenberg points out, the gay community 'tends to view its naked political self-interest as lying somewhere in bed with' the most successful male-stream pornographers (p. 257).

But, as gay critics of gay porn have pointed out, there is good reason for gay men themselves to be concerned about pornography. So important is it said by many gay commentators to be to gay male sexuality that it might perhaps be considered to be the DNA of that sexuality. One gay writer says, for instance, 'I want to tell you that I would have no sexual life if it weren't for pornography' (Weinstein 1991: 277). Gay male porn sets the scene and the rules for the problematic behaviours that cause harm to gay men's health and self-esteem, particularly those gay men who least represent the racial and appearance norms of pornography. Porn also seems to have very negative consequences for those gay men impelled by the desire to be liked, or by the need to advertise the work in prostitution by which they survive, to be used in its production. Whilst it remains the holy of holies of gay male sexual culture, the interests of most gay men, as well as the interests of women's, lesbian and gay liberation, will continue to be very seriously undermined.

Self-Harm or Social Change? Sadomasochism, Cutting and Piercing in Lesbian and Gay Culture

Since the 1960s substantial parts of the male gay community have developed sadomasochism as the focus of their sexual practice, and given it a politics and a spirituality that render SM distinctively gay. Chris Woods from the UK, for instance, in his critique of the direction of queer culture and politics in the 1990s, argues that SM 'which in reality only appeals to a minority, has been so normalised within our communities that to express opposition is to fail as a homosexual' (Woods 1995: 54). So influential has SM become in the gay male community that its symbols have been adopted as the symbols of gayness – i.e. black leather and piercings. In the 1980s some parts of the lesbian community also adopted SM sexuality, in a way that emerges from, and copies quite precisely, the forms of that practice in the gay male community. The defenders of sadomasochism argue that it should be treated as a private matter of no concern to the state. They argue that it should not be susceptible to political criticism from within the lesbian and gay community either. Pat (now Patrick) Califia, for instance, who learnt SM from gay male and straight practitioners, and then promoted the practice to lesbians, says: 'Women and gays who are hostile to other sexual minorities are siding with fascism' (Califia 1994: 164). I will suggest that, on the contrary, sadomasochism needs to be understood both as a practice that affirms masculinity for gay men who feel they have been shut out of masculine status and as a practice of self-mutilation which arises from abuse and oppression. It needs to be seen in the context of a range of self-mutilating behaviours such as cutting and piercing which are now being analysed by some feminist theorists as related to the inferior status of women and of homosexuals, groups which act out upon their bodies the woman-hating and gay-hating of the societies they inhabit (Jeffreys 2000). The implications of the celebration of SM and other forms of self-mutilation within lesbian and gay communities are very worrying, both for the futures of lesbians and gay men and for all women.

Sadomasochism and gay masculinity

Ian Young sees the development of SM as a symptom of the disaster that overcame gay men after Stonewall – i.e. the development of practices that inscribe the oppression they have suffered into a commercial sex culture. As an example of the seriousness of the disaster, he describes an event celebrated in *Dungeonmaster* magazine in the 1980s in which four men nailed their 'cock-heads to a butcher block with stainless steel needles' whilst the SM pornographer and *Advocate* editor John Preston took photographs. He is distressed at the development of fisting as a signature gay sexual practice. He shows the extremity of the danger of the practice for health in that fisters will frequently not eat for two days before an 'engagement', use diet pills, douche for two to three hours, take pain-killers and deep muscle relaxants and then put a pound in weight of lubrication into the anus to allow the fists entry. The hydrogenated fats in the lubricants, he says, apart from the other harmful elements of this scenario, cause damage to the immune system. 'The fisting lifestyle, facilitated by medicinal and recreational drugs, entailed a massive assault, not only on the delicate membranes of the rectal mucosa but also on the immune system' (Young 1995: 174).

The sociologist Martin Levine attributes the development of gay sadomasochism to the cult of gay masculinity that developed in response to the 'butch shift' in the 1970s (Levine 1998). Sadomasochism was adopted as the ultimate in masculine sexual practice, which would demonstrate that gay men were not nellies, but 'real men'. 'The masculine erotic script', he explains, 'led clones to become more sexually adventurous than other gay men, to experiment with a variety of fringe sexual practices such as S/M and leather sex' (p. 95). The leather scene was seen as 'archetypically masculine, mainly because it is organized around stereotypically male role performances (dominance, control, endurance) and symbols (whips, chains, leather)'. Thus, in order to 'butch sex up', clones 'engaged in sadomasochistic practices' (p. 95). It was not just the tops in SM who established their masculinity through the practice, because 'Within the S/M community, it is seen as highly masculine to be a superb bottom, to be able to take an enormous amount of sexual activity and pain' (p. 98).

Interestingly, it is not just the critics of SM who identify it as creating masculinity for gay men. Its practitioners see it that way too, and there is no irony in their advocacy. John Preston, for instance, derived his living from SM pornography, as well as being a faithful practitioner in the role of sadist, sometimes professionally. He tells us that SM is a 'ritual of manhood, especially for gay men' (Preston 1993: 17). He says that SM sex clubs were 'cathedrals where acolytes were able to find and serve their priests in a public display of overt masculinity that was characterized by the need to have a community witness the event' (p. 17). He writes about SM clubs as 'The Theater of Sexual Initiation', in which the audience is crucial.

For Preston, public SM sex in clubs is how gay men can demonstrate that they are 'real men', by acting out 'male sex essential'. It is the way they can overcome the stereotypes of being 'less than totally manly', in public displays of 'traditional masculinity in order to allow them to integrate a self-image as being manly' (p. 50). Preston explains that gay men need rituals of initiation into manhood which are denied to them by their gayness. He quotes Robert Bly, the proponent of essentialist 'Iron John' masculinity for straight men. Bly is a mytho-poetic writer – i.e. he supports his schemes for men to become more manly with ideas from myth and legend. His work is recognized by pro-feminist men's movement theorists as explicitly anti-feminist (Kimmell 1995; Messner 1997). Gay men need the sort of rituals that straight men find in the military or in competitive sport, Preston says; and public SM sex is the equivalent gay initiation ritual into manhood: 'It is the way gay men accomplish their gender needs of leaving adolescence and entering male adulthood' (Preston 1993: 59).

He quotes Jungian psychology on the need for men to 'achieve maturity . . . (by) a public embracing of male icons' (p. 51). Gay men also need to act out, he says, because they have often been sexually repressed in the early parts of their lives. Preston describes the action that took place at one of the 'amphitheaters' of SM, the Mineshaft in the mid-1970s. The activities at the Mineshaft were 'devoted to initiating a male into the camaraderie of the group, something that had to be observed by the group' (p. 52). Men entering the Mineshaft were supposed to be traditionally manly. They would not get in wearing perfume, including after-shave lotions, because these signified 'society's feminization of men' (p. 53). Inside there was 'hardly any conversation to disrupt the mood' (p. 54). Laughter was certainly not allowed. The activities included fistfucking, in which the fist and forearm are inserted into the anus, and water sports. Equipment was provided for fisting, so that 'a man could climb into the sling, attach his feet to stirrup-like appendages that lifted his limbs up and apart, and offer his exposed anus to his accomplice' (p. 54). There was a bathtub for those who wanted to be urinated on, and some men might spend an entire night in the tub. There were stocks, chains and manacles, and a cross. The club owner employed professional sex industry dominators, and coaches were paid to show novices the ropes. This was a practice that developed as part of the sex industry, and depended upon creating acolytes for future profits. Clubs such as this disappeared for some years after the AIDS epidemic developed, but were reinvented as 'safe-sex' clubs.

Preston echoes Levine in asserting that the bottom in the SM sex club is no less masculine than the top. Preston explains that the bottom proves his masculinity by endurance. 'The men who climb into the sling to be fist-fucked are *enduring* the act, and they have an audience to prove that they passed the test' (p. 60). The gay man being flagellated is 'the Sioux Indian enduring hooks in his chest; this is the walk across hot coals in Polynesia; this is the way a male can enter manhood'. The bottom is 'man enough' to 'suck cock in public', and 'invites the audience to watch him as he gets on his knees in front of another man dressed in the attire of overt masculinity: the leather of the biker, the uniform of the military man, the outfit of the athlete, all of them garb of this community's expression of masculinity' (p. 60).

Another 'fascinating element' of the activities of such clubs, Preston tells us, is that the punishment that the bottom endures needs to be administered by an older man. Thus *Drummer* magazine, to which he attributes the 'codification of the icons of the sex clubs', has promoted the idea that 'daddies' should 'initiate their "Boys" into adulthood' (p. 61). When an older man is fisting a younger man, he is 'passing on the ancient rites of the tribe. He is making sure that the passage to malehood is done appropriately and with ample regard to the rules of the clan' (p. 62). Though, as Preston admits, some men may just go to SM clubs for the sake of anonymous sex, the true 'celebrants' are those who go as 'aspirant and mentor, the teacher and student and the gathering of a tribe of men', so that 'Rough male sexuality, including public acts of bondage, flagellation, fist-fucking, and cocksucking, give the supplicant a means to show his tribe that he is ready to become a man' (p. 62).

Sadomasochism as New Age religion

For a good number of its adherents, gay male SM is regarded as a religion, or at least part of their spiritual practice. Preston uses religious language when describing SM. Ivo Dominguez in his odd little ode to the New Age possibilities of gay male SM, *Beneath the Skins: The New Spirit and Politics of the Kink Community*, is another who does so (Dominguez 1994). He explains, 'I am a spiritual person, and I believe strongly in the essential health and rightness of my Kink sexuality' (p. 11). He says that he is a Wiccan priest. Like Preston, he sees SM as providing an important ritual for gay men, and as having 'tribal' roots, for, 'Unlike our tribal forbears we have little exposure to meaningful rituals in daily life' (p. 58).

He spells out the common justification for the gay community welcoming sadomasochists. They are an oppressed community, just like 'Women, People of Color, and Gay/Lesbian people', and must be mainstreamed into lesbian and gay organizations, marches and culture. Those who are critical he accuses of 'leatherphobia that is homophobia's first cousin' (p. 14). This is an interesting tactic of those who oppose criticism of any aspect of gay or lesbian behaviour. Such criticism, sometimes called 'biphobia' when applied to bisexuality or transphobia when applied to transsexual surgery, is likened to a mental illness, which tends to discourage ordinary discussion. The practices themselves are seen as natural, inevitable and always with us, rather than historically contingent and socially constructed. Acceptance is seen as the only correct approach. Dominguez, for instance, tells us that there 'have always been Leather/SM/Fetish people' (p. 13), the denizens of his 'kink community'.

He too sees SM as being about masculinity, but calls it 'butch'. He is intolerant of those who are so bold as to make a political criticism of this masculinity: 'There are prudish, anti-sex feminists, radical faeries espousing sissy fascism, and Leftist demagogues who would theorize or deconstruct *butch* out of existence, were it possible to do so' (p. 58). His confident masculine bias is clear in his description of a religious experience which he had at a ritual when three men acted out the gay male archetypes: drag queen, leatherman and teacher/priest. Both drag queen and leatherman are forms of identity created specifically out of male domination, and depend upon the existence of a subordinate class of women. But as the men acted their parts, so 'real magic happened', and people came close to tears (p. 72). The archetypes are the three faces of the 'Queer god', so no wonder lesbians have some difficulties feeling integrated into queer culture. The leatherman archetype turns out to be rather alarming for anyone concerned to counter aggressive masculinity rather than worship it:

> He is the wild man. The animal powers course through his being.... He marks his territory with piss, with cum, with the red welt of his whip.... He is the irresponsible force of Eros and the sour sweat stink of panic offered as incense to a universe too vast to be comprehended.... With his strop, he hones the knife's edge that free will dances upon. (p. 75)

The leatherman represents precisely the forces of male dominance that are presently causing not just destruction to individual women in the form of physical and sexual violence, but destruction to the environment. It may be necessary for those who are concerned to create a different kind of world to be leatherphobic in a serious way.

Lesbians imitate gay SM

The lesbians who were to promote sadomasochism in the lesbian community, such as Pat (now Patrick) Califia, learnt their practice in mixed settings with straight and particularly with gay men. Califia acted as a fister to gay men, and gained whatever pleasures of dominance are to be milked from such power over men. Such lesbians were avid and precise learners. They read *Drummer*, the male gay SM magazine, and gay male porn, and were happy to explain that they learnt everything therein and are lost in admiration. However, for lesbians SM does not offer quite the same political pay-off. Through SM, lesbians can achieve a temporary masculine power, but this power does not last outside the sex venue. Walking down the street, a butch man retains masculinity, whereas a woman does not.

Gayle Rubin, the influential lesbian theorist of SM, says that gay men had an SM subculture before lesbians had even imagined such a development (Gomez et al. 1998). Rubin, like the other lesbians she converses with in the collection *Opposite Sex*, reproaches lesbian feminism for being timid and narrow about sex, so that adventurous lesbians had to learn from men. Though it might seem clear from such straightforward remarks that lesbians did indeed learn SM from gay men, Rubin expresses annoyance that I should draw such inferences. She accuses me of exemplifying the view that 'blames gay men for all the lesbian behavior that's considered reprehensible' (p. 124). No, she says; lesbians and gay men have had an equal influence on each other. It is instructive to try to imagine the ways in which lesbians have helped construct gay male sex, politics or life-style. Not much comes to mind. Indeed, Jewelle Gomez, the lesbian poet, says, in the same discussion with Rubin and Amber Hollibaugh, that she has learned much from gay men, but does not think that this works the other way round, partly because gay men have a much higher 'ick' factor – i.e. find lesbians disgusting.

Meanwhile Amber Hollibaugh is determined to make lesbians into simulacra of gay men. She says she is 'incredibly interested in their sexuality, because I really feel like it's information about my own':

> Amber: I feel like a lot of the themes of sexual desire are similar, even if the sexual practices are different. Like semen is not the same . . . . But my girlfriend fucks me and we talk about her cock getting hard. It's like an important piece of our lives. And it's amazing that there's nothing correspondingly interesting, intrinsically interesting to men, or worth investigating about my sexuality. (p. 128)

Hollibaugh shows no awareness of the insights of feminist writers over thirty years that suggest that it is men's desires and ideologies, particularly complete obsession with the penis as the fulcrum of sex, that have structured how women are to do sex, and how they are always to experience a lack of the real equipment.

The lesbians in this conversation seem to feel no humiliation in being an admiration society for gay men. They function as the lesbian auxiliary, like the women who make sandwiches for straight men in their churches and sports. Yet the volume in which this drooling sycophancy occurs contains the famous essay 'The ick factor' (Rofes 1998b), in which Eric Rofes proclaims that one-third of gay men feel sick if they see naked women's bodies or think of lesbians doing sex. There is no equality here.

Lesbian sadomasochism and child sexual abuse

One factor which enabled sadomasochism to be taken up by sections of the lesbian community is the prevalence of histories of child sexual abuse. It is likely that child sexual abuse also influences the attraction of gay men to sadomasochism, but what is significant about SM amongst lesbians is that the connection with sexual abuse is very much an open secret. I can remember comments from the floor at conferences in the 1980s, when I or others criticized sadomasochism, which defended the practice as efficacious for incest survivors who were unable to access sexual pleasure in any other way. Quite detailed rationales were offered, such as that sadomasochism was cathartic, and would help incest survivors come to terms with their abuse through recycling it.

Lesbians involved in the 'daddy' scene within sadomasochism are remarkably straightforward about the origins of the practice in child sex abuse. Daddy dykes act out the role of the often very abusive father towards other lesbians who take on the roles of daughter or son. This is a practice which has been copied directly from gay male sadomasochism too. Daddy dykes explain that they got ideas for the practice from the male gay SM magazine *Drummer*. Lesbians did not invent it. But it has a particular resonance for lesbians who are incest survivors. The winner of the first annual Dyke Daddy Contest in San Francisco 1992 stated that 'Some people have been incested and are really into playing daddy. It helps them deal with their childhood experiences' (Due 1994: 196). Another daddy explains that she has 'had girlfriends who haven't known they were incest survivors until they discovered it with me .... We've had to be OK with the fact that it's hot. I think you have to rip the scab off and let it bleed before it can be healed' (p. 198).

Julia Penelope, the US lesbian feminist theorist, demonstrates considerable insight about the attraction of SM for lesbians. In her critiques of the acting out of hierarchies derived from the hetero-patriarchy for the purposes of sexual excitement, she uses her own experience to write incisively about the ways in which butch/femme role-playing and sadomasochism are connected with child sexual abuse. She explains that the ideology of sadomasochism and the 'polarities that make it "work"' incorporate our experience of power and control as children. Sado-masochism depends upon our memories of the power differential that exists between those who have power, adults, and those who don't, children, and our experi-ence of the violent acts adults committed against us because they could' (Penelope 1992: 120).

SM practitioners often talk of pain being necessary to enable them to overcome the barriers built up to survive sexual abuse. Penelope explains: 'And I also know the origins of my own wall – I built it as a last defence to protect my autonomy and sense of self against the perpetual assaults of adult predators' (p. 123). It is only 'extreme pain', she says, that can 'get through that numbing' (p. 127). She says that sadomasochism is a 'constructed' desire, learnt by the child who interprets abuse as love, since that is all she is receiving from the abusive father. Thus, 'In the mind of the beaten child, violence as an exercise of control equals love. In the mind of the raped daughter, sex as an exercise of power equals love' (p. 128).

Cutting, piercing and self-mutilation

The cutting and piercing industry which developed in the 1990s originates, to a large extent, in gay sadomasochism. Extreme forms of self-mutilation became signals of gay identity and rites of passage for many young lesbians and gay men. Cutters and piercers in city centre shops are paid to cut up the bodies of these young people in order that they may express their identities. The studio sites linked to the website of the *Body Modification Ezine* all provide photographs of their work, which includes the carving of wings on the full extent of women's backs or other pictures into arms, stomachs and calves, and an extraordinary array of piercings of all parts of the body. Some of the 'artwork' is labelled 'fresh' in reference to the blood. Some of these web pages have rainbow flags and the slogan 'Out and proud' at the bottom of the page. The cutters know where their bread is buttered, and frequently they are themselves gay or lesbian. The industry of mutilation then went on to draw in young heterosexual women, abused young men, some of whom see themselves as sexually neuter, and the physically disabled. Sadomasochism in queer circles is not hermetically sealed away from straight society, but has considerable impact on what is considered ordinary sex or ordinary body decoration therein. Gay SM practitioners, for instance, in their roles as creators of a piercing and cutting industry, in the creation of mutilation pornography for straight male audiences, and in the celebration of mutilation and SM themes in the fashion industry, have an influence in the cultural normalization of self-mutilation. This has particular implications for women.

The industry of self-mutilation that has developed out of gay sadomasochism exploits the practice of self-mutilation in which young women cut and burn their bodies in private. What is generally referred to as self-mutilation in mental health literature comprises attacks on the skin or bodily organs such as the eyes or genitals, usually conducted in private and with the object of alleviating some mental distress (Favazza 1998). It can include head-banging, hitting and self-biting, 'enucleation, castration, and limb amputation', but most commonly 'refers to acts such as hair-pulling, skin scratching and nail-biting . . . as well as to skin-cutting, carving, burning, needle sticking, bone breaking, and interference with wound healing, which comprise the episodic and repetitive subtypes' (p. x). In psychiatric literature, these practices are seen as symptoms or features of 'a number of mental disorders such as borderline, histrionic, and anti-social personality disorders' (p. x).

Most varieties of self-mutilation are far more prevalent in females. The SAFE, Self-Abuse Finally Ends, programme in the USA which treats self-mutilators, for instance, sees females overwhelmingly (Strong 1998: 187). Feminist researchers who have worked with or interviewed self-mutilators have found one explanation in a particular aspect of male dominance, men's sexual abuse of children. Marilee Strong found a very clear connection amongst the self-injurers she interviewed for her landmark feminist approach to the issue, *A Bright Red Scream*. Nearly all of the more than fifty self-injurers she interviewed had suffered some form of child abuse or neglect

(Strong 1998: p. xvii). Cutting is explained as a way of dealing with the dissociation which is frequently a consequence of childhood sexual abuse. A study of women Special Hospital patients gives strong evidence of the links between mutilation and childhood abuse, not all of it sexual. Some 92 per cent of patients said that their self-harming was linked to previous life experiences, including in rank order (1) sexual abuse; (2) family stress, rejection or blame; (3) physical, emotional and psychological abuse; (4) illness of a family member or close friend; (5) bullying at school and leaving school (Liebling et al. 1997: 429).

When referring to practices of mutilation which, though often pursued by the mutilated, are carried out by another, I use the term 'self-mutilation' by proxy. I think that it is a useful term to apply to a range of practices in which another person is employed, such as a top in sadomasochism, a cosmetic surgeon, a piercing practitioner or a surgeon who performs transsexual surgery, to perform the mutilation desired by the victim. Though the cutting in these contexts is carried out under the aegis of medicine or beauty, or even sexual liberation, it often replicates quite precisely the techniques employed by solitary self-mutilators. Self-mutilation by proxy is linked to self-mutilation in private, by the fact that it is practised overwhelmingly by groups within society with unequal access to power or influence as a result of their sex, their sexuality or their disability. The proxies, generally for profit, though in the case of sadomasochism it may be simply for personal gratification, re-enact upon the bodies of the oppressed the violence that many of them suffered in childhood or adulthood from men.

'Body modification', as the practices of mutilation are called by those who profit from it, has been developed in the last ten to fifteen years into a burgeoning industry. One force behind this phenomenon is gay sadomasochism; the other is punk culture. Martin Levine tells us that tattoos and piercings were part of the image of gay men who aspired to masculinity in the fashionable gay bars and clubs of the 1970s (Levine 1998). He considers that the cult of masculinity amongst gay men expanded outwards to influence fashion and design in the malestream world through gay designers and photographers. Thus, 'many of these gay fads and fashions of the 1970s have become institutionalized in a more generalized, sexually fluid, youth culture. What gay men wore in the late 1970s is today's trendiest haute couture' (p. 5). Gay fashion designers promoted gay sadomasochist practices to an audience of young heterosexual women by using pierced women on catwalks in the early Nineties. As Marilee Strong puts it: 'Jean-Paul Gaultier, the late Gianni Versace, and other designers have built entire collections around tattoo designs, piercings, tribal decorations, and bondage wear' (Strong 1998: 137). Piercing is just one of the practices relayed through gay fashion designers that have become *de rigeur* for women, though designed originally to enhance the femininity or masculinity of gay men.

From the two major routes of gay sadomasochism and punk adornment developed the cottage industry of self-mutilation in which practitioners carry out piercings, cuttings, brandings and tattoos in studios internationally, which are advertised on the Internet. The customer base is potentially very large indeed, since it includes not just a generation of young people who have been taught that piercing is chic, but also the millions of serious cutters who have previously cut up in secret and in shame, and now have access to public approbation.

Fakir Musafar is the figure most frequently cited as the father of the 'body modification movement'. Musafar, who was originally an ad executive, developed his practice in a gay male SM group in California in the 1970s. He has been spectacularly successful in promoting mutilation to lesbians, gay men and other socially despised groups, using a pseudo-spirituality to appeal to his customers. He purports to be replicating the rites of other cultures in piercings. Though keen to promote piercing as a spiritual experience, he none the less gives examples of women using it as part of their attempt to recover from sexual abuse. He quotes the words of a piercee whose sentiments were 'common especially among women who had been raped': 'I'm getting pierced to reclaim my body. I've been used and abused. My body was taken by another without my consent. Now, by this ritual of piercing, I claim my body back as my own. I heal my wounds' (Musafar 1996: 329).

Musafar's reach extends beyond lesbians and gay men through his magazine *Body Play*, which is body modification pornography aimed at male readers. It features female African children who have suffered genital mutilation, women whose bodies have been contorted by corsets, who have had ribs removed to make tiny waists, and women who have used torture instruments on their feet to enable them to fit into impossibly high heels. The women in the magazine have breast cuttings and other forms of cuttings and piercings. The magazine is written as if these women just happen to be doing these interesting things to their bodies for the male voyeurs who happen upon them, rather than as a classic sex industry magazine. Its content is more disturbing than much pornography, because the injuries sustained are so severe. What Musafar's magazine demonstrates is that gay male sadomasochism can play a significant role in servicing and constructing men's pornographic ownership and destruction of women.

Since Musafar was a self-mutilator as a child, piercing his own penis at age thirteen (Myers 1995: 163), it is very possible that he was responding to abuse, rather than making a commercial decision in taking up the profitable enterprise that his mutilation practice has become. At a series of mutilation workshops for lesbian and gay sadomasochists described by James Myers, Musafar was one of the professionals who was branding participants. The ordinary collateral damage that results when commercial mutilation is carried out is treated very casually by Musafar. Whilst branding a lesbian, 'Musafar inadvertently brushed the edge of her left foot with a "cooled" brand as he returned it to the torch for renewed heating. Musafar rubbed some Vaseline on the brand and the foot burn, and the volunteer sat up and put her low-cut boot back on. The audience applauded' (p. 166).

Jim Ward was another mutilator practising at the workshop. He has been involved in piercing since the mid-1970s, and quickly extended his lucrative practice beyond gay men. As well as a piercing shop and business called Gauntlet, he set up *Piercing Fans International Quarterly*, which includes much mutilatory pornography directed at straight men, in which women receive wounds which, in some stories, sound too severe for survival (see Jeffreys 1990a: 218–21). Gay mutilators like Ward and Musafar influence male-stream pornography. They teach straight men practices of mutilation to try out on women for their own sexual excitement.

Another professional at the workshop was Raelynn Gallina. She explains that her lesbian customers are likely to be sexual abuse victims. 'Piercing is really a rite of passage. Maybe a woman is an incest victim and wants to reclaim her body' (Myers 1995: 167). Her first volunteer for nipple piercing was 'an achondroplastic dwarf in her thirties', who had a clearly visible recent cutting on her breast saying "The bottom from Hell" (p. 168). Gallina moved on to do a cutting workshop in which, having cut up a woman's back, she 'then ignited a fresh rinsing of alcohol with her cigarette lighter. A loud poof was heard, and a bluish flame danced across the entire left side of Rosie's back' (p. 171). The flash and burn were repeated twice more.

The invention by lesbians and gay men of practices of extremely serious self-harm should be a matter of concern to those still interested in lesbian and gay liberation. Some of those being injured have clearly suffered male violence in youth or adulthood. Others have just suffered the oppression, brutalizing and bullying that comes with the turf for many young lesbians and gay men. In a legal theory collection on human rights, Rhoda Howard writes most interestingly about the way in which self-mutilatory practices – and she means such women's practices as cosmetics, high-heeled shoes and eating disorders – arise from a socially despised status. Her understanding of such status includes homosexual men. As she explains:

> Inequalities between the two sexes are not simply a matter of ana-
> chronistic customs surviving into the modern era. They are deeply
> rooted in women's symbolic meaning and in the almost universal
> tendency to degrade them, even in the liberal Western world. Like
> other degraded social categories such as homosexuals, blacks and
> Jews... women experience inferiorization in everyday life. (Howard
> 1993: 514)

Gay men are a socially degraded group by any standards, and have been immensely influential in disseminating the practices of self-mutilation. Men's involvement in self-mutilation can also be explained through understanding the effects of child sexual abuse. Though there is considerable evidence for links between childhood sexual abuse and self-mutilation in women, such evidence is harder to come by for men. However, in a recent collection, *Gay Men and Childhood Sexual Trauma*, therapists discuss the ways in which child sexual abuse causes gay men to pursue in adulthood self-destructive sexual practices (Cassese 2000). There is anecdotal evidence, moreover, in the stories which gay sadomasochists, pornographers and transsexuals tell about their lives (Preston 1993). It seems likely that where membership of a despised group such as that of women, lesbians or gay men is combined with the experience of child sexual abuse, some of the more extreme forms of self-mutilation which threaten actual self-annihilation may be embarked upon.

Sadomasochism and the law: implications for opposing violence against women

SM practitioners are at risk of prosecution for the injuries they inflict upon one another. A famous case in the UK, *R. v Brown*, or the Spanner case, in which gay male sadomasochists were prosecuted for actual bodily harm and for aiding and abetting bodily harm, has led to a campaign to protect practitioners from legal penalties. The Spanner Trust in the UK, an organization that represents the interests of gay male sadomasochists, seeks to change the law to protect SM practice by making 'consent' a defence in the case of actual bodily harm. The Trust had enough political clout with John Major's Conservative government to get special legislation drawn up to this end. The legislation was later dropped because of a feminist outcry. Feminist anti-violence organizations have pointed out that such a change would create significant obstacles in the way of women's chances of getting their complaints of battery and sexual violence by men taken seriously.

The Spanner Trust was set up to fund and support the appeal of the gay men who were convicted in the Spanner case. Its title comes from the name given by police to an operation which involved the seizure of video films made during sadomasochistic encounters involving as many as forty-seven gay men. As a result, several men were charged with a series of offences, including assault and wounding. The acts in question are described in the text of the European Court judgment on this case:

> The acts consisted in the main of maltreatment of the genitalia (with, for example, hot wax, sandpaper, fish hooks and needles) and ritualistic beatings either with the assailant's bare hands or a variety of implements, including stinging nettles, spiked belts and a cat-o'-nine tails. There were instances of branding and infliction of injuries which resulted in the flow of blood and which left scarring. (European Court Judgment 1997: para. 8)

In December 1990 sixteen of the men pleaded guilty and received jail sentences, suspended sentences or were fined. Some of these men then appealed against their convictions and sentences. The convictions were upheld, though the sentences were reduced on the grounds that the men may not have known that the practices were illegal. The grounds upon which the House of Lords in 1993 upheld the convictions were that consent cannot be a defence in the case of assault that causes actual bodily harm or injuries of a lasting nature. A further appeal to the European Court failed in 1997.

In response to the exhaustion of all the appeal processes, pro-SM lobbyists in the UK chose to pursue a change in British law. They were remarkably successful, to the extent that a Home Office consultation paper was drawn up, which recommended changing the law to address their concerns. The consultation paper on 'Consent and the Criminal Law' was sent to gay groups for comment in 1996. It introduced the principle of consent to assault, which had not previously existed, so that sadomasochists could not be found guilty of a crime so long as their victims 'consented'. The Law Commission document proposed that 'the consensual infliction of injury that falls short of seriously disabling injury should in general be lawful'. An injury was considered to be serious if it

(a) causes serious distress, and
(b) involves loss of a bodily member or organ, or permanent bodily injury, or permanent functional impairment, or severe or prolonged pain, or serious impairment of mental health, or prolonged unconsciousness;

and an effect is permanent regardless of whether or not it is remediable by surgery (Hackett 1997).

The document called for views on the burden of proof that should be required as to the consent of the victim. Two possibilities were put forward. According to the first, it would be up to the defence to prove 'on the balance of probabilities' that the person injured 'consented to injury of the type caused, or (in the case of injury recklessly caused) to the risk of such injury or to the act or omission causing the injury'. According to the second, it should be up to the prosecution to prove 'beyond reasonable doubt, that the person did not so consent'. In the latter case the batterer could plead mistaken belief in consent, suggesting that 'it is the state of mind of the perpetrator rather than the acts themselves or the effects on the victim that should be considered' (p. 2). It is this last suggestion that would be likely to have the most serious impact on the possibility of women proving acts of domestic violence.

Feminist anti-violence groups were not consulted, and they found out rather late about the document. Many then sent in submissions declaring their outrage and grievous concern that the notion of consent to assault would strip away protection from women battered by male partners. The batterers would be able to argue that they had genuinely believed their partners to be consenting to the battery. As West Yorkshire Justice for Women put it, 'The proposals put the interests of a few sado-masochists above those of hundreds of thousands of women. At a time when we are finally succeeding in getting the police to bring prosecutions for domestic violence, these proposals, if they become law, will make it much more difficult to get convictions' (Justice for Women 1996: 1). The feminist outrage does seem to have been effective in stopping the proposals from being pursued at this time. It is worrying that they could have been drawn up and sent out for comment without any consideration for, or attempt to consult, those for whom they held most serious implications – namely, women's organizations involved in fighting men's violence against women. It seems likely that gay sadomasochists cannot protect their 'right' to sexually violent and exploitative practices without endangering women's safety. The celebration of 'consensual' violence is inextricably linked to non-consensual violence.

The Spanner Trust has not given up its advocacy of gay SM rights. The Home Office in 2001 published a paper for comment, summing up its suggestions for changing the law on sexual offences. The consultation paper is wide-ranging, and includes much that is to the advantage of women and gay men. It does not recommend any change in the law on consent. The Spanner Trust's submission in response expresses disappointment that its concerns have not been met. It argues that SM 'is an integral part of sexuality for a significant part of the population and therefore should have been considered in the Review' (Spanner Trust 2001: para. 3).

The Spanner Trust's argument as to the effect of the ruling in the Spanner case is a little contradictory. The Trust argues that the criminal status of SM will mean that those who 'suffer injury' in SM and need medical attention 'may be discouraged from seeking such attention, thus potentially exacerbating a minor injury into a serious one' (para. 17). Thus it agrees that serious injury can occur. But it asserts that serious injury could happen only 'if there is an accident or if it arises from some unforeseen consequences'. The Trust continues to demand a change in the law of consent, so that there can be 'consent to physical injury, not amounting to serious injury, caused either directly or indirectly during any consensual sexual activity'. It concludes that the current law on SM is 'a gross intrusion into a person's sexual activity', and that there is 'no good reason to prohibit consenting adults from inflicting non-serious injuries for the purposes of sexual gratification'. It is unfortunate that the recognition of the infliction of injury as 'sexual expression' and its protection in law have become significant items on the queer political agenda in the UK. Gay liberation was, to its original visionaries, about creating positive change and the elimination of oppressive hierarchies of sex and gender. In the Spanner Trust version, gay liberation has become the defence of the right of some men to injure others enough to need medical attention at sex parties.

Though the majority of queer theorists, such as Carl Stychin (1995) in the UK and the Sex Panic grouping in the USA, defend SM as simply a form of sexual expression that requires protection, not all gay commentators whole-heartedly approve of sadomasochism. Chris Woods in the UK, in his critical commentary entitled *State of the Queer Nation*, is more ambivalent. He explains that the Spanner defendants were not revolutionaries involved in the promotion of sexual freedom or a 'sophisticated urban coterie', but rather 'middle-aged, pre-liberation homosexual males, some of whom despised themselves so much that their pursuit of SM was an attempt at self-obliteration' (Woods 1995: 53). Woods had interviewed the leading defendant, a man regarded by the gay community as a 'martyr', and found that he talked of his psychotherapy and the fact that he was doing SM 'due to a painful relationship with my father.... At one point I even got into the idea of being tortured to death. At the back of my mind I knew that wasn't natural.' The interviewee commented that 'If you meet someone who's mentally fucked up, then torturing them is only going to make things worse. One of X's boys was quite mixed up. He didn't need torturing, he needed help' (p. 53)

Sadomasochism, self-mutilation and internalized oppression

Chris Woods sees SM as reflecting the damage suffered by gay men and lesbians from the 'hypocrisy and hostility of society'. In the 1970s, he says, it was understood that people could suffer 'internalised homophobia, self-hatred brought on people both by the horrors of external oppression and the requirements of an often-brutal scene'

(Woods 1995: 54). Now it was taboo to suggest that role-playing and the 'scene' both arose from and reinforced the harm suffered from the oppression of homosexuality. The result is that 'as an antidote to our communities' failings, or as a badge of political nous, we encourage the pursuit of pain and abuse' (p. 54). Woods's insight into the connection between the practice of SM and the oppression suffered by gay men and lesbians is an important one. It is echoed by the sociologist Stephen O. Murray in his critique of queer theory. He points out that many of the practices labelled 'transgressive' in queer theory may in fact be the result of oppression rather than an antidote to it: 'I think that we need fewer celebrations of "transgression" and more analysis of how subalterns reproduce their own subordination, both intra-psychically (call it self-hatred, with "self" being a kind of person) and interpersonally (call it socialization)' (Murray 1997).

This analysis works well for sadomasochism and other practices of self-mutilation common in gay culture, such as cutting, piercing and tattooing. It also helps in understanding self-destructive practices that queer theory has not yet got around to celebrating as transgressive, such as alcohol and drug abuse and suicide. In a volume on the alarming rates of suicide amongst gay youth, Paul Gibson explains that as a result of receiving hatred and punishment for their gayness,

> Some gay youth have an uncaring approach to life that reflects a "suicidal script". They are more prone to self-destructive behavior because of the severity of the problems they have experienced throughout their lives and specifically in relation to their sexual orientation. Contracting AIDS becomes for them the fulfilment of a life of pain and suffering they no longer want to cope with. They feel that they deserve to die. (Gibson 1994: 53)

As well as leading to reckless behaviour over HIV/AIDS infection, such attitudes can lead to a reckless approach to the injuries of sadomasochism. Lesbians and gay men who have suffered multiple forms of abuse may not be in a good position to exercise 'consent', because they do not have enough self-love to want to protect their bodies and lives. It is precisely these 'uncaring' people who are most likely to be attracted to forms of self-mutilation by proxy.

David Plummer's fascinating research on the effects of homophobia in Australia demonstrates very well, through interviews with young men, how those who do not fit ideals of heterosexual masculinity are abused and bullied in school, and particularly in sports (Plummer 1999). He quotes a 1994 survey to show one dimension of the oppression of gay men and lesbians: harassment in public places. The survey, which took place in Sydney, found that 'both gay men and lesbians were at least five times more likely to experience verbal harassment in a twelve-month period than the "general community" had ever experienced' (Plummer 1999: 11). The 139 gay men in the sample were 'at least four times more likely than the general Sydney adult male population to experience an assault in a twelve-month period' (p. 11). Plummer's understanding of homophobia is a broad one. He understands it to represent the forces of hatred unleashed for any deviation by boys from the script of heterosexual masculinity. The homophobia manifests in teasing, bullying and violence, and, he argues, it constructs both homosexuality and heterosexuality and polices the boundaries. 'In effect, homophobia precedes sexual identity, separates erotic practice, links difference with sexuality and thereby creates homosexual and heterosexual identities' (p. 214). The enforcers harass such behaviours as 'crying, being academic, not playing football, being girlish, being a loner' (p. 295). The harassment causes some boys to feel 'different', which can then be interpreted by them as being homosexual. Similarly, heterosexual identities are constructed to escape the harassment. This understanding of 'homophobia' as the punishing and disciplining forces that shape the construction of sexuality under male dominance broadens our understanding of anti-gay oppression, whilst illuminating the suffering of the boys who do not fit in and are likely to end up gay.

Sadomasochism and other forms of self-harm should be seen as the result of oppressive forces such as sexual abuse, bullying, physical violence, hatred and contempt, rather than celebrated as 'transgressive' or even as signature gay practices. The celebration of damage should not be a sign of gayness. Another reason why sadomasochism is a matter of concern for feminists is because the influence of gay SM is not confined to the lesbian and gay community. The practices and fashions extend outwards into the heterosexual malestream world, so the cult of commercial cutting up can affect a whole generation of young heterosexual women, who will never know why belly button piercing happens to be fashionable. In the long run the fashionability of SM for influential gay lobbyists is likely to affect the fate of all women who suffer violence from men, if the lobbyists are successful in gaining a change in the law on consent. Not only is there nothing revolutionary about sadomasochism; it is an unsustainable practice. Serious social change such that masculinity is eroded as a social good, and gay men no longer act out their pain by slicing each other's bodies, will cause the practice to die out. Meanwhile the promotion of sadomasochism can usefully be combatted in many ways, by upholding the current laws on consent or strengthening them in women's interests, by expelling SM organizations from community facilities, and by opposing the celebration of the practice in lesbian and gay media and lesbian and gay space.

FTM Transsexualism and the Destruction of Lesbians

In the late 1980s and 1990s an epidemic of female-to-male (FTM) transsexualism began in Western countries. Women who had previously identified as butch lesbians, or been afraid to identify as lesbians despite loving women, began to opt for surgical mutilation. I call this the destruction of lesbians, because lesbians are physically destroyed in this surgery, and their lesbianism is removed along with female body parts. The lesbianism of their female partners is severely tested too, as they struggle to adjust to loving surgically constructed 'men' or leave. The FTMs are having double mastectomies and hysterectomies, and sometimes phalloplasties, which create lumps of inactive tissue in the genital area. They inject lifelong male hormones, with worrying effects upon their health. This issue has become, I suggest, an emergency for lesbian politics. In the 1970s, when radical lesbian and gay movements began, there was a strong awareness of the barbaric methods by which the medical profession in the twentieth century had sought to eradicate lesbianism, such as incarceration in mental hospitals, electric shock treatment and lobotomies (Katz 1978). At that time it was thought that a brand new day had dawned, in which these cruel forms of control would be ended, so that lesbians could live happily in their lesbian bodies. Transsexual surgery on lesbians, as a burgeoning practice, clearly shows that this optimism was unrealistic. In the twenty-first century the methods being used to get rid of lesbians are very much more cruel than we could have imagined thirty years ago.

The major stumbling block in the way of recognizing this state of emergency is the enthusiasm with which queer theory and politics have celebrated transsexual surgery. Transsexuals are accepted as an unproblematic category in the queer coalition of LGBT, represented as revolutionaries or quintessentially queer (Stryker 1998; Halberstam 1994). Few voices have been raised in protest, perhaps because those who have spoken out are accused of 'transphobia' and reviled. One notable exception is the inspirational US lesbian feminist singer and song-writer, Alix Dobkin, who has had the courage to speak out against FTM transsexualism in her concern for what is happening to young lesbians in her community (Dobkin 2000). In this chapter I will look at what is happening in this epidemic, and place it within its historical and political context in the oppression of lesbians. I will refer to FTMs with female pronouns and to MTFs with male pronouns in order to highlight their sex classes of origin. Use of the pronouns of the political class to which these people wish to be reassigned makes political analysis very difficult.

When lesbian feminists first became concerned about the issue of transsexualism, it was clear that the vast majority of those being 'reassigned' were men. Transsexualism was analysed as a form of social control and as creating the profits of a medical empire (Raymond 1994), but not as constituting a serious problem for lesbians. The picture has changed, however. In the late 1980s and the 1990s lesbians began to 'transition', as the aspirants call the process of changing from lesbians to FTMs, and the numbers, to judge by the websites, conferences and organizations now being set up, are escalating. The FTM Network in the UK, founded by Stephen Whittle, a self-help group for 'trans men', started in 1990, and now has 700 members in the UK and members in another twenty countries (Whittle 2000). Loree Cook-Daniels, in the USA, whose lover is an FTM, explains that she thought her situation unique until she talked to her friends and discovered that out of the first thirty coupled lesbian friends she talked to, three said that one of the partners 'felt she was also a female-to-male transsexual (FTM)', and a fourth that 'she had struggled with the question for many years before deciding to keep her female body and role' (Cook-Daniels 1998). Sadly, Cook-Daniels's FTM partner committed suicide in 2000. A recent phenomenon is the 'transitioning' of lesbians to become 'gay men'. This does seem to be a new development, and is particularly common amongst lesbians who have spent years practising sadomasochism, often with gay men. Linnea Due, co-editor of the anthology *Dagger: On Butch Women* (1994), quotes the FTM David Harrison as saying that close to half of the 250 FTMs at a 1995 US conference on the issue were gay-identified (quoted in Due 1998: 210).

FTM transsexualism is a vital issue for lesbian politics, because the vast majority of the women who transition have identified as lesbians, or at least lived within the lesbian community and conducted relationships with lesbians. The attribution of masculinity to lesbians historically has formed a major tool of control. Lesbian feminists in the 1970s developed a sophisticated critique of the ways in which masculine scholarship and culture sought to disparage or disappear lesbians by portraying them as masculine or really wanting to be men. Many lesbians in the 1980s and 1990s rejected the understandings of feminism, and developed fashionable sadomasochism and butch/femme role-playing out of which the phenomenon of FTM transsexualism has arisen. Most of those who transition, despite their histories of lesbianism and fervent declarations, in some cases, that they were proud lesbians and would not have considered trans-sexing only a couple of years before, tend to seek a clear-cut distinction between themselves and lesbians. This is necessary because they wish to consider themselves 'men', and any connection with their earlier lesbianism would tend to undermine this understanding. Thus FTM activists tend to stress that 'There is no correlation between sexual orientation and gender identity' (Amboyz 2000).

Holly Devor's study of the FTM phenomenon, which was carried out through interviewing forty-five FTMs, does not support the idea that there is such a distinction (Devor 1999). The vast majority of her interviewees had been, and were presently, involved in relationships with women at the time of their 'transition'. Nineteen participants had been involved in sexual relationships with other females during adolescence. Ten of her participants found lovers and identities among women who defined themselves as lesbian feminists during the 1970s and 1980s. Devor attributes some of the blame for these women deciding that they must be 'men' instead of lesbians to the influence of lesbian feminism on the construction of lesbian identity. Lesbian feminists saw the imposition of gender roles as the foundation of male supremacy, and were therefore critical of lesbians who took on such roles. According to Holly Devor, this made the lesbian feminist-influenced community a less friendly place for lesbians who like to trick themselves out with masculinity and see themselves as butch. When they felt excluded from the lesbian feminist community, then the only alternative was to actually become men. She explains that participants in her research who had 'been drawn to lesbian identities on the basis of older definitions of lesbians', which included masculinity, felt 'ashamed, embarrassed, or disgusted by the specifically female aspects of their bodies and therefore had little desire to join with their companions in the glorification of their womanhood' (Devor 1999: 343). Their discomfort in a lesbian community which now rejected 'masculine' lesbians was alleviated by the discovery of the 'socially available concept of female-to-male transsexualism'.

Judith Halberstam, who identifies herself as a transgender butch, and C. Jacob Hale, who identifies herself as FTM, are concerned at the ways in which false distinctions may be being created in aid of asserting the uniqueness of those who decide to call themselves FTM. They explain that 'FTMs complained that butches (seen unequivocally as lesbian women or as just "playing" with gender) were incorrectly identifying themselves as transgendered or transitioning. Some FTMs felt that their transsexual or male seriousness and uniqueness were being diluted by the presence of butches' (Halberstam and Hale 1998: 283). Hale argues that there is only the difference of self-identification between those who call themselves butch and those who decide they are FTM. She says that, 'Contemporaneously, self-identification as butch or ftm is the only characteristic that distinguishes some butches from some ftms' (Hale 1998: 325). She explains that a hierarchy has been created in which lesbians, both butch and those who decide they are FTM, compete to be more masculine than each other: 'the guy with the biggest dick wins' (p. 327). This should create some difficulties for the surgeons and sexologists who have previously prided themselves on being able to tell the difference between real transsexuals who deserve surgery and others. The pretence that there are 'real' ones is now hard to maintain.

Halberstam explains that 'the distinctions between some transsexuals and lesbians may at times become quite blurry. Many FTMs do come out as lesbians before they come out as transsexuals' (Halberstam 1998b: 293). Many identified as butch in the lesbian community before transitioning, and continue to want to maintain their ties to that community. But many of the writings and stories of FTMs try 'to cast the lesbian pasts of FTMs as instances of mistaken identities or as efforts to find temporary refuge within some queer

gender-variant notion of ''butchness'' ' (p. 294). She says that Internet FTM sites offer tips for FTMs so that they will not be suspected of
being just butch lesbians, such as dressing in a preppy manner rather
than in black leather jackets. She seems concerned that FTMs are
seen as outperforming butches (like herself) in transgression, the
pinnacle of queer politics: 'FTMs are often cast as those who cross
borders (of sex, gender, bodily coherence), while butches are left as
those who stay in one place' (p. 304). In the battle to be more
masculine than thou, these lesbians seem to be battling over the
scarce goods of masculine power and privilege. If too many lesbians
were to claim them, then the value of the goods might decrease.
Halberstam suggests why some butches might not wish to be so
transgressive as to transition. Some lack the money, and some are
attached to 'gender queerness'. Others don't think it is worth it as
long as functional penises remain a technological impossibility.
Others, like herself, may simply prefer to be a butch, or transgender,
without becoming a 'man'.

Since so many of the writings of the current transgender activists
make it clear that transsexualism is in fact an extension of butchness,
rather than a distinct phenomenon, it is useful to examine the development of the cult of lesbian role-playing in the 1980s, in order to
understand how this occurred. For our critiques of this development
in lesbian culture, Halberstam calls the lesbian feminist philosopher
Marilyn Frye and me 'sex-negative' (see Jeffreys 1989; Halberstam
1998b: 308). Now it seems that we might have been underestimating
the damaging effect of the promotion of role-playing in that period.
FTM transsexualism is a very serious result.

Butch-femme role-playing

The lesbian liberation movement that exploded into life in the USA
in the late Sixties and continued around the Western world was
founded upon the rejection of the 'sex roles', as they were called, of
heterosexist culture. The movers and shakers of lesbian liberation
criticized the acting out of the sex roles of heterosexual culture by
lesbians, called lesbian role-playing. Lesbian liberation exemplified
the feminist idea that women could reinvent themselves and throw
off the yoke of expected behaviours, whether these were based upon
dominant masculinity or subordinate femininity. Lesbians were free

to create a quite new form of womanhood that would explode this binary division and allow women to find new ways of being, beyond gender. The construction of equal relationships outside the role-playing of male dominance and female subordination has been one of the aspects of lesbian feminism that has inspired most pride and been most attractive to other women (Gottschalk 2000).

In the 1980s, however, butch/femme role-playing, aping the most exaggerated versions of femininity and masculinity available in heterosexual culture, became fashionable in some influential sections of the lesbian community. Lesbians such as Merrill Mushroom, Joan Nestle and Amber Hollibaugh popularized role-playing as a form of watered-down sadomasochism in which lesbians could experience the delights of eroticized dominance and submission (see Jeffreys 1989). The celebration of masculinity came to dominate areas of lesbian culture such as the new lesbian pornography and the drag king phenomenon in which lesbians publicly imitated gay men and received prizes for the exactitude of their imitations (Volcano and Halberstam 1999). By the 1990s, some lesbians claimed that authentic butchness could be realized only through undergoing surgical or chemical self-mutilation to turn lesbians into straight or gay men.

The butch/femme role-playing that became fashionable in the 1980s was not very sophisticated. The model of femininity and masculinity that the main American proponents of role-playing have adopted, as exemplified in the anthology *The Femme Mystique* (Newman 1995), is an exaggerated version of the sort of heterosexual dynamics that exist in 1950s Hollywood movies or old-fashioned romance novels. The femininity adopted by femmes involved an inequality – doing most of the housework – and an acquired powerlessness that would probably have no appeal for heterosexual women in the present. Kelly Conway says that she was raised by two butches and then learnt to be femme. She was taught by a girl-friend 'the erotic dynamic of butch-femme. It turned me on when she opened doors for me' (Conway 1995: 301). Despite having had to be taught, she none the less claims that femmeness is her 'real' self: 'Today I know that to be butch or femme is not to play a role but to express one's self' (p. 302). Her motivation appears to be a kind of romantic masochism. 'I am in constant awe of my butch: her strength and intelligence, and the power in her ability to be so gentle. . . . It is liberating to be able to turn to strong arms during a nightmare, delegate spider patrol, and allow myself to be vulnerable and nurturing' (p. 302).

Housework is divided by strict role-players along extremely rigid gender lines, according to rules they have imitated or invented. Thus Kelly cooks for her butch, who takes out the rubbish. 'Jill has garbage and bug duty...I have made our relationship the number-one priority in my life. I love to cook for her, nurture her, and make our home comfortable.... The look on her face when she comes home and the house smells like home cooking and I'm dressed like dessert makes it all worthwhile' (p. 302). Most of the femmes in the *Femme Mystique* anthology agree, for some reason, that butches must take out the rubbish. Theresa Carilli, writing as a butch, tells us that 'Femmes pay particular attention to color schemes' (Carilli 1995: 151). Femmes do most of the housework and the most tedious parts: 'Femmes love tasks which are never finished. Often you might find her vacuuming and revacuuming' (p. 151) and they 'also enjoy washing dishes' (p. 152). The anthology's title, *The Femme Mystique*, alludes to the classic feminist text of 1963, Betty Friedan's *The Feminine Mystique* (1965). But Friedan's book criticizes precisely the confining expectations that the role-playing anthology celebrates.

The unequal power dynamics set up by such role-playing create the foundation for a sexual interaction based upon dominance and submission. Lesbian feminists are attacked for promoting a form of egalitarian sexuality. Liz O'Lexa, for instance, attacks feminists because they 'won't take the responsibility for sex...don't believe in courtship...don't believe in one who says no and one who says yes' (O'Lexa 1995: 213). Lesbian feminists opposed the heterosexual dynamic in which males are imbued with the sexual initiative and women are given only the power to say yes or no. In the SM sexual practice of role-playing, butches are strong and femmes surrender; as O'Lexa puts it, 'let me feel all your strength, let me submit to you, be the butch for me'(p. 213).

Not surprisingly, the femmes seem to experience the traditional ills associated with the subordinate role of women. Sue O'Sullivan's article on this theme is an example of what may soon become a flood of femme complaint as the excitement of sadomasochism wears off (O'Sullivan 1999). The femme problems that she articulates sound not dissimilar to the criticisms that heterosexual women made of the negative effects upon their lives of similarly exaggerated masculine/feminine role-playing in the 1960s. Sue O'Sullivan, who came out as a lesbian and then as a femme in the UK, is now very disillusioned with her choice. She explains why she chose to be a femme. She 'fell into swooning love with butch lesbians' (p. 465). She was identified as a femme by those around her. She wanted for some reason to be rebellious 'against feminism' and 'the rest of the world'. She loved dressing up and wearing hats, and she thought it 'made some sense'.

She learned the rules of femmeness from heterosexual romances read in childhood: 'My daydreams were fuelled by historical romances. I devoured *Gone With the Wind* when I was ten' (p. 466). She now sees old-fashioned heterosexual role-playing as having formed the model for her lesbian version: 'I managed to avoid confronting just how much my early visions of heterosexuality informed my lesbian relationships. I was overly confident that lesbian feminism changed the names of the games' (p. 467). She wonders whether she needed 'an othering' in order to allow herself to feel desire for women and to fit her desire 'into a recognizable scenario'. She suggests that her femmeness may represent 'the romantic script of an older generation of women, including lesbians' (p. 470).

She says it is time to 'reassess and admit personally' that the celebration of butch/femme role-playing often hides 'sadder realities' (p. 467). One of these realities is that some femmes are willing to be bullied by butches, and some butches are willing to bully. The determination to see lesbian role-playing as having nothing to do with heterosexuality, she considers, has made it more difficult to recognize its 'underside', which is ill-treatment of femmes by butches. She conducted a workshop on femmeness, and found that femmes 'described dismissive treatment by butch lesbians in their personal and social lives' (p. 470). As a result of feeling the emotional pain of being on the wrong end of too many romantic butch/femme relationships, she is sick of lesbian role-playing, which 'too often feels repetitive, compulsive and boringly predictable' (p. 467). She is sick of 'suits' and 'hanging on the arm of a butch', and the 'idea' that 'butch lesbians automatically swagger in a sexy way', and the 'self-conscious display of lesbian masculinity'. Instead of being sexually attractive to her, these things now often seem 'silly'.

Physical, as well as emotional, violence is apparently associated with lesbian role-playing. 'Butch' Sally Munt ponders: 'I wonder how to question how we can critically perceive hostility as a transformational crucible. There is violence in butch/femme, the violence of differentiation, supposedly necessary for the generation of desire. Butch/femme is precious, but it is also fraught' (Munt 1998: 9). It will be no surprise to any feminists who have worked on the issue of violence against women that dominance/submission dynamics in relationships are likely to result in physical violence. Lesbian role-playing seems to be no different.

Those lesbians who choose to be femmes have some responsibility for the FTM phenomenon. Femmes help to construct butches. They seek to satisfy the masochistic desires they developed whilst growing up in subordinate girlhood. Girls learn to love and have sexual feelings in a position of low status, and the eroticization of powerlessness is a normal part of the construction of femininity. Instead of seeking to change these feelings, women like Heather Findlay, editor of the US lesbian magazine *Girlfriends*, a femme who has had two lovers transition to become FTMs, indulge them. Her experience is evidence of just how common transsexualism has become in some parts of the lesbian community. She says she is sorry to have been born at a historical moment where medical technologies have made it so easy to 'change one's sex' (Findlay 1998: 136). She says she 'half-jokes' with friends that 'I'm experiencing what is becoming an occupational hazard for femmes at the close of the twentieth century: don't blink, because when you open your eyes your butch will have kissed her elbow and turned into a man' (p. 136). She wants her girl-friends to be masculine, because that is sexy for her, but wants them to stop short of actually becoming men.

Findlay does not see herself as having any responsibility for the tragedy of what happens to her lovers. Instead, she laments the problems caused her by having a girl-friend transition. She rejected Sue when she became John, but found that she had to 'come out as a lesbian all over again' (p. 142). People ask her why she doesn't want to be with her girl-friend now that she is a 'man'. She says: 'Today I got all pissed off, thinking, *It's like lesbianism 101. Everybody wants to know why you don't want to be with men. Men, men, men.* It doesn't occur to anyone to ask you why it is you love women' (p. 143). She says she feels 'bowled over by the realization that I've been living publicly as a lesbian for thirteen years, I'm a "professional lesbian" even, and yet on some deeper (unconscious?) level, I was fucking *straight*' (p. 145). When lesbians decide they are men, they destroy the lesbianism, and therefore the identity, of their lovers, unless those lovers, like Findlay, get out and start all over again. Some butches are now taking things a little too far, so that they are no longer exciting to their femme admirers but exasperating instead. The bleak realities of transsexualism do not yet seem to have dented the enthusiasm of femmes such as Findlay, though the pain and misery that FTMs go through ought perhaps to encourage a reconsideration.

FTM technologies and health

Both FTMs and MTFs are accessing surgery, silicone and hormones both from ordinary doctors and surgeons and from unofficial or criminal sources. Many cannot afford the surgery and hormones through regular channels. Many FTMs admit that they do not really see themselves as men, so would not be accepted as fitting the criteria set up by the sexological gatekeepers. Stephen Whittle, founder of the British FTM Network, is excited that a broad transgender community is now developing in the UK that is not limited to traditional sexological definitions. She says: 'Testosterone is a positive way for some women to affirm who they are – not just through butching it up on the bar scene but for themselves. We are seeing many more who don't actually want to become men, but who find their own expression' (Brosnan 1996: 41). Transition has evolved to resemble more familiar forms of cosmetic surgery, with FTMs acquiring operations and body-altering drugs in an *ad hoc* way. Some FTMs seem to be cosmetic surgery junkies. Della Grace, for instance, had had silicone implants to 'even up breast size' before she decided to transition, and then had to consider breast reduction (Brosnan 1996). Both forms of surgery derive from societal prescriptions for acceptable femininity and masculinity.

For the sexologists the horse of transsexualism has well and truly bolted. They may still be getting large profits from those who use their services, but they are no longer in control of the labelling. Only half of the participants in Devor's study went to gender identity clinics, and many of those got *ad hoc* treatments from general practitioners and plastic surgeons of testosterone and breast and womb removal. One speaks of having her breasts off in an 'assembly line' in a doctor's surgery, with terrible results (Devor 1999: 399). Cheapness is an important consideration, because FTM surgery is expensive. Estimates range from US$50,000 (Cook-Daniels 2000) to US$77,000 (Mason 2001). Costs like these drive aspirants to back-street surgery and the illegal drug trade. Such costs also suggest that the profits of drug companies and surgeons are important factors behind the contemporary promotion of transsexualism as a solution for unhappy lesbians.

Some of the lesbians wanting to transition have been exploring alternatives to genital surgery by modifying their bodies with piercings that Loren Cameron describes as 'relatively inexpensive and accessible'. 'The subject in one photograph has been taking testosterone: his clitoral enlargement is hormonally induced. Through a series of piercings, he is gradually pulling his larger outer labia together with several rings. By doing so, he hopes to produce a scrotum-like appearance and place more visual emphasis on his enlarged clitoris' (Cameron 1996: 54). Some aspirants select self-help treatments which are much cheaper, such as clitoral pumps, which are supposed to enlarge the clitoris (Hernandez 1998).

For those who have surgery to construct a phalloplasty – and most of Devor's participants did not bother with this – the pain and long-term damage to health, through a series of operations which create serious wounds, are considerable. The following description was given to a UK FTM, Raymond Thompson, by the surgeon who examined her before the first operation.

> 'We'll cut here,' he said to his assistant, drawing a ten-inch line from my groin, along the crease of my leg, to the side of my hip, 'and here,' and he made another line, parallel to the first line, but four and a half inches above.... 'We cut along these two lines and then lift the four and a half inch wide band of flesh and skin, along with an artery, up and away from your leg. We then make a coil, or a tube, by rolling it up lengthwise and stitching the length of the coil at the back. Both ends of this tube, your penis, will still be attached at your groin and your hip respectively, but the middle will be free and separated from your body'. (Thompson 1995: 286)

Whilst she was still in hospital, she suffered an infection in the newly constructed penis, and death of tissue due to poor blood supply. This was dealt with by very large doses of antibiotics. Once out of hospital, she had to live with the constructed penis attached to hip and leg for six months, during which she suffered great pain, walked with a limp, and was unable to have her cats on her lap. Then she returned to the hospital to have her phalloplasty detached from her leg in two stages. Prior to the second detaching operation, Thompson was told by the doctor that her 'penis' might go black at the end, and that she might lose some of it if the blood supply was not good enough. In fact, she did not lose any of it. For just one aspect of FTM transition, this woman had three major operations over many months and was in pain, taking large amounts of drugs and unable to work in between. Thompson's mother found a love letter she had written to a girl when she was eleven, telling her not to tell anyone about her feelings for girls, or 'there'll be murders'. This helped her to decide that she was really a boy. The surgery can be seen as just a continuation of the savage punishment she was to receive in life for her lesbianism.

There are serious health problems associated with both regular and under-the-counter surgeries and drugs. The negative health effects are rarely mentioned, such as hair loss and acne, or the physical deformations that result from the use of chemicals. Monthly injections of Sustanon, for instance, which is testosterone in a peanut oil base, can lead to 'hair loss, acne and enlarged jaw bones' (Brosnan 1996: 39). The surgery can lead to serious losses. Mastectomy can cause permanent loss of feeling in the nipples (Devor 1999: 480).

According to Dallas Denny (2000), an MTF psychologist who founded, and is executive director of, The American Educational Gender Information Service, transgendered youth are at particular risk of exploitation, with serious health risks. Young males and females seeking to change their bodies become victims of 'unscrupulous "practitioners" who perform quasi-medical services in exchange for money'. They feminize or masculinize their bodies with injections of hormones and liquid silicone. The hormones are often from forged prescriptions, and are injected in large quantities, sometimes into the genital and breast areas. The use of androgens can cause liver damage, and requires monitoring through blood tests. Many of those self-administering are street youth, prostitutes or those familiar with other forms of self-mutilation and not protective of their bodies in any way.

Queer theory justifications

Considering the pain, expense and sheer misery involved in transsexualism, it might be expected that academic lesbians would be critical of the project of acquiring masculinity. But no critique has emerged. Instead, in the 1990s some academic lesbians took up fashionable butchness, and found it necessary to justify their choice with complex language and ideas from queer theory. They sought to make the pursuit of masculinity seem like a heroic quest. Sally Munt is a UK lesbian academic who says that in her thirties she 'found a gender I could live in, and it found me' (Munt 1998: 2). Munt explains that she seeks to imitate her working-class father who taught her how to tie a tie. Despite the knowledge of women like Munt that she has exercised choice, and that gender is socially constructed, there is a tendency to make the role-playing sound somehow inevitable and beyond conscious control. Munt, when defending her choice, creates a kind of romance-novel excitement: 'Femme shame can emerge when what she really, really wants is the (lesbian) cock, but is not allowed to show it, or say it' (p. 5). But her writing is laced with more academic language. Thus she says that butch/femme role-playing is 'a tangible articulation, a form of lesbian desire which rubs up against us and becomes us, in our particular daily practices, in our mannerisms, in our deportment, in our sexual responses, in the diaphonous but ordinary dispositions of our days' (p. 3). For a lot of women, being rubbed up against is not an attractive idea, but suggests frotteurism in the London Underground. When a particular kind of sexual attraction is glorified with academic language and turned into a theory, it can be hard to criticize. Political analysis is detumescent, spoils the game, and is much resented.

Munt represents role-playing as revolutionary heroism, in which the lesbian feminists who are critical of role-playing are the enemy to be vanquished. 'Reclaiming a debased identity, and reconstructing a new self as a survivor, are replete with the symbolism of heroism. It is a movement of struggle, re-appropriation, and triumph. During the 1980s and 1990s we have reclaimed butch/femme as the erotic symbol *par excellence*' (p. 4). She allows herself a moment of self-doubt, and asks whether 'we have appropriated heterosexual gender binarism because of its pretensions to sexual realness' (p. 5). All the sound and fury of heroic confrontation does not fit well with this understanding that role-players may really just be trying to fit their sexual practice into a heterosexual model, because they do not feel up to a sexuality of equality. She has other concerns too. She wonders why the model for butchness must be working class, like her father. Lesbians fought to get lesbian studies into the academy, and it is a tragedy that the influence that has been gained should be used to promote the tawdry excitements of dominant/submissive sex.

Another lesbian who seeks to support her choice of butchness with academic queer arguments is Judith Halberstam (1998a). She says:

'I am using the topic of female masculinity to explore a queer subject position that can successfully challenge hegemonic models of gender conformity' (p. 9). The title of Judith Halberstam's book *Female Masculinity* suggests that the adoption of butchness is a form of social climbing. It is helpful to imagine substituting for Halberstam's title ones which show other oppressed groups seeking to emulate the behaviour and manners of the groups that oppress them – 'Working-Class Middle Classness', for instance, or 'Aboriginal Whiteness'. Halberstam's individualist solution to the oppression of women is to seek to move into the oppressor class, rather than to work collectively with the oppressed to end the system of oppression.

She writes: 'I was a masculine girl, and I am a masculine woman' (p. xii). Her book is an attempt to make her project of adopting masculinity seem politically and academically respectable. She grew up as a 'tomboy', as so many lesbians and even many heterosexual women have always done, but chose in adulthood to adopt a style of butchness that replicates precisely the working-class masculinity favoured by 1970s gay men. The photograph of her on the back cover shows that the masculinity she has adopted is the gay ideal of tough working class masculinity as described by Levine in *Gay Macho*: 'tight black tee shirt; faded, skin-tight, straight-legged Levis; work boots; and a black leather motorcycle jacket. All of these styles call for short hair, muscular bodies' (Levine 1998: 39). Halberstam crouches on the back cover of her book in cut-off black Tshirt, jeans, boots, cropped hair, looking like the sort of lad on the street whom it would be safest to avoid.

She writes of her indignation that the contributions that women have made to the construction of masculinity, historically and in the present, have been ignored. Masculinity still, she complains, gets associated solely with men, with no recognition that women can be masculine just as easily, and with no connection whatsoever to men or male power. Women can, and historically have, invented masculinity, she says, all by themselves. She believes that female masculinity has been ignored with 'clearly ideological motivations', and that this has 'sustained the complex social structures that wed masculinity to maleness and to power and domination' (Halberstam 1998a: 2). There is no reason, she considers, to connect masculinity with men at all; indeed, 'Masculinity, this book will claim, becomes legible as masculinity where and when it leaves the white male middle-class body' (p. 2). She doesn't believe that masculinity is biological, otherwise butches like herself might have difficulty having a piece of it. It is socially constructed, and somehow a choice.

The problem with her formulation – and it is a major one – is that masculinity cannot exist without femininity. On its own, masculinity has no meaning, because it is but one half of a set of power relations. Masculinity pertains to male dominance as femininity pertains to female subordination. In the queer, postmodern theory which informs Halberstam, masculinity has slipped its moorings from any connection with the power relations of male supremacy, and has floated off on its own as a sort of fashion accessory. As Halberstam laments, 'historically it has become difficult, if not impossible, to untangle masculinity from the oppression of women' (p. 4). This may be because the behaviour of the dominant in a system of domination actually would not have any meaning, could not even be envisioned, if that system of domination did not exist. Could the behaviour of slave-masters be invented in the absence of slaves, for instance? Halberstam essentializes masculinity into something which just *is*. Halberstam says that female masculinity should be discussed as if neither men nor male dominance existed, and lesbians were doing this out of a clear blue sky: 'I believe it is both helpful and important to contextualize a discussion of female and lesbian masculinities in direct opposition to a more generalized discussion of masculinity within culture' (p. 15).

She does show some understanding that femininity is not empowering in the way that masculinity is. She loathes femininity, which she sees as constricting women. Scholars, she says, 'have long pointed out that femininity tends to be associated with passivity and inactivity, with various forms of unhealthy body manipulations from anorexia to high-heeled shoes' (p. 268). So damaging to women and girls does she consider femininity to be that: 'It seems to me that at least early on in life, girls should avoid femininity. Perhaps femininity and its accessories should be chosen later on, like a sex toy or a hairstyle' (p. 268). But toxic femininity is not just a sex toy. It represents the subordination in opposition to which masculinity is constructed. In order for Halberstam to have masculinity, the majority of women must continue to be relegated to precisely the femininity she despises. Halberstam says that she 'personally experienced adolescence as the shrinking of my world' (p. 267). That shrinking is common to the experience of women, however, and most women who seek to understand and oppose it become feminists and challenge the male domination that is responsible. Halberstam eschews feminism, and adopts the individualist solution of getting some masculinity for herself.

Reasons for transsexualism

Academic queer theory's explanations of the desirability and transgressive nature of 'performing' or otherwise acquiring masculinity are somewhat discredited by the very humdrum reasons given by nonacademic lesbians who decide to 'transition'. The reasons given by FTMs relate straightforwardly to the oppression of women and lesbians and to child sexual abuse. The commonest reason given by FTMs for their decision to transition is discomfort with lesbianism and the idea that they would feel more comfortable loving women if they were not in a woman's body. This is what gay liberationists called 'internalized homophobia', or a hatred of one's same-sex attractions absorbed from the lesbian- and gay-hating culture. This problem was supposed to be solved by the promotion of gay pride. Transsexualism is the opposite of gay pride. Hatred of her own lesbianism is the motivation given by Mark Rees, the famous UK FTM who took the UK government to the European Court for the right to marry as a man in 1984 and failed. She makes it totally clear that as a working-class woman with no role models, attraction to women meant she had to become a man. She was in the Navy as a young woman and writes: 'My extreme horror of a physical relationship was not because of the fear of Service disapproval – others had risked it – but because of my abhorrence of my own body, being seen as a woman and unable to have a normal heterosexual relationship with a female' (Rees 1996: 59).

Holly Devor comments on the role of 'rampant homophobia' in the lives of her participants. It was responsible for 'temporarily derailing' their interests in 'pursuing sexual relations with females'. In some cases 'homophobic misinformation' was responsible for 'the idea in adolescent participants' minds that if they were sexually interested in women, then they either were or should be men' (Devor 1999: 302). Some put off having any relationships with women until after surgery, so that they would experience less psychological discomfort. Her participants did not want to be 'transgressive' but 'normal', and lesbianism did not fit with that ideal. They aspired to transsexual surgery because it would make them normal. Stan explains that she 'just could not tolerate being a lesbian...I couldn't consider myself that bad, that sinful' (p. 335). She wanted to be 'normal' and have a 'white picket fence'. Then she could get married, and 'People could be proud of us'. This impulse towards fitting in is a far cry from the embracing of transgression which some more public queer exponents of transsexualism express. It doesn't look very revolutionary.

It is clear from Devor's work that the availability of a surgical solution, which she shows was discovered by her interviewees from popular culture, enabled precisely those lesbians who had been 'stone butches' in the 1950s to opt to become 'men'. The transsexual solution was discovered by Devor's younger participants on 'television talk and news magazine shows in the late 1970s and the 1980s which featured transsexual guests or stories' (p. 353). Robin, for instance, describes an experience very similar to that described by 1950s stone butches, the same hatred of her female body and determination to do sex like a man and not be touched. '[M]ost of the time I wanted to be on top . . . For lack of words, riding her. And she didn't enjoy that. When I was with her . . . she wanted to touch me and I allowed her to touch me . . . . I didn't like my body, didn't like my breasts, didn't like it when she touched me or made love to me' (p. 338).

Many accounts of lesbian history describe how some women who loved women in the days before feminism offered an alternative way to be a lesbian, suffered agonies of discomfort about having female bodies (Davis and Kennedy 1991). They bound their breasts, and would not let their female partners touch their bodies lest they be reminded that they were female. Julia Penelope (1984) writes movingly about how her stone butchness was connected with her incest experience. With the help of feminism and an incest survivors' consciousness-raising group, Penelope learnt to feel comfortable in her female body and engage in mutual love-making. Feminism offered a solution to the problem of butchness for many lesbians in the 1970s. The solution that became popular in the 1990s was not reclaiming their female bodies, but cutting them up.

FTMs do not usually mention child sexual abuse as a reason for their desire to transition, probably because this would not support the notion that they were 'really' men, or engaged in a positive transformation. But many accounts of transitioning make it clear that child sexual abuse plays an important role. I have argued else-where that transsexual surgery needs to be understood as a form of self-mutilation by proxy, in which self-mutilators engage someone else to perform the mutilation (Jeffreys 2000). Feminist commentators are showing that self-mutilation is strongly linked with child sexual abuse (Strong 1998). Butch lesbianism, a usual precursor to FTM transsexualism, is explained by Sara Cytron as a rejection of the femininity that caused her to be abused.

> I had come to associate my girlness with being invaded, flooded, and overwhelmed. If no one else was home, my father would ask me to lie down on him. He would hold me tightly, fervently, talking rapturously of how he loved me. I would feel his hot, close breath, the moistness of his lips, the faintly spicy smell of his skin. . . . He'd pull down my shorts so he could tuck my shirt into my underwear. (Cytron 1999: 211)

She learnt to associate being female with danger, and 'wanted to be *near* femininity, though I dreaded inhabiting it' (p. 212). She learnt to dissociate from her body and feelings, to 'escape how beaten and obliterated I felt' (p. 217).

Dallas Denny, in his health report on transgendered youth, comments that 'Many adult transgendered and transsexual people report having been repeatedly beaten or sexually abused while in the home' (Denny 2000: 3). Holly Devor (1999) found that 53 per cent reported that they had been abused by males in childhood; 16 per cent reported physical abuse by their mothers; and 60.5 per cent reported abuse before their teenage years. The transsexualism of these abused lesbians originated in a desire to exit the body that was associated with abuse, the female body, and aspiration to the body of the abuser that represented power. 'Many of those who suffered under their fathers' reigns spoke of wanting to hold power like their father when they were older' (Devor 1999: 141). They learnt, Devor says, 'that men are people of great importance and power who can hurt and control others but who can rarely be hurt or controlled themselves' (p. 141).

For Sara Cytron it was not sexual abuse alone that caused her to adopt masculinity, but also a resentment of the powerlessness that being a girl represented. She hated family parties because the privilege of boys was particularly clear. They could 'be dressed up but still retain themselves and their dignity. They could be cleaned and combed out of respect for an occasion without serving as delicacies for the consumption of others' (Cytron 1999: 213). The men's roles at these parties were a great deal more exciting than those reserved for females. Men 'made the speeches and told the jokes', while 'the women laughed and applauded them' (p. 214). Judith Halberstam also writes, in explanation of her adoption of butchness, of the desire to escape the constraints of femininity, particularly in adolescence. She says she had adolescent rage about the demands placed upon her 'to be a girl in conventional ways' (Halberstam 1999: 154). She explains that adolescence was a 'crisis' for girls, because whilst for boys it represented 'an ascension to some version...of social power', for girls it was a 'lesson in restraint, punishment, and repression' (p. 156).

Some FTMs are quite explicit about envying the power and privilege of men and wanting to possess them. Loren Cameron identifies as a transsexual man. She has published a book, entitled *Body Alchemy*, of photographs and vignettes of a number of lesbians who have transgendered through chemicals and/or surgery, many to 'become' gay men. She recognizes that her identity as a man is largely chemically constructed, as she explains: 'Discontinuing the testosterone isn't really an option since so much of my identity hinges on it' (Cameron 1996: 20). Yet discontinuance might be desirable, since she is already experiencing damaging mood swings. She hankers after the power and authority that come with manliness. As a small woman, she feels vulnerable, and even testosterone cannot relieve this.

> So much about my coming to manhood has been about a quest for size. I mean, I really need to be a big man. All of the men I've looked to as role models have been body-builders and athletes. They seem like gods and great beasts to me in their huge and beautiful bodies. I envy them. I want to be like them. They look so virile and invincible. (p. 85)

She says that as her muscles grow, 'being five foot three doesn't feel quite so small' (p. 85). Her doubtfulness about whether 'I'll ever feel safe in this body' suggests that she might have some experience of female vulnerability to male violence (p. 85).

The biographical statements provided by the other women in the anthology show that they also want male power. Shadow Morton, for instance, is a lesbian who has 'been a gay man for about the last three years' (p. 81). She feels powerful when cruising on the street as a gay man: 'Sex is a lot more fun for me now . . . .When I'm cruising on the street, I have a sense of predatory power and that I'm in complete control' (p. 81). Jeffrey Shevlowitz explains that as a Jew she experienced particular restrictions because she was a girl.

> I never even wanted to go to Hebrew school until I could go to a synagogue and be treated as a man there. For me, it [Bar Mitzvah] was an affirmation of my heritage and of who I am now. Traditionally, a young boy says during the ceremony, "Today I am a man." I always felt that this would be the perfect experience for me. (p. 34)

Judith Halberstam quotes a woman who runs drag king workshops, in which women learn to dress up as masculine gay men on a temporary basis, as saying that the reasons for cross-dressing lie in wanting to experience 'male authority and territory and entitlement' (Halberstam 1998a: 252). For some FTMs gay masculinity was recognized as the ultimate form of masculinity. One of Holly Devor's interviewees speaks of what she found in the cruising grounds of public toilets:

> It's such an education. . . .First of all, it's like a very intense male bonding thing. . . . Because it's the ultimate in masculinity (being gay). . . . They're more men than anybody, 'cause they're totally homoerotic. How much more masculine can you get? They're not even interested in women. They're just interested in men. It's incredible. I love it. And, of course, it's risky and it's a real adventure. (Devor 1999: 504)

This helps to explain why an increasing number of FTMs who want to reject their femaleness as completely as possible decide that they are 'gay men'.

Involvement in sadomasochism is an antecedent to transsexualism for many lesbians (Due 1998). Most prominent lesbians who are transitioning have experience of sadomasochism, and the connection seems to lie in the practice of dissociation from the body and the destruction of body boundaries that takes place. The MTF Susan Stryker, in explaining his transsexualism, explains that SM offered an effective alternative to transsexualism when he was unable to access 'transsexual technologies'. SM created a dissociative relationship with his body which made it possible for him to transition 'to an extent that made my body seem as inherently unstable as a blob of gelatin wrapped in rubber bands, I realized that I *was* a mean femme top' (Stryker 1998: 149).

Another explanation for the decision to transition is ageing. Some butch lesbians, for instance, speak of finding the menopause intolerable. One of Devor's interviewees says that she could not tolerate ageing because it made her look more like a woman: 'there's absolutely no future in being a very masculine lesbian.... It was great, up to, say, five years ago.... I'm getting older, and it's showing. Up til then, I got away with [it].... I was young looking.... I looked more like a boy' (Devor 1999: 330). A corporate vice-president explains that she also looked like a boy when young and could not see herself 'becoming an old woman': 'I'd try to imagine myself as a fifty-year-old woman, and there would be nothing there, nothing to see. One day I tried to imagine myself as a fifty-year-old man, and I was amazed to see someone, a man with strong shoulders and graying hair, a neat beard, a handsome face; it was me...time to grow up' (p. 341).

One of the FTMs whom Devor interviewed said that the critical moment of decision was when she was offered female hormones to deal with menopausal symptoms. Pat Califia, the SM activist, says the same thing, 'I had a breakdown in my doctor's office and started to cry, I realised that I just could not do it, I could not put oestrogen in my body on purpose' (quoted in Hawker 2000). Heather Findlay explains that ageing was the catalyst in the case of one of her two lovers who became FTMs. Sue, who became John, said 'he was always, always a boy in his mind, that he could kind of pull that off when he was young and gay, but he *really* couldn't bear to grow up into an old woman' (Findlay 1998: 144). Older women in male supremacist societies are of such low value that they become invisible. For lesbians who already chafed at their subordinate female status, ageing was the last straw.

The reasons listed here show that the lesbians who transition do so because they wish to escape women's subordination. There is copious feminist analysis of the range of forms of women's oppression which these FTMs describe. It is compulsory heterosexuality, aimed at rendering unto men women's bodies and labours, that causes these women to want so desperately to be normal and to feel unable to love women without cutting up their bodies. Anne Menasche's enlightening research on why many lesbians choose to abandon their love for women and relate to men, *Leaving the Life* (1998), analyses the reasons behind that choice, using the words of twenty-six 'lesbians who left'. They speak of the pressures to conform of family, work and religion, of just wanting to feel normal, of not being able to relate affectionately to girl-friends in public, and the views of sexologists.

All these pressures work on FTMs too. They also 'leave the life', but instead of leaving it to relate to men, they leave to 'become' men. There are extra pressures that drive FTMs that also stem from the oppression of women, child sexual abuse, hatred of female body parts, fear of being socially despised as a woman and particularly an ageing woman, and the allure of male power which they believe can be attained by imitating a male body. Some of the advantages of male power are achieved, such as feeling safer in the street, the delights of being able to feel powerful over and dominate women in relationships, and to feel superior to women. But the extra income and social dominance that males enjoy is unlikely to be acquired so easily. The glamour that gay men possess in a mixed gay culture by virtue of their power over community resources, particularly media, their money and dominance in all gatherings and institutions are extra factors that affect many FTMs. Gay men are their point of reference, rather than straight ones, and male dominance still works to keep the women who relate to them in thrall and looking up to men; so for gay-orientated FTMs it is gay men who must be imitated. What this sad litany of the forms and effects of women's subordination tells us is that lesbian feminism, far from being irrelevant, as those lesbians who rushed into the arms of queer men to escape it suggest, is as vital as it has ever been to lesbian existence. Queer politics, which celebrates transsexualism, should be seen not just as unsympathetic to lesbianism, but as being in direct opposition to lesbian survival.

Lesbian Feminism and Social Transformation

In the foundational texts of lesbian feminism such as *Sappho Was a Right-on Woman* (Abbott and Love 1972) and 'The Woman-Identified Woman' (Radicalesbians 1999, 1st published 1970), lesbianism is represented as the very model of liberation for women. Lesbian feminist writers explain that lesbians have the independence and equality that heterosexual women hanker after. Lesbians are celebrated as strong, woman-loving and possessed of an egalitarian ethics and practice developed in opposition to the dominance/submission, woman-hating ethics of heterosexuality (Daly 1979). As lesbian feminism developed as a movement in the 1970s, lesbians wrote and thought of themselves as the vanguard of social transformation. Lesbianism gave to feminists an egalitarian ideal which illuminated the oppressive nature of the political institution of heterosexuality, and offered a revolutionary alternative. As the lesbian feminist philosopher Adrienne Rich wrote in 1979: 'To the historical feminist demand for equal humanity, for a world free of domination through violence, lesbian/feminism has joined the more radical concept of woman-centered vision, a view of society whose goal is not equality but utter transformation' (Rich 1979: 229). Lesbian feminists were proud of their choice to love women and immensely proud to be model revolutionaries, living the revolution now.

This pride and self-confidence was shattered in the 1980s, as a lesbian sexual revolution took place (Jeffreys 1993), and as a class of lesbian sex industry entrepreneurs began to promote lesbian

pornography, lesbian strip-tease, sadomasochism and even prostitution. These new sexual libertarian lesbians derided lesbian feminists
for their anti-sex puritanism and particularly for their practice of
equality, which was said to be non-sexy and unsustainable (Nicholls
1987; Stack 1985). Queer and postmodern lesbians continued the
assault. They held up gay men as their model for sex and transgression, and questioned whether it was possible or reasonable to even
use the word or notion of 'lesbianism' (Butler 1990; Lamos 1994).

But the lesbian alternative, as a way to create personal and political
equality, has lost none of its cogency. Now that a considerable
number of gay theorists and activists are questioning the destructive
nature of malestream gay culture and sexual practice, the lesbian
alternative is becoming more and more relevant. Research into the
dynamics of hetero-relating suggests that women are still savagely
disadvantaged in relationships with men (Bittman and Pixley 1997;
Pocock 2000). Women are still overwhelmingly those responsible for
all forms of domestic labour, including sexual and emotional labour.
Men have changed little in their behaviour. They exploit women's
labour, and make only a small contribution of their own. Some
dominant gay male forms of intimacy, as we have seen in this book,
suffer from serious problems of eroticized inequality. The lesbian
alternative needs to be given centre stage, rather than being shuffled
off into the wings of history.

In this chapter I shall explain why a gay equality project which
seeks to protect a 'private' sphere of sexual exploitation from political scrutiny, whilst demanding equal access to heterosexual privileges which derive precisely from women's subordination, cannot
advantage lesbians or any other women. I shall suggest that lesbian
feminism, which seeks to create an equality in the 'private' sphere of
sexual and intimate relationships, should be seen as the vanguard of
lesbian and gay politics and of general social transformation.

Lesbians and the equality agenda

Fundamental to a radical and lesbian feminist politics is the understanding that 'the personal is political'. This phrase has two inter-
related meanings. It means that the political power structures of the
'public' world are reflected in the private world. Thus, for women in
particular, the 'private' world of heterosexuality is not a realm of

personal security, a haven from a heartless world, but an intimate realm in which their work is extracted and their bodies, sexuality and emotions are constrained and exploited for the benefits of individual men and the male supremacist political system. The very concept of 'privacy', as Catharine MacKinnon so cogently expresses it, 'has shielded the place of battery, marital rape, and women's exploited labor' (MacKinnon 1987: 101). But the phrase has a complementary meaning, which is that the 'public' world of male power, the world of corporations, militaries and parliaments is founded upon this private subordination. The edifice of masculine power relations, from aggressive nuclear posturing to take-over bids, is constructed on the basis of its distinctiveness from the 'feminine' sphere and based upon the world of women which nurtures and services that male power. Transformation of the public world of masculine aggression, therefore, requires transformation of the relations that take place in 'private'. Public equality cannot derive from private slavery.

It is this understanding that differentiates radical feminist and radical lesbian politics from liberal feminist politics. Whereas liberal politics seeks equality in the public realm, radical feminist politics points out that a public realm constructed specifically from women's private subordination can never offer women 'equality'. This radical feminist approach casts great doubt upon lesbian and gay equality politics in which lesbians seek to be the equals of gay men, or attain some equality alongside gay men, with the privileges that heterosexual men derive from their dominance.

Catharine MacKinnon explains clearly why a policy of equal opportunity will not help women in general. One problem is that the world that men have created is organized around their biology and their dominant class status. The public world is organized such that men always have the advantage, she argues, of an affirmative action programme.

> Men's physiology defines most sports, their health needs largely define insurance coverage, their socially designed biographies define workplace expectations and successful career patterns, their perspectives and concerns define quality in scholarship, their experiences and obsessions define merit, their military service defines citizenship, their presence defines family, their inability to get along with one another – their wars and rulerships – defines history, their image defines god, and

their genitals define sex. These are the standards that are presented as gender neutral. For each of men's differences from women, what amounts to an affirmative action plan is in effect, otherwise known as the male-dominant structure and values of American society. (MacKinnon 1989: 224)

No kind of equality for women is possible within a political system set up entirely for men's advantage. One arena in which women cannot achieve 'equality', for instance, is the parliamentary system. Tess Kingham, a British Labour ex-MP, has described her despair at the relentless and impenetrably masculine British parliament, where MPs from the two main political parties engage in 'willy-jousting' (Kingham 2001). Opposition MPs, she says, spent days and nights 'endlessly thrusting their groins around the Chamber in mock combat with Labour ministers – achieving absolutely nothing', and Parliament was simply a 'boys' public school debating club'. Only dramatic transformation could create a political environment in which women could be 'equal'. However, for gay men, who are likely to be in politics and all the echelons of power already, the problem may be simply that they cannot be comfortably 'out'. For gay men, equality with straight men in an affirmative action programme is possible once the prejudice that prevents 'outness' is overcome. For women the problem is very different.

It is aggressive masculinity that shapes the institutions of male supremacy such as parliaments. As Germaine Greer points out, 'Masculinity is a system. It is the complex of learned behaviours and subtly coded interactions that forms the connective tissue of corporate society' (Greer 1999: 294). When women try to enter these 'masculine hierarchies', they constitute 'exported tissue, in constant danger of provoking an inflammatory response and summary rejection' (p. 294). The shaping of the corporate world by masculinity means that any aspirations towards equality in that sphere are cruel to women, requiring them to 'duplicate behaviours that they find profoundly alien and disturbing' (p. 309). Men like the masculine world they have built for themselves, she argues, and had they not enjoyed 'what they euphemistically call the "cut and thrust" – the sanctioned brutalities of corporate life – such behaviour would never have been institutionalized and women would not now be struggling with it' (p. 309).

Greer describes the behaviours of males in the heterosexual male-stream in a way which seems particularly apt to the behaviour of male gay sadomasochists in sex clubs too.

> Wherever men are gathered together, in the pool hall, at a restaurant, you can see the wannabes waiting on the dominant males, studying their reactions, gauging when to defer and when to challenge. There will always be one man who can silence the other with a look; most will defer... and there will be the junior males, who seek to ingratiate themselves by stepping and fetching, and grooming the silverback. The presence of women in such groups distracts the men from the work in hand – if they acknowledge women's presence, which they usually don't. (p. 293)

It is clear from such insights why gay men might wish to protect the all-male character of their sex clubs. Women would simply destroy the dynamics, or perhaps find them hilarious.

Men's studies theorists have pointed out that the aggressive competitive masculinity that structures men's institutions and political and economic systems not only excludes women, but has toxic social effects in terms of inequality and warfare. Andy Metcalf writes of how aggressive masculinity constructs the economy through notions such as that 'in the market place only the fittest should survive, and that a hard, lean industrial sector is necessary' (Metcalf 1985: 11). Michael Kimmel explains that 'American aggression and violence conform to this compulsive masculinity, a socially constructed gender identity that is manifest both in individual behaviour and in foreign and domestic policies' (Kimmel 1987: 237).

Gay male sex culture reproduces precisely the codes of masculine dominance of the malestream world. Gay men's sex clubs, and particularly SM clubs and parties, are organized very strictly according to masculine, aggressive, willy-jousting hierarchy. They are a very explicit version of the masculinity that presents a threat militarily, economically and sexually to women and men internationally. As Metcalf goes on to explain, male sexuality is not 'purely a private affair', but 'suffuses public life'. He argues that 'the alternative starts with acknowledging our need to change' (Metcalf 1985: 14).

Equality in systems built upon aggressive masculinity is not open to women unless they seek to outbutch the men, as sadomasochists such as Pat Califia have done. But once these women become older, just outbutching men does not suffice and they have had to engage in self-mutilation in an attempt to become men. This is not a form of 'equality' which offers any future for women who choose to remain in women's bodies. Whereas gay men can aspire to become integrated as equals into the public world of male dominance – indeed, are likely to be there already – this is hardly a reasonable expectation for lesbians, because lesbians are women.

There are two main versions of equality to which gay theorists and activists subscribe. Gay conservatives such as the contributors to the American Independent Gay Forum, a 'moderate conservative' group set up in 1999 to co-ordinate gays with centrist politics, from Log Cabin (gay Republicans) to free-market libertarians, want to fit gay men into an already existing America which they consider pretty much perfect. Thus they want access for gay men to goods such as marriage, which have been unfairly permitted only to heterosexuals. They are 'pro-family', so have no critique of marriage from a feminist or any other perspective. Queer activists are likely to criticize this version of the equality agenda. Queer theorists of the Sex Panic variety, such as Michael Warner, have no truck with campaigning for marriage rights (Warner 1999). They consider the promiscuity of gay men to be revolutionary in itself. Their demand is for the kind of sexual freedom engaged in by upper-class heterosexual men in periods of history when men were allowed even more unalloyed privilege to abuse women, men such as those involved in the eighteenth-century Hellfire Club in Britain, or the hero of left revolutionaries of sexuality, the Marquis de Sade.

Such conservative and queer positions can be seen to represent the major two positions within patriarchal thought about sexuality. One is to maintain marriage because of its benefits to society – read male dominance – whilst allowing men to play around on the side as usual, whereas the other is to celebrate men's sexual freedom and create a society in which men can sexually use all others in any way possible. Queer demands for sexual freedom also represent an attempt to gain for gay men the rights to the expression of male sexual aggression and exploitation in the public and private worlds that were gained for heterosexual men in the sexual revolution of the 1970s (Jeffreys 1990a). I have written elsewhere about the ways in which the 'sexual revolution' inscribed straight men's sexual rights to a sexuality of inequality, and to sexual exploitation in pornography and prostitution. In this 'revolution', women's rights to bodily integrity and equality were overruled (Jeffreys 1997a). This sexual

freedom of straight men is constructed out of women's subordination. The gay demand for equality with straight men's sexual freedom depends equally upon women's subordination.

Marriage and other heterosexual privileges

The equality agenda of gay politics is most problematic where it
involves the very foundations of women's historical oppression, the
exchange of women between men for labour and reproduction in
marriage. Gay equality politics demands, for instance, the right for
gay men to marry, and includes the buying of women's bodies in
reproductive surrogacy so that they may acquire offspring. Jonathan
Rauch of Log Cabin expresses the conservative position on gay
marriage succinctly. He says that a 'principled social-conservative
position could be pro-family without being anti-gay', because it
would 'encourage both straights and gays to settle down in committed relationships and acknowledge the real advantages for children of
two-parent families' (Rauch 1994: 1). His views are those of malestream old-fashioned and anti-feminist conservatism, as in seeing the
'enemies of the state' and of the 'family' as 'Divorce, illegitimacy and
infidelity' (p. 2). Andrew Sullivan argues in favour of gay marriage
that marriage is 'a fundamental mark of citizenship' (Sullivan 2000).
It is for this very reason, the importance of marriage to citizenship,
that feminist critics have argued that women have a second-class
citizenship. Women receive citizenship vicariously through men
when they marry, and are prevented from obtaining its benefits by
the toils of housework (Lister 1997).

There is no space here to engage in a full discussion of this issue,
which has received a good deal of attention in the last decade in
lesbian and gay literature. The feminist critique of marriage is hardly
mentioned, however, and seems little understood. Marriage is not on
the agenda of lesbian feminism, because it symbolizes and constructs
women's subordination. The most profound feminist critique of
marriage is that of Carole Pateman, in her book *The Sexual Contract*.
Pateman points out that 'Until late into the nineteenth century the
legal and civil position of a wife resembled that of a slave. Under
the common law doctrine of coverture, a wife, like a slave, was civilly
dead' (Pateman 1988: 119). Like a slave, she was brought to life
by being given a name by her master, which is how women come

to lose their own names upon marriage. Under coverture, a woman had to live where her husband demanded. He owned her earnings and her children, 'just as the children of the female slave belonged to her master' (p. 121). Through to the nineteenth century, wives could be, and were still, sold by their husbands. Ursula Vogel, in her compelling work on the connection between women's reduced citizenship and marriage, explains that by the end of the nineteenth century, 'marriage alone...had retained some of the peculiar attributes of feudal bondage. It had remained a status relationship in which a husband, *qua* husband, had certain proprietary rights to the person of his wife' (Vogel 1994: 79). The US lesbian legal theorist Ruthann Robson argues for the general abolition of marriage, saying that 'lesbian survival is not furthered by embracing the law's rule of marriage. Our legal energy is better directed at abolishing marriage as a state institution and *spouse* as a legal category' (Robson 1992: 127).

Though the right to gay marriage has been a controversial issue, and subject to heated debate, another example of heterosexual privilege, reproductive surrogacy, has not. This may be because it does not have to be campaigned for as a right. It is already available to gay men in the USA. But a lesbian feminist perspective would suggest that it should not be available to anyone, because this is a privilege which specifically arises from, and constitutes, the exploitation of women. Whereas gay marriage simply supports an oppressive institution, gay use of reproductive surrogates directly enacts the oppression of women.

Reproductive surrogacy is an offshoot of the profitable reproductive technology industry. Feminist theorists and activists in groups such as FINNRAGE have campaigned against the marketing of these technologies, on the grounds that the procedures constitute violence against women, that they are experimental technologies, and that the surgeons, often trained on cows, are experimenting on women (Corea 1990; Rowlands 1992). But it is reproductive surrogacy which has been the cause of most concern amongst feminist critics of these new technologies. The 'Baby M' case in the USA, in which the purchasing father enforced his rights through the courts to gain custody of the child from her mother, was the focus of much feminist theorizing on the damage done to women and children through this practice (Chesler 1990). In reproductive surrogacy, women are paid to carry embryos. The eggs of the 'surrogate' mother may be combined with semen from the purchasing 'father', or the egg too may be bought in. In either case, feminists argue, women's bodies are being turned into the property of men who have ownership rights over them for the period of the pregnancy and then buy the baby that is born. Janice Raymond calls surrogacy 'reproductive slavery' (Raymond 1990: 110). The 'surrogate' mothers are poor and often Third World women who need the money. They suffer the invasive surgeries and drugs of IVF, and have to be examined throughout the pregnancy and agree that an abortion will be carried out if the child is not as the purchaser requires. Thus women's bodies and children are placed on the market. In countries like Australia, commercial surrogacy of this kind is outlawed. In the state of Victoria altruistic surrogacy is outlawed too. This is based upon an understanding that women can suffer pressure to bear babies for others, but then find that they cannot bear the emotional pain of relinquishment, which can be similar to the pain experienced by mothers forced to give up their babies for adoption.

In the USA, commercial surrogacy, in which women sign enforceable contracts to bear and hand over babies, is legal, and gay men are now availing themselves of this, renting women's bodies and buying their offspring. Men in the USA who have no female partner can pay surrogacy agencies to find and pay women to produce children for them in their wombs. One such agency, which markets itself directly to gay men, is called Growing Generations: Surrogacy for the Gay Community. It claims to be the 'first and only gay and lesbian owned surrogacy firm exclusively serving the gay community worldwide'. The agency employs a network of physicians, psychologists, and attorneys, and supplies 'responsible surrogates and egg donors'. They offer a 'traditional program', in which a surrogate mother, 'using her own eggs, is artificially inseminated with the semen of the prospective father'. In the 'gestational surrogacy program', there is 'both an egg donor and a gestational surrogate'. The gay male clients can select 'from a wide range of committed and responsible surrogates and egg donors'. To help the men select, the 'surrogates' are shown in a group photograph smiling for the camera. They are put through 'in-depth medical and psychological evaluation'. As the agency's website proclaims, 'Our surrogates are between the ages of 21–36, healthy, financially secure, and have at least one child of their own. Many of our surrogates and egg donors are college educated and have active professional lives. They are special women who have chosen to help the gay community realize the joys that a child can bring to life' (Growing Generations 2001).

One of the agency's team of surrogate mothers says, 'I was always extra proud to share that I was having a baby for a single gay man.' Lest any of these selfless women should find it hard to hand over their babies after birth, the agency will refer clients to lawyers who will help them in 'establishing or confirming your parental rights'. It is interesting that the agency says that the women are psychologically tested but makes no mention of any testing of the male buyers, or any preparation of them for the demands their purchases may make on their patience or time.

The reason why these women are willing to become surrogates is likely to be the money they are paid. The woman receives US$18,000 for carrying the baby plus extra one-off payments for invasive IVF procedures. She has to submit to health checks to ensure that the product is turning out according to the contract. This is not a great deal of money for a nine-month job, but may seem like a lot to a poorly paid or unemployed woman, or one who is in debt. The web page makes the process sound warm and cuddly:

> Most of Growing Generations' surrogates develop a close bond with their intended parents starting with their first meeting. This continues through the birth and oftentimes beyond. Your journey with your intended parents in creating a child will leave you with cherished lifelong memories. The surrogacy process is a happy, joyful and rewarding experience that is built on respect, friendship and teamwork.

In fact, it is a commercial enterprise of baby-selling in which the interests of the relinquishing mothers and their children are sidelined or guarded against. The fact that gay men are participating in the trade in women's bodies should not be a matter for celebration, but one for serious concern. Equality in sexual exploitation is one way in which gay men's interests lie in direct contradiction to the interests of women.

Sexual freedom

Queer activists tend to seek a different platform of rights – namely, the rights involved in 'sexual freedom' – but these too can be seen to arise from patriarchy. The patriarchal notion and practice of sexual freedom to which queer theorists subscribe arise from the male sex right, which is well described by Carole Pateman. She sees 'The husband's conjugal right' – i.e. his sexual ownership of his wife's body in marriage – as 'the clearest example of the way in which the modern origin of political right as sex-right is translated through the marriage contract into the right of every member of the fraternity in daily life' (Pateman 1988: 123). This is an important understanding for male sexual freedom politics, straight or gay.

Men's sexual freedom has depended, and still does to a large extent, upon their ownership of women's bodies. Men have bought, sold and traded women as things to be used. Women are still regularly raped in marriage, even though most Western countries have now changed their laws to recognize that wives have a right not to be raped (Russell 1990). Women are still bought and sold in marriage in many countries, and in the vast majority of countries of the world their bodies are still legally owned by their husbands. In prostitution and pornography, the mail-order bride business and reproductive surrogacy, the international trade in women is a burgeoning industry (Hughes and Roche 1999). Men's ownership of women's bodies has been the substrate on which their idea of sexual freedom was born and given its meaning. This is why it includes the right to buy access to women, men and children as an important way of demonstrating that freedom (Kappeler 1990). At the base of men's sexual freedom agenda is the concept of the rights of the male individual. Pateman points out that women cannot gain recognition as individuals, since the very concept of the 'individual' is male.

> The conclusion is easy to draw that the denial of civil equality to women means that the feminist aspiration must be to win acknowledgment for women as 'individuals'. Such an aspiration can never be fulfilled.... The individual is masculine.... The 'individual' is a man who makes use of a woman's body (sexual property); the converse is much harder to imagine. (Pateman 1988: 185)

The gay version of sexual freedom originates in the same masculine privilege.

Michael Warner is an exemplary exponent of queer sexual freedom politics. He is the influential queer theorist who provided much of the inspiration for the Sex Panic group's defence of public sex. He is the editor of the foundationalist queer text *Fear of a Queer Planet* (1993), and a Professor of English at Rutgers University, where he teaches Queer Studies. His book *The Trouble with Normal* (1999) is a response to the most influential American gay conservative, Andrew Sullivan, and his book *Virtually Normal* (1996). Warner argues that queer politics should be about fighting sexual shame and celebrating a public sexual culture of bathhouses, pornography theatres and stores, and prostitution. His understanding of sexuality is a specifically masculine one of risk-taking. The masculine sexuality of risk is precisely what feminists have struggled to change because of the consequences it has for unwanted pregnancies, sexually transmitted diseases, and violence. Warner writes:

> The appeal of queer sex, for many, lies in its ability to shed the responsibilizing frames of good, right-thinking people.... There is no sublimity without danger, without the scary ability to imagine ourselves and everything we hold dear, at least for a moment, as relatively valueless. In this context, the pursuit of dangerous sex is not as simple as mere thrill seeking or self-destructiveness. In many cases it may represent deep and mostly unconscious thinking, about desire and the conditions that make life a value. (Warner 1999: 213)

The creation of this kind of politics based upon sexual freedom is rather old-fashioned. It replicates the sexual freedom politics of the 1960s which gave straight men access to the sexual exploitation of women in pornography and prostitution (Jeffreys 1990a).

Michael Bronski, the queer cultural critic, proposes a similar sexual freedom agenda. He uses Freud's notion of sexual repression being at the basis of the creation of civilization in his book *The Pleasure Principle* (1998). He also sees sexual freedom as the fount and aim of gay politics: 'Complete freedom of expression for gay sexuality is the keystone of gay freedom, for it is homosexual sexual activity that makes gay people different' (Bronski 1998: 184). He considers that gay men's freedom to do whatever they like sexually, in public or private, paid or free, will guarantee the freedom of everyone in the future. It is that simple. Gay men will take responsibility for releasing the pleasure principle, civilization will be overturned, and everyone will be free. This is a quintessentially masculine agenda. Feminist theorists have pointed out that the sex of the present is constructed from male dominance and female subordination and will have to change for women to be free, rather than de-repressed (MacKinnon 1989; Jeffreys 1990a).

Some gay conservatives join the queer sex panickers in excoriating feminists for their criticism of gay men's sexual freedom prerogative. Stephen Miller, for instance, in his article 'Masculinity under siege' is as gung-ho on this issue as Michael Warner, and he attacks John Stoltenberg for his 'contempt of raw, aggressive, combustible masculinity' (Miller 1994: 2). Even those conservative gay men, such as Andrew Sullivan, who seem more publicly devoted to traditional pro-family policies than others seem to make exceptions for their own private sexual interests. Andrew Sullivan was involved in a media controversy in June 2001 when it was discovered that he had advertised on a barebacking site under the pseudonym RawMuscle-Glutes, as an HIV-positive man, seeking 'bi-scenes, one-on-ones, three-ways, groups, parties, orgies and gang bangs' and warning off 'fats and fems' from responding (Kim 2001; Signorile 2001). Sullivan's inclusion of bisexuality in his barebacking practice makes it clear that the barebacking agenda is one of direct relevance to women. Since he is the most famous exponent of pro-family gay conservatism, this is all something of an embarrassment for those associated with this position. What it does demonstrate is that there is not necessarily any gap between libertarian and pro-family gay political commentators in private practice, though there may be considerable public hypocrisy.

Lesbians as the 'vanguard of change'

There is no future for lesbians in seeking equality either with men in the gay sexual culture or public world or with men in general in the malestream world of the state, the military sports and the economy, because these public worlds are constructed out of male dominance and female subordination. Lesbians are women, and the future of lesbians is embedded in the future of women. The private world from which men's public privilege, forms of organization, behaviour and sexual 'freedom' are constructed must be changed, in order for a public world to be created in which women and men can share politically and socially. Lesbians offer a model in their modes of sexual and emotional relating of the egalitarian intimate relations upon which transformation of the public world can be based. In this lesbians are, as the UK lesbian sociologist Gillian Dunne argues, the 'vanguard of change' (Dunne 1997, 2000).

In sexuality in particular, lesbians have offered an egalitarian alternative. For men, sexual practice constructs and confirms manhood (Stoltenberg 1990). This fundamental connection explains the forms of much male sexual behaviour, the obsession with penile penetration, goal orientation, penis size, frequency and conquest. This masculine sexuality, as many gay male critics have recently pointed out, is the sexuality of the dominant gay male sexual culture as well as of heterosexual male culture. In lesbian relationships there is no necessity for either partner to assert manhood through sex, and sex is likely to take very different forms, or even to seem relatively unimportant. Lesbians have a history of engaging in sexual relationships on more egalitarian terms than gay men or heterosexuals. Research comparing lesbian and gay experience found that lesbians had much longer relationships, did vastly less casual sex or cruising, and chose partners who were closer to them in age and occupation (Bell and Weinberg 1978; Gagnon and Simon 1973). Lesbian feminist researchers have pointed out that many lesbians have the ability to sustain long-term, passionate but non-genital sexual relationships, despite assumptions by sex therapists and other members of their communities that such women are not properly lovers, because they do not follow a hetero-patriarchal model (Rothblum and Brehony 1993; Rothblum 1994).

Nett Hart explains how lesbians can offer a way out of the sexuality of risk and danger that is so highly valued under male dominance. Her title 'From an eroticism of difference to an intimacy of equals' encapsulates her argument about what lesbians have to offer (Hart 1996). The eroticism of difference is a patriarchally constructed desire which arises from the power difference between women and men – what I call 'heterosexual desire' (Jeffreys 1990a). Such an eroticism values the danger and risk involved in sex with strangers or others who cannot really be known. Intimacy creates sexual difficulties for those who can only respond sexually to 'difference'. Hart asks whether the lesbian experience of being able to eroticize intimacy offers a new way forward: 'What if lesbians accepted as our central task not only the recontextualising of sexual relationship but a reformulation of desire' (Hart 1996: 69).

One reason why lesbian sexual practice differs so much from the sexual practice of gay men may be that lesbians do not suffer, as gay men apparently do, from 'shame'. Michael Warner claims that gay men are much afflicted by 'shame' about sex, and that this can be resolved only through public sex, in which men will find that everyone is a 'bottom', and not feel the shame of being one so badly (Warner 1999). The different constructions of lesbian and gay sexuality are the result of the different political positions that lesbians and gay men occupy in relation to male supremacy. Gay male 'shame' is about being a bottom – i.e. an effeminized male who has lost heterosexual male power and privilege. The situation of lesbians is very different. Since women are already in the subordinate class, lesbians do not fall, but may rise into equality in love with no requirement that anyone should play bottom.

The lesbian potential for egalitarian love-making was attacked with fury in the 1980s by lesbian sadomasochists and sex therapists trained in the regulations of male supremacist sexuality. The bisexual sex therapist Margaret Nicholls, for instance, attacked lesbian feminists for egalitarian sexual practice, or what she calls 'politically correct lesbian lovemaking'. She derides what other lesbians might delight in: 'Two women lie side by side (tops or bottoms are strictly forbidden – lesbians must be non-hierarchical); they touch each other gently and sweetly all over their bodies for several hours' (Nicholls 1987: 97). If lesbian love-making had not offered the delights of equality, then such a vigorous repudiation would not have been necessary.

The lesbians who chose to serve the sexual ideology of male supremacy through the sex industry or sex therapy waged a battle royal to overcome what they saw as the anti-sexual egalitarianism of lesbian practice and lesbian feminism in particular. They struggled against lesbian resistance and lack of interest, as male sexologists have struggled for over a century to get women in heterosexuality to be enthusiastic about female subordination in sex (Jeffreys 1990a, 1997b). The size of the struggle suggests the size of the problem of lesbian egalitarian sexual culture. Though this onslaught was quite successful in eliminating lesbian feminist ideas about sex from public discussion, it was clearly not as successful in changing practice, as indicated by the lack of enthusiasm amongst lesbians for public sex in sex clubs today.

Another way in which lesbian feminist self-confidence was undermined in the 1980 and 1990s was through the destruction of the identity 'lesbian' in postmodern and queer theory. Postmodernists attacked 'identity' politics as essentialist – i.e. as implying some essence of lesbianism, whether biologically, spiritually or otherwise constructed, which constrained how women who saw themselves as lesbians could be. Postmodern and queer theorists required lesbians to be ruthlessly deconstructive of lesbian identity. Judith Butler, whose work has been most influential in creating this radical uncertainty about what a lesbian is, writes that she suffers great anxiety when requested to give a talk as a lesbian: 'To write or speak as a lesbian appears a paradoxical appearance of this "I," one which feels neither true nor false' (Butler 1991: 13).

At present, the constructed category 'lesbian' does exist, and hundreds of thousands of women choose to live their lives within it. More pressing than the constrictions of the category itself are likely to be the pressures that are exerted upon these women to cease their love of women and return to the polite servicing of men in heterosexuality that they have deserted. So strong are these pressures, as we have seen in this book, that many lesbians are undergoing savage surgical and chemical treatments that destroy their lesbian bodies and deconstruct their lesbian identities rather too effectively. In such a state of emergency, the identity 'lesbian' needs to be employed politically, rather than abandoned. But the identity 'lesbian' is important in another way. This identity under which women live out sexual and emotional relationships with other women offers an alternative which can be counterposed right now to the institutionalized heterosexuality which organizes and maintains male dominance. Heterosexuality is constructed, and so is the lesbian alternative. Nothing is 'natural' here; but in order to undermine male dominance, the lesbian alternative – indeed the lesbian vanguard – has a crucial role to play.

There is a dawning recognition amongst some gay male critics of the destructive nature of gay men's sexual and emotional lives that lesbians offer a positive alternative. Gabriel Rotello, for instance, argues that to make gay culture 'sustainable', it needs to 'create an honored place for relationships and fidelity' and a 'new gay ideal that validates and supports relationships rather than one that validates and honors sexual adventurism, sexual consumerism and risk taking'. The model for this, he says, is not necessarily a heterosexual one, since 'one could just as accurately say that the values I'm talking about are found in the lesbian world more than among heterosexuals. Indeed, if gay men want a model at all, the lesbian model seems much more appropriate to our condition than a heterosexual model, since lesbians are in much the same political and social boat as gay men'.

(Rotello 1997: 245). Recent British research on how lesbians live their lives supports the idea that lesbians can offer a new model. Research by Jeffrey Weeks, Catherine Donovan and Brian Heaphy on 'Families of Choice: the structure and meanings of non-heterosexual relationships' found that lesbians positively chose lesbianism 'as a conscious alternative to subordination to men' (Weeks 2000: 221). Lesbians interviewed in the study spoke of being stronger since coming out as lesbians, and of the positive value of escaping the 'essential power imbalance' and roles of heterosexuality.

Gillian Dunne's work on the relationship and work lives of lesbians produced similar findings (Dunne 1997, 2000). Her work is inspiring in the picture it offers of how lesbian lives can serve as an attainable alternative to the heterosexual model. Dunne is a UK lesbian sociologist who has carried out extensive research through interviews with lesbians about how they came to be lesbians, how they conduct their relationships and their work lives, and specifically who does what in terms of housework and child care. She, like other researchers (see Gottschalk 2000), found that women see coming to lesbianism as 'empowering', because they can throw off the constraints of hetero-relating and the inequality that is inherent in it.

Dunne's interviewees said that it was precisely the 'role play' of heterosexuality, rather than individual men, that was the problem (Dunne 1997: 113). Women in lesbian relationships engaged 'in an unusual amount of creativity' as they invented ways of relating in the absence of a role-playing script (p. 184). Dunne's findings of more egalitarian home lives than the heterosexual norm confirmed other research findings that lesbians were less inclined towards role-playing than either gay men or heterosexual couples, and that it was 'rare to find one partner in a lesbian relationship performing mostly "masculine" or mostly "feminine" tasks' (p. 204). It was the rejection by lesbians of the restrictions of femininity and the embrace of 'broader gender self-concepts and capabilities' that meant they did not seek to unite with men to fill the gap that gender role-playing creates, and were 'less likely to find relationships with the masculine "other" based on eroticized power difference and, once again, role-playing "an erotic experience"'.

Dunne argues that 'gender inequalities in the labour market' cannot be understood 'without reference to the organization of work in the home' (p. 136). Men's contribution to work in the home, 'domestic and caring work', has not increased; so, Dunne comments, 'the gender of the person with whom women form or intend to form relationships matters'. She points out that if 'men's ability to retain their labour market advantage rests largely on their capacity to appropriate the unwaged labour of women', then heterosexuality should be understood as central to 'providing the logic that translates women's labour into men's material advantage' (p. 137).

Dunne found many commonalities in respondents' autobiographies, but one of the most 'striking' was 'the relationship between lesbianism and empowerment' (p. 136). The lesbians in her study gained financial self-reliance, and found it was easier to be part of the paid work-force, because they gained 'more egalitarian domestic arrangements . . . the recognition of their right to work, and the encouragement they often experienced from partners' (p. 139). She concludes that sexuality cannot reasonably be understood as 'an individual choice' or 'private issue' once 'the relationship between a lesbian lifestyle and material empowerment' is recognized (p. 145). Thus lesbian experience may 'provide new insights about the work process and feminist aims in relation to improving women's life chances' (p. 146). Lesbian experience, she argues, should not be seen as private and personal, or divorced from its 'wider social and material context', but rather as a way of living in equality which affects the whole way public/private, home life and work are done (Dunne 2000: 135).

The lesbian versus the queer agenda

Many of the demands of both conservative gay and queer politics serve to retain the structures and practices of male domination and integrate gay men into them. But, as John Stoltenberg points out, 'A political movement trying to erode homophobia while leaving male supremacy and misogyny in place won't work. Gay liberation without sexual justice can't possibly happen. Gay rights without women's rights is a male-supremacist reform' (Stoltenberg 1991: 253). Gay or queer equality demands which privatize sexuality and intimate relationships provide obstacles in the way of lesbian and women's liberation. The sexual freedom demands to protect gay porn, to protection from prosecution for injuries inflicted in practices of self-mutilation by proxy, to protect sex clubs and prostitution and the right to act out sexually in public places in which women might like to wander, are in conflict with women's interests. Women, including lesbians, need the reconstruction of sexuality to end men's violence; they need freedom from the sexual exploitation of the sex industry and freedom to use public space. Equality demands and practices which support the sale and exchange of women's bodies in marriage and reproductive surrogacy are in conflict with women's interests in demolishing the institutionalized sale and exchange that form the framework of male supremacy. The interests of all women, including lesbians, will not be served by an extension of a privatized sexual practice of dominance and submission to more and more areas of public space, but rather by the extension of an intimate equality into the public world. The lesbian vanguard is well suited to leading the social transformation which will accomplish this end.

References

Abbott, Sidney and Love, Barbara 1972: *Sappho Was a Right-On Woman: A Liberated View of Lesbianism*. New York: Stein and Day.

Adams, Matt 1999: *Hustlers, Escorts, Porn Stars: The Insider's Guide to Male Prostitution in America*. Las Vegas: Matt Adams, Insiders' Guide.

Alexander, Priscilla 1996: Bathhouses and brothels: symbolic sites in discourse and practice. In Dangerous Bedfellows (eds.), *Policing Public Sex*, Boston: South End Press, 221–50.

Amboyz 2000: What is FTM? www.amboyz.org/articles/whatf2m.html

Amis, Martin 2001: A rough trade. Martin Amis reports from the high-risk, increasingly violent world of the pornography industry. *Guardian Weekend*, Saturday, 17 March.

Ayres, Tony 1999: China doll – the experience of being a gay Chinese Australian. In Peter A. Jackson and Gerard Sullivan (eds), *Multicultural Queer: Australian Narratives*, Binghamton, NY: Harrington Park Press, 87–98.

Bar On, Bat-Ami 1994: The feminist sexuality debates and the transformation of the political. In Claudia Card (ed.), *Adventures in Lesbian Philosophy*, Bloomington and Indianapolis: Indiana University Press, 51–63.

Barry, Kathleen 1979: *Female Sexual Slavery*. Englewood Cliffs, NJ: Prentice-Hall.

Bedoya, Roberto, Ried-Pharr, Robert and Rofes, Eric 1998: If two men are having lesbian sex together . . . In Sara Miles and Eric Rofes (eds), *Opposite Sex: Gay Men on Lesbians, Lesbians on Gay Men*, New York: New York University Press, 222–51.

Bell, Alan P. and Weinberg, Martin S. 1978: *Homosexualities: A Study of Diversity among Men and Women*. New York: Simon and Schuster.

Bell, David and Binnie, Jon 2000: *The Sexual Citizen: Queer Politics and Beyond*. Cambridge: Polity.

Bell, Diane and Klein, Renate (eds) 1996: *Radically Speaking: Feminism Reclaimed*. Melbourne: Spinifex Press.

Bittman, Michael and Pixley, Jocelyn 1997: *The Double Life of the Family*. Sydney: Allen and Unwin.

Brodribb, Somer 1992: *Nothing Mat(t)ers: A Feminist Critique of Postmodernism*. Melbourne: Spinifex Press.

Bronski, Michael 1998: *The Pleasure Principle: Sex, Backlash, and the Struggle for Gay Freedom*. New York: St Martin's Press.

Brosnan, Julia 1996: Julia Brosnan talks to lesbians who choose to take testosterone. *Diva*, August, 39–41.

Bunch, Charlotte 2000: Lesbians in revolt. In Barbara A. Crow (ed.), *Radical Feminism: A Documentary Reader*, New York: New York University Press, 332–6. (1st published 1972.)

Burana, Lily, Roxxie and Linnea Due (eds) 1994: *Dagger: On Butch Women*. San Francisco: Cleis Press.

Burger, John R. 1995: *One-Handed Histories: The Eroto-Politics of Gay Male Video Pornography*. New York: Harrington Park Press.

Burgess, Christian 1999: Internal and external stress factors associated with the identity development of transgendered youth. In Gerald P. Mallon (ed.), *Social Services with Transgendered Youth*, Binghamton, NY: Harrington Park Press, 35–48.

Burstyn, Varda (ed.) 1985: *Women Against Censorship*. Vancouver: Douglas and McIntyre.

Butler, Judith 1990: *Gender Trouble: Feminism and the Subversion of Identity*. London and New York: Routledge.

Butler, Judith 1991: Imitation and gender insubordination. In Diana Fuss (ed.), *Inside Out: Lesbian Theories, Gay Theories*, New York: Routledge, 13–31.

Butler, Judith 1994: Against proper objects. *Differences: A Journal of Feminist Cultural Studies*, 6 (Summer–Fall), *Feminism Meets Queer Theory*, 1–26.

Califia, Pat 1994: A secret side of lesbian sexuality. In Pat Califia, *Public Sex: The Culture of Radical Sex*, Pittsburgh and San Francisco: Cleis Press, 157–64.

Cameron, Loren 1996: *Body Alchemy*. Pittsburgh: Cleis Press.

Carbery, Graham 1992: Some Melbourne beats: a 'map' of a subculture from the 1930s to the 1950s. In Roberta Aldrich and Garry Wotherspoon (eds), *Gay Perspectives: Essays in Australian Gay Culture*, Sydney: Department of Economic History, University of Sydney, 131–46.

Carilli, Theresa 1995: The care and feeding of femme. In Leslea Newman (ed.), *The Femme Mystique*, Boston: Alyson Publications, 150–2.

Case, Sue-Ellen 1997: Toward a butch-feminist retro-future. In Dana Heller (ed.), *Cross Purposes: Lesbians, Feminists, and the Limits of Alliance*, Bloomington, Ind.: Indiana University Press, 205–20.

Cassese, James (ed.) 2000: *Gay Men and Childhood Sexual Trauma: Integrating the Shattered Self*. New York: Harrington Park Press.

Chesler, Phyllis 1990: Mothers on trial: custody and the "Baby M" case. In Dorchen Leidholdt and Janice G. Raymond (eds), *The Sexual Liberals and the Attack on Feminism*, New York: Pergamon Press, 95–102.

Clarke, Cheryl 1999: Lesbianism: an act of resistance. In Larry Gross and James D. Woods (eds), *The Columbia Reader on Lesbians and Gay Men in Media, Society, and Politics*, New York: Columbia University Press, 565–70. (1st published 1981.)

Clatts, Michael C. 1999: Ethnographic observations of men who have sex with men in public: toward an ecology of sexual action. In William L. Leap (ed.), *Public Sex: Gay Space*, New York: Columbia University Press, 141–56.

Connell, Robert 1995: *Masculinities: Knowledge, Power and Social Change*. Cambridge: Polity.

Conway, Kelly 1995: Stop me before I bake again. In Leslea Newman (ed.), *The Femme Mystique*, Boston: Alyson Publications, 300–2.

Cook-Daniels, Loree 1998: Trans-positioned. First published in *Circles Magazine*, Boulder, Colo. *http://members.aol.com/ ht a/marcellecd/Transpositioned.html*. Consulted 14 August 2000.

Cook-Daniels, Loree 2000: Hope the blood never washes off your hands: transgender parenting crossing the lines. In Jess Wells (ed.), *Home Fronts: Controversies in Nontraditional Parenting*, Los Angeles: Alyson Books, 9–24.

Corea, Gena 1990: The new reproductive technologies. In Dorchen Leidholdt and Janice G. Raymond (eds), *The Sexual Liberals and the Attack on Feminism*, New York: Pergamon Press, 85–94.

Crain, Caleb 1997: Pleasure principles: queer theorists and gay journalists wrestle over the politics of sex. *Lingua Franca: The Review of Academic Life*, 7 (8), 26–37.

Crimp, Douglas 1997: Randy Shilts's miserable failure. In Martin Duberman (ed.), *A Queer World: The Center for Lesbian and Gay Studies Reader*, New York: New York University Press, 641–8.

Cytron, Sara with Harriet Malinowitz 1999: Butch in a Tutu. In Matthew Rottnek (ed.), *Sissies and Tomboys: Gender Nonconformity and Homosexual Childhood*, New York: New York University Press, 209–25.

Daly, Mary 1979: *Gyn/Ecology: The Metaethics of Radical Feminism*. London: The Women's Press.

Dangerous Bedfellows (ed.) 1996: *Policing Public Sex*. Boston: South End Press.

Davis, Madeline and Kennedy, Elizabeth Lapovsky 1991: Oral history and the study of sexuality in the lesbian community: Buffalo, New York, 1940–1960. In Martin Duberman, Martin Bauml, Martha Vicinus, and

George Chauncey (eds), *Hidden from History: Reclaiming the Gay and Lesbian Past*, Harmondsworth: Penguin Books, 426–40.

De Lauretis, Teresa 1997: Fem/les scramble. In Dana Heller (ed.), *Cross Purposes: Lesbians, Feminists, and the Limits of Alliance*, Bloomington, Ind.: Indiana University Press, 42–8.

Delphy, Christine 1993: Rethinking sex and gender. *Women's Studies International Forum*, 16 (1), 1–9.

D'Emilio, John 1998: *Sexual Politics, Sexual Communities: The Making of a Homosexual Minority in the United States, 1940–1970*. Chicago: University of Chicago Press. (1st published 1983.)

D'Emilio, John 1992: Foreword. In Karla Jay and Allen Young (eds), *Out of the Closets: Voices of Gay Liberation*, London: Gay Men's Press, pp. xi–xxx.

Denny, Dallas 2000: Transgendered youth at risk for exploitation, HIV, hate crimes. www.amboyz.org/articles/youthrisk.html. Consulted 14 August 2000.

Devor, Holly 1999: *FTM: Female-to-Male Transsexuals in Society*. Bloomington and Indianapolis: Indiana University Press.

Diaman, N. A. 1992: On sex roles and equality. In Karla Jay and Allen Young (eds), *Out of the Closets: Voices of Gay Liberation*, London: Gay Men's Press, 262–3. (1st published 1972.)

Dobkin, Alix 2000: The Emperor's new gender. *Off Our Backs*, April. www.rapereliefshelter.bc.ca/issues/

Dominguez Jr, Ivo 1994: *Beneath the Skins: The New Spirit and Politics of the Kink Community*. Los Angeles: Daedalus.

Due, Linnea 1994: Dyke daddies. In Lily Burana, Roxxie and Linnea Due (eds), *Dagger: On Butch Women*, San Francisco: Cleis Press, 195–203.

Due, Linnea 1998: Crossing over. In Sara Miles and Eric Rofes (eds), *Opposite Sex: Gay Men on Lesbians, Lesbians on Gay Men*, New York: New York University Press, 201–21.

Duggan, Lisa 1995: Making it perfectly queer. In Lisa Duggan and Nan D. Hunter (eds), *Sex Wars*, New York and London: Routledge, 155–72.

Duggan, Lisa and Hunter, Nan D. (eds) 1995: *Sex Wars*. New York and London: Routledge.

Dunne, Gillian A. 1997: *Lesbian Lifestyles: Women's Work and the Politics of Sexuality*. Basingstoke and London: Macmillan.

Dunne, Gillian A. 2000: Lesbians as authentic workers? Institutional heterosexuality and the reproduction of gender inequalities. *Sexualities*, 3 (2), 133–48.

Dworkin, Andrea 1981: *Pornography: Men Possessing Women*. London: The Women's Press.

Edmonson, Roger 1998: *Casey Donovan, Boy in the Sand: All-American Sex Star*. Los Angeles and New York: Alyson Books.

Edmonson, Roger 2000: *Clone: The Life and Legacy of Al Parker, Gay Superstar.* Los Angeles and New York: Alyson Books.

Ellis, Henry Havelock 1913: *Studies in the Psychology of Sex,* vol. 2: *Sexual Inversion.* Philadelphia: F. A. Davis. (1st published 1903.)

Epstein, Steven 1996: A queer encounter: sociology and the study of sexuality. In Steven Seidman (ed.), *Queer Theory/Sociology,* Cambridge, MA: Blackwell, 144–67.

European Court Judgment, 1997: Case of *Laskey, Jaggard and Brown v. The United Kingdom* (109/1995/615/703–705), Strasbourg, February. www.spannertrust.org/documents/eurofinal.

Evans, David 1993: *Sexual Citizenship: The Material Construction of Sexualities.* London: Routledge.

Everywoman 1988: *Pornography and Sexual Violence: Evidence of Harm.* London: Everywoman Ltd.

Faderman, Lillian 1984: *Surpassing the Love of Men.* London: Junction Books.

Faderman, Lillian 1997: Afterword. In Dana Heller (ed.), *Cross Purposes: Lesbians, Feminists, and the Limits of Alliance,* Bloomington, Ind.: Indiana University Press, 221–9.

Favazza, Armando 1998: Introduction. In Marilee Strong, *A Bright Red Scream: Self-Mutilation and the Language of Pain,* New York: Viking, pp. ix–xiv.

Figes, Eva 1970: *Patriarchal Attitudes: Women in Society.* London: Faber.

Findlay, Heather 1998: Losing Sue. In Sally R. Munt (ed.), *Butch/Femme: Inside Lesbian Gender,* London: Cassell, 133–46.

Foreman, Martin (ed.) 1999: *AIDS and Men: Taking Risks or Taking Responsibility?* London: The Panos Institute and Zed Books.

Friedan, Betty 1965: *The Feminine Mystique.* Harmondsworth: Penguin Books.

Frye, Marilyn 1983: *The Politics of Reality: Essays in Feminist Theory.* New York: The Crossing Press.

Fung, Richard 1999: Looking for my penis: the eroticized Asian in gay video porn. In Larry Gross and James D. Woods (eds), *The Columbia Reader on Lesbians and Gay Men in Media, Society and Politics,* New York: Columbia University Press, 517–25. (1st published 1988.)

Gagnon, John H. and Simon, William 1973: *Sexual Conduct.* London: Hutchinson.

Gamson, Joshua 1996: Must identity movements self-destruct?: a queer dilemma. In Steven Seidman (ed.), *Queer Theory/Sociology,* Cambridge, MA: Blackwell, 395–420.

Gay Revolutionary Party Women's Caucus 1992: In Karla Jay and Allen Young (eds), *Out of the Closets: Voices of Gay Liberation,* London: Gay Men's Press, 177–81. (1st published 1972.)

GenderPAC www.gpac.org/gpac/index.html. Consulted 18 March 2001.

Gibson, Barbara 1996: *Male Order: Life Stories from Boys Who Sell Sex.* London: Cassell.

Gibson, Paul 1994: Gay male and lesbian youth suicide. In Gary Remafedi (ed.), *Death by Denial: Studies of Suicide in Gay and Lesbian Teenagers,* Boston: Alyson Publications, 15–68.

Gomez, Jewelle, Hollibaugh, Amber and Rubin, Gayle 1998: Another place to breathe. In Sara Miles and Eric Rofes (eds), *Opposite Sex: Gay Men on Lesbians, Lesbians on Gay Men,* New York: New York University Press, 105–38.

Gopalkrishnan, Carl 2000: A sociological analysis of gay racism and its effect on Asian men in HIV social research. Unpublished honours thesis, Department of Sociology, Murdoch University.

Gottschalk, Lorene 2000: Feminism and the construction of lesbianism: a comparison of lesbians' experiences in feminist and non-feminist contexts. Unpublished Ph.D. thesis. University of Melbourne, Department of Political Science.

Greer, Germaine 1999: *The Whole Woman.* London: Doubleday.

Growing Generations 2001: www.growinggenerations.com. Consulted March 2001.

Hackett, Louise 1997: *Consent in the Criminal Law.* The Law Commission Consultation Paper 139. Leeds: Civil and Criminal Justice Working Group.

Halberstam, Judith 1994: FtoM: the making of female masculinity. In Laura Doan (ed.), *The Lesbian Postmodern,* New York: Columbia University Press, 210–28.

Halberstam, Judith 1998a: *Female Masculinity.* Durham, NC, and London: Duke University Press.

Halberstam, Judith 1998b: Transgender butch. *GLQ: A Journal of Lesbian and Gay Studies,* 4 (2), 287–310.

Halberstam, Judith 1999: Oh bondage up yours! Female masculinity and the tomboy. In Matthew Rottnek (ed.), *Sissies and Tomboys: Gender Nonconformity and Homosexual Childhood,* New York: New York University Press, 153–79.

Halberstam, Judith and Hale, C. Jacob 1998: Butch/FTM border wars. *GLQ: A Journal of Lesbian and Gay Studies,* 4 (2), 283–6.

Hale, C. Jacob 1998: Consuming the living, dis(re)membering the dead in the butch/FTM borderlands. *GLQ: A Journal of Lesbian and Gay Studies,* 4 (2), 311–48.

Hanisch, Carol 1970: The personal is the political. In Shulamith Firestone (ed.), *Notes from the Second Year,* New York: Radical Feminism, 76–8.

Hart, Nett 1996: From an eroticism of difference to an intimacy of equals: a radical feminist lesbian separatist perspective on sexuality. In Lilian Mohin (ed.), *An Intimacy of Equals: Lesbian Feminist Ethics*, London: Onlywomen Press, 69–77.

Hawker, Philippa 2000: In touch with the feminist side. *The Age Today Section*, Tuesday, 2 May, 3.

Heller, Dana (ed.) 1997: *Cross Purposes: Lesbians, Feminists, and the Limits of Alliance*, Bloomington, Ind.: Indiana University Press, 1–16.

Herman, Judith 1994: *Trauma and Recovery: From Domestic Abuse to Political Terror*. London: Pandora.

Hernandez, Michael M. 1998: Transsexuality: GONNA PUMP YOU UP! *FTM Newsletter* # 41, June. http://www.koan.com/~lbear/pump.html. Consulted 14 August 2000.

Hocquenghem, Guy 1978: *Homosexual Desire*. London: Alyson and Busby. (1st published 1972.)

Hodges, Andrew and Hutter, David 1999: With downcast gays: aspects of homosexual self-oppression. In Larry Gross and James D. Woods (eds), *The Columbia Reader on Lesbians and Gay Men in Media, Society and Politics*, New York: Columbia University Press, 551–61. (1st published 1974.)

Hoffman, Wayne 1996: Skipping the life fantastic: coming of age in the sexual devolution. In Dangerous Bedfellows (ed.), *Policing Public Sex*, Boston: South End Press, 337–54.

Hogan, Christopher 1996: What we write about when we write about porn. In Michael Bronski (ed.), *Taking Liberties: Gay Men's Essays on Politics, Culture, Sex*, New York: Masquerade Books, 229–46.

Howard, Rhoda E. 1993: Health costs of social degradation and female self-mutilation in North America. In K. Mahoney and P. Mahoney (eds), *Human Rights in the Twenty-First Century*, Dordrecht, Boston and London: Martinus Nijhoff, 503–16.

Hughes, Donna and Roche, Claire (eds) 1999: *Making the Harm Visible: Global Sexual Exploitation of Women and Girls*. Kingston, RI: Coalition Against Trafficking in Women.

Humphries, Martin 1985: Gay machismo. In Andy Metcalf and Martin Humphries (eds), *The Sexuality of Men*, London: Pluto Press, 70–84.

Isherwood, Charles 1996: *Wonder Bread and Ecstasy: The Life and Death of Joey Stefano*. Los Angeles: Alyson Publications.

Jagose, Annamarie 1998: *Queer Theory*. Melbourne: Melbourne University Press. (1st published 1996.)

Jay, Karla and Young, Allen 1992: Introduction to the second edition. In Karla Jay and Allen Young (eds), *Out of the Closets: Voices of Gay Liberation*, London: Gay Men's Press, pp. vii–lix.

Jeffreys, Sheila 1989: Butch and femme: now and then. In Lesbian History Group (ed.), *Not a Passing Phase: Reclaiming Lesbians in History 1840–1985*, London: The Women's Press, 158–87.

Jeffreys, Sheila 1990a: *Anticlimax: A Feminist Perspective on the Sexual Revolution*. London: The Women's Press; New York: New York University Press, 1991.

Jeffreys, Sheila 1990b: Eroticizing women's subordination. In Dorchen Leidholdt and Janice G. Raymond (eds), *The Sexual Liberals and the Attack on Feminism*, New York: Pergamon Press, 132–5.

Jeffreys, Sheila 1993: *The Lesbian Heresy: A Feminist Perspective on the Lesbian Sexual Revolution*. Melbourne: Spinifex Press.

Jeffreys, Sheila 1994: The queer disappearance of lesbians. *Women's Studies International Forum*, 17 (5), 459–72.

Jeffreys, Sheila 1997a: *The Idea of Prostitution*. Melbourne: Spinifex Press.

Jeffreys, Sheila 1997b: *The Spinster and her Enemies*. Melbourne: Spinifex Press. (1st published 1985.)

Jeffreys, Sheila 1997c: Transgender activism. *Journal of Lesbian Studies*, 1 (3/4), 55–74.

Jeffreys, Sheila 1999: Bisexual politics: a superior form of feminism? *Women's Studies International Forum*, 22 (3), 273–86.

Jeffreys, Sheila 2000: 'Body art': cutting, tattooing and piercing from a feminist perspective. *Feminism and Psychology*, 10 (4), 409–29.

Jensen, Robert 1998: Getting it up for politics: gay male sexuality and radical lesbian feminism. In Sara Miles and Eric Rofes (eds), *Opposite Sex: Gay Men on Lesbians, Lesbians on Gay Men*, New York: New York University Press, 146–70.

Justice for Women 1996: Response to Consultation Paper no. 139, Consent and the Criminal Law. London: Justice for Women.

Kappeler, Susanne 1990: Liberals, libertarianism, and the liberal arts establishment. In Dorchen Leidholdt and Janice G. Raymond (eds), *The Sexual Liberals and the Attack on Feminism*, New York: Pergamon Press, 175–83.

Katz, Jonathan 1978: *American History: Lesbians and Gay Men in the USA*. New York: Avon Books.

Kendall, Christopher N. 1997: Gay male pornography after Little Sisters Book and Art Emporium: a call for gay male cooperation in the struggle for sex equality. *Wisconsin Women's Law Journal*, 12 (21), 21–82.

Kendall, Christopher N. 1999: Gay Male pornography/gay male community: power without consent, mimicry without subversion. In Joseph A. Kuypers (ed.), *Men and Power*, Halifax, Nova Scotia: Fernwood Publishing, 157–72.

Kim, Richard 2001: Andrew Sullivan overexposed. *The Nation*, June. www.thenation.com/doc.mhtml?i = special&s = kim20010605.

Kimmel, Michael 1987: The cult of masculinity: American social character and the legacy of the cowboy. In Michael Kaufman (ed.), *Beyond Patriarchy*, Toronto and New York: Oxford University Press, 235–49.

Kimmel, Michael S. 1995: *The Politics of Manhood: Profeminist Men Respond to the Mythopoetic Men's Movement*. Philadelphia: Temple University Press.

Kingham, Tess 2001: Cheesed off by willy-jousters in a pointless parliament. *The Guardian*, Wednesday, 20 June.

Kirsch, Max H. 2000: *Queer Theory and Social Change*. London and New York: Routledge.

Kitzinger, Celia 1997: Lesbians and psychology: straightening us out? In Gabrielle Griffin and Sonya Andermahr (eds), *Straight Studies Modified: Lesbian Interventions in the Academy*, London: Continuum International Publishing Group, 157–67.

Klein, Viola 1971: *The Feminine Character: History of an Ideology*. London: Routledge and Kegan Paul. (1st published 1946.)

Kramer, Larry 1978: *Faggots*. New York: Random House.

Lamos, Colleen 1994: The postmodern lesbian position: *on our backs*. In Laura Doan (ed.), *The Lesbian Postmodern*, New York: Columbia University Press, 85–103.

Leap, William L. (ed.) 1999: *Public Sex: Gay Space*. New York: Columbia University Press.

Leigh, Carol 1996: P.I.M.P. (Prostitutes in Municipal Politics). In Dangerous Bedfellows (ed.), *Policing Public Sex*, Boston: South End Press, 251–62.

Levine, Martin P. 1998: *Gay Macho: The Life and Death of the Homosexual Clone*. New York: New York University Press.

Levine, Martin and Kimmell, Michael 1998: Men and AIDS. In Martin Levine, *Gay Macho: The Life and Death of the Homosexual Clone*, New York: New York University Press, 143–57. (1st published 1989.)

Lewins, Frank 1995: *Transsexualism in Society: A Sociology of Male-to-Female Transsexuals*. Melbourne: MacMillan Education.

Liebling, Helen, Chipchase, Hazel and Velangi, Rebecca (1997). Why do women harm themselves? – Surviving special hospitals. *Feminism and Psychology*, 7 (3), 427–37.

Linden, Robin, Pagano, Darlene, Russell, Diana E. H. and Star, Susan Leigh 1982: *Against Sadomasochism*. East Palo Alto, Calif.: Frog in the Well.

Lister, Ruth 1997: *Citizenship: Feminist Perspectives*. Basingstoke and London: Macmillan.

Lothstein, Leslie Martin 1983: *Female-to-Male Transsexualism*. Boston and London: Routledge and Kegan Paul.

MacKinnon, Catharine A. 1987: *Feminism Unmodified*. Cambridge, Mass.: Harvard University Press.

MacKinnon, Catharine A. 1989: *Towards a Feminist Theory of the State*. Cambridge, Mass.: Harvard University Press.

MacKinnon, Catharine A. and Dworkin, Andrea (eds) 1997: *In Harm's Way: The Pornography and Civil Rights Hearings*. Cambridge, Mass.: Harvard University Press.

Mallinger, Scott 1998: About anal sex, barebacking: slogans aren't enough. *Badpuppy Gay Today*, Monday, 6 April. http://gaytoday.badpuppy.com/ garchive/viewpoint/040698v:htm.

Mallon, Gerald P. 1999: Practice with transgendered children. In Gerald P. Mallon (ed.), *Social Services with Transgendered Youth*, Binghamton, New York: Harrington Park Press, 49–64.

Mason, Margie 2001: Sex-change benefits may be approved. *New York Times*, 16 February.

Menasche, Anne E. 1998: *Leaving the Life: Lesbians, Ex-Lesbians and the Heterosexual Imperative*. London: Onlywomen Press.

Messner, Michael A. 1997: *Politics of Masculinities: Men in Movements*. Thousand Oaks, Calif.: Sage.

Metcalf, Andy 1985: Introduction. In Andy Metcalf and Martin Humphries (eds), *The Sexuality of Men*, London: Pluto Press, 1–14.

Miles, Sara and Rofes, Eric (eds) 1998: *Opposite Sex: Gay Men on Lesbians, Lesbians on Gay Men*. New York: New York University Press.

Miller, Stephen 1994: Masculinity under siege. *Christopher Street*, issue 209, January. www.indegayforum.org/articles/miller63.html.

Millett, Kate 1977: *Sexual Politics*. London: Virago.

Minter, Shannon 1999: Diagnosis and treatment of gender identity disorder in children. In Matthew Rottnek (ed.), *Sissies and Tomboys: Gender Nonconformity and Homosexual Childhood*, New York: New York University Press, 9–33.

More, Kate 1999: Never mind the bollocks: 2 Judith Butler on transsexuality. In Kate More and Stephen Whittle (eds), *Reclaiming Genders: Transsexual Grammars at the Fin de siècle*, London: Cassell, 285–302.

Munoz, Jose Esteban 1996: Ghosts of public sex: utopian longings, queer memories. In Dangerous Bedfellows (ed.), *Policing Public Sex*, Boston: South End Press, 355–72.

Munt, Sally R. 1998: Introduction. In Sally R. Munt. (ed.), *Butch/femme: Inside Lesbian Gender*, London: Cassell, 1–11.

Murray, Stephen O. 1997: Five reasons I don't take 'queer theory' seriously. Paper presented at the 1997 annual meeting of the Pacific Sociological Association in San Diego, California. www.indegayforum.org/articles/ murray4.html.

Musafar, Fakir 1996: Body play: state of grace or sickness? In Armando Favazza, *Bodies Under Siege: Self-Mutilation and Body Modification in Culture and Psychiatry*, Baltimore and London: Johns Hopkins University Press, 325–34.

Myers, James 1995: Nonmainstream body modification: genital piercing, branding, burning and cutting. In Thomas S. Weinberg (ed.), *S&M: Studies in Dominance and Submission*, New York: Prometheus Books, 151–94.

Nestle, Joan 1987: *A Restricted Country*. London: Sheba.

Newman, Leslea (ed.) 1995: *The Femme Mystique*. Boston: Alyson Publications.

Nicholls, Margaret 1987: Lesbian sexuality: issues and developing theory. In Boston Lesbian Psychologies Collective (eds.), *Lesbian Psychologies*, Urbana, Ill.: University of Illinois Press, 97–125.

Nicholson, Linda (ed.) 1990: *Feminism/Postmodernism*. New York: Routledge.

Odets, Walt 1995: *In the Shadow of the Epidemic*. Durham, NC: Duke University Press.

O'Hara, Scott 1997: *Autopornography: A Memoir of Life in the Lust Lane*. Binghamton, NY: Harrington Park Press.

O'Hara, Scott 1999: *Rarely Pure and Never Simple: Selected Essays of Scott O'Hara*. New York and London: Harrington Park Press.

O'Lexa, Liz 1995: Let me be the femme. In Leslea Newman (ed.), *The Femme Mystique*, Boston: Alyson Publications, 213–15.

Osborne, Duncan 2001: More alarming CDC data on gay black infections. *Lesbian and Gay New York*. www.lgny.com/HIV.HTM. Consulted 26 June 2001.

O'Sullivan, Kimberley 1997: Dangerous desire: lesbianism as sex or politics. In Jill Julius Matthews (ed.), *Sex in Public: Australian Sexual Cultures*, St Leonards, New South Wales: Allen and Unwin, 114–26.

O'Sullivan, Sue 1999: I don't want you anymore: butch/femme disappointments. *Sexualities*, 2 (4), 465–73.

Pateman, Carole 1988: *The Sexual Contract*. Cambridge: Polity.

Pazos, Sophia 1999: Practice with female-to-male transgendered youth. In Gerald P. Mallon (ed.), *Social Services with Transgendered Youth*, Binghamton, NY: Harrington Park Press, 65–82.

Pendleton, Eva 1996: Domesticating partnerships. In Dangerous Bedfellows (ed.), *Policing Public Sex*, Boston: South End Press, 373–94.

Penelope, Julia 1984: Whose past are we reclaiming? *Common Lives, Lesbian Lives*, no. 13.

Penelope, Julia 1992: Controlling interests, consuming passions: sexual metaphors. In Julia Penelope, *Call Me Lesbian: Lesbian Lives, Lesbian Theory*, Freedom, Calif.: The Crossing Press, 113–31. (1st published 1987.)

Perkins, Roberta and Bennett, Gary 1985. *Being a Prostitute*. St Leonards, New South Wales: Allen and Unwin.

Phelan, Shane 1994: *Getting Specific: Postmodern Lesbian Politics*. Minneapolis: University of Minnesota Press.

Plummer, David 1999: *One of the Boys: Masculinity, Homophobia, and Modern Manhood*. Binghamton, NY: Harrington Park Press.

Pocock, Barbara 2000: *Having a Life: Work, Family, Fairness and Community in 2000*. Adelaide: Centre for Labour Research, Adelaide University.

Power, Lisa 1995: *No Bath but Plenty of Bubbles: An Oral History of the Gay Liberation Front from 1970–1973*. London: Cassell.

Preston, John 1984: *I Once Had a Master and Other Tales of Erotic Love*. Boston: Alyson Publications.

Preston, John 1993: *My Life as a Pornographer and Other Indecent Acts*. New York: Masquerade Books Inc.

Radicalesbians 1999: The woman-identified woman. In Larry Gross and James D. Woods (eds), *The Columbia Reader on Lesbians and Gay Men in Media, Society and Politics*, New York: Columbia University Press, 562–4. (1st published 1970.)

Ramakers, Micha 2000: *Dirty Pictures*. New York: St Martin's Press.

Rauch, Jonathan 1994: A pro-gay, pro-family policy. *Wall Street Journal*, 29 November. www.indegayforum.org/articles/rauch13.html.

Raymond, Janice G. 1986: *A Passion for Friends: Toward a Philosophy of Female Affection*. Boston: Beacon Press.

Raymond, Janice G. 1990: Sexual and reproductive liberalism. In Dorchen Leidholdt and Janice G. Raymond (eds), *The Sexual Liberals and the Attack on Feminism*, New York: Pergamon Press, 103–11.

Raymond, Janice G. 1994: *The Transsexual Empire*. New York: Teachers' College Press. (1st published 1979.)

Rechy, John 1981: *The Sexual Outlaw*. London: Futura. (1st published 1977.)

Redstockings 2000: Redstockings manifesto. In Barbara A. Crow (ed.), *Radical Feminism: A Documentary Reader*, New York: New York University Press, 223–5. (1st published 1969.)

Rees, Mark 1996: *Dear Sir or Madam: The Autobiography of a Female-to-Male Transsexual*. London: Cassell.

Remafedi, Gary 1994: *Death by Denial: Studies of Suicide in Gay and Lesbian Teenagers*. Boston: Alyson Publications.

Rich, Adrienne 1979: The meaning of our love for women is what we have constantly to expand. In Adrienne Rich, *On Lies, Secrets and Silence: Selected Prose 1966–1978*, New York and London: W.W. Norton and Company, 223–30. (1st published 1977.)

Rich, Adrienne 1993: Compulsory heterosexuality and lesbian existence. In H. Abelove, M. A. Barale and D. M. Halperin (eds), *The Lesbian and Gay Studies Reader*, London: Routledge, 227–54. (1st published 1982.)

Richardson, Diane (ed.) 1996: *Theorising Heterosexuality*. Buckingham, UK: Open University Press.

Richardson, Diane 2000a: Claiming citizenship? Sexuality, citizenship and lesbian/feminist theory. *Sexualities*, 3 (2), 271–88.

Richardson, Diane 2000b: *Rethinking Sexuality*. London: Sage.

Robson, Ruthann 1992: *Lesbian (Out)Law: Survival under the Rule of Law*. Ithaca, NY: Firebrand Books.

Rofes, Eric 1997: The emerging sex panic targeting gay men. Speech given at the National Gay and Lesbian Task Force's Creating Change Conference in San Diego, 16 November. http://www.managingdesire.org/sexpanic/ rofessexpanic.html. Consulted 20 May 2001.

Rofes, Eric 1998a: *Dry Bones Breathe: Gay Men Creating Post-AIDS Identities and Culture*. New York and London: Harrington Park Press.

Rofes, Eric 1998b: The ick factor: flesh, fluids, and cross-gender revulsion. In Sara Miles and Eric Rofes (eds), *Opposite Sex: Gay Men on Lesbians, Lesbians on Gay Men*, New York: New York University Press, 44–65.

Rotello, Gabriel 1997: *Sexual Ecology: AIDS and the Destiny of Gay Men*. New York: Dutton.

Rothblum, Esther D. 1994: Transforming lesbian sexuality. *Psychology of Women Quarterly*, 18, 627–41.

Rothblum, Esther D. and Brehony, K. A. (eds) 1993: *Boston Marriages: Romantic but Asexual Relationships among Contemporary Lesbians*. Amherst: University of Massachusetts Press.

Rottnek, Matthew (ed.) 1999: *Sissies and Tomboys: Gender Nonconformity and Homosexual Childhood*. New York: New York University Press.

Rowlands, Robyn 1992: *Living Laboratories: Women and Reproductive Technologies*. Sydney: Pan MacMillan.

Rowse, A. L. 1977: *Homosexuals in History*. London: Weidenfeld and Nicolson.

Rubin, Gayle 1984: Thinking sex. In Carole Vance (ed.), *Pleasure and Danger*, New York: Routledge, 267–319.

Russell, Diana 1990: *Rape in Marriage*. Bloomington, Ind.: Indiana University Press.

Russell, Diana 1995: The making of a whore. *Violence against Women*, 1, 77–98.

Saxe, Lorena Leigh 1994: Sadomasochism and exclusion. In Claudia Card (ed.), *Adventures in Lesbian Philosophy*, Bloomington and Indianapolis: Indiana University Press, 64–80.

Sedgwick, Eve Kosofsky 1985: *Between Men: English Literature and Male Homosocial Desire*. New York: Columbia University Press.

Sedgwick, Eve Kosofsky 1999: *A Dialogue on Love*. Boston: Beacon Press.

Shiers, John 1980: Two steps forward, one step back. In Gay Left Collective (eds.), *Homosexuality: Power and Politics*, London: Alison and Busby, 140–56.

Shilts, Randy 1987: *And the Band Played On: Politics, People and the AIDS Epidemic*. New York: St Martin's Press.

Signorile, Signorile 1998a: *Life Outside: The Signorile Report on Gay Men: Sex, Drugs, Muscles, and the Passages of Life*. New York: HarperCollins.

Signorile, Michelangelo 1998b: Sex panic! and paranoia. *Out Magazine*, April. http://www.signorile.com/col-sexpanic.html. Consulted 20 May 2001.

Signorile, Michelangelo 2001: The contradictory faces of Andrew Sullivan. *LGNY: The Paper for Lesbian and Gay New York*, issue 159, 25 May–7 June.

Smyth, Cherry 1992: *Lesbians Talk: Queer Notions*. London: Scarlet Press.

Spanner Trust 2001: Spanner Trust submission to the Home Office Review Board on Sexual Offences. BM99, London, WC1N3XX, England. www.spannertrust.org/documents/sexualoffencesreview.asp.

Stack, Carolyn 1985: Lesbian sexual problems. *Bad Attitude*, Spring.

Stoltenberg, John 1990: *Refusing to Be a Man*. London: Fontana.

Stoltenberg, John 1991: Gays and the propornography movement: having the hots for sex discrimination. In Michael S. Kimmel (ed.), *Men Confront Pornography*, New York: Meridian, 248–62.

Strong, Marilee 1998: *A Bright Red Scream: Self-Mutilation and the Language of Pain*. With an Introduction by Armando Favazza. New York: Viking.

Strubbe, Bill 1997: Getting a grip on the ick factor. *Outrage*, no. 168, May, 42–7.

Stryker, Susan 1998: An Introduction. *GLQ: A Journal of Lesbian and Gay Studies*, 4 (2): *The Transgender Issue*, 145–58.

Stychin, Carl F. 1995: *Law's Desire. Sexuality and the Limits of Justice*. London and New York: Routledge.

Sullivan, Andrew 1996: *Virtually Normal: An Argument about Homosexuality*. London: Picador.

Sullivan, Andrew 2000: Why 'civil union' isn't marriage. *The New Republic*, 8 May 2000. www.indegayforum.org/articles/sullivan4.html.

Swann, Stephanie and Herbert, Sarah E. 1999: Ethical issues in the mental health treatment of gender dysphoric adolescents. In Gerald P. Mallon (ed.), *Social Services with Transgendered Youth*, New York: Harrington Park Press, 19–34.

Thomas, Kendall 1996: Going public: a conversation with Lidell Jackson and Jocelyn Taylor. In Dangerous Bedfellows (ed.), *Policing Public Sex*, Boston: South End Press, 53–72.

Thompson, Denise 1985: *Flaws in the Social Fabric*. Sydney: George Allen and Unwin.

Thompson, Raymond 1995: *What Took you so Long? A Girl's Journey to Manhood*. Harmondsworth: Penguin Books.

Tucker, Scott 1991: Radical feminism and gay male porn. In Michael S. Kimmel (ed.), *Men Confront Pornography*, New York: Meridian, 263–76.

Tucker, Scott 1997: *The Queer Question: Essays on Desire and Democracy*. Boston: South End Press.

Vaid, Urvashi 1995: *Virtual Equality: The Mainstreaming of Lesbian and Gay Liberation*. New York: Anchor Books, Doubleday.

Vance, Carole A. (ed.) 1984: *Pleasure and Danger: Exploring Female Sexuality*. London: Routledge and Kegan Paul.

Vogel, Ursula 1994: Marriage and the boundaries of citizenship. In Bart van Steenbergen (ed.), *The Condition of Citizenship*, London: Sage, 77–89.

Volcano, Del Lagrace and Halberstam, Judith "Jack" 1999: *The Drag King Book*. London: Serpent's Tail.

Walter, Aubrey (ed.) 1980: *Come Together*. London: Gay Men's Press.

Walters, Suzanna Danuta 1996: From here to queer: radical feminism, postmodernism, and the lesbian menace (or, why can't a woman be more like a fag?). *Signs*, 21(4), 830–69.

Warner, Michael 1993: *Fear of a Queer Planet: Queer Politics and Social Theory*. Minneapolis: University of Minnesota Press.

Warner, Michael 1999: *The Trouble with Normal: Sex, Politics, and the Ethics of Queer Life*. New York: The Free Press.

Watney, Simon 1992: Queerspeak: the latest word. *Outrage*, April, 19–22.

Weedon, Chris 1987: *Feminist Practice and Poststructuralist Theory*. Oxford: Basil Blackwell.

Weeks, Jeffrey 1985: *Sexuality and its Discontents*. London: Routledge and Kegan Paul.

Weeks, Jeffrey 2000: *Making Sexual History*. Cambridge: Polity.

Weinberg, Thomas S. (ed.) 1995: *S&M: Studies in Dominance and Submission*. New York: Prometheus Books.

Weinstein, Jeff 1991: What porn did. In Michael S. Kimmel (ed.), *Men Confront Pornography*, New York: Meridian, 277–80.

Whittle, Stephen 2000: Press for change. PFC vice-president. http://www.pfc.org.uk/campaign/people/swhittle.htm. Consulted 14 August 2000.

Wilkinson, Sue and Kitzinger, Celia (eds) 1993: *Heterosexuality: A Feminism and Psychology Reader*. London: Sage.

Wilkinson, Sue and Kitzinger, Celia 1996: The queer backlash. In Diane Bell and Renate Klein (eds), *Radically Speaking: Feminism Reclaimed*, Melbourne: Spinifex Press, 375–82.

Wilson, Angelia (ed.) 1995: *A Simple Matter of Justice: Theorizing Lesbian and Gay Politics*. London: Cassell.

Wittig, Monique 1992: *The Straight Mind and Other Essays*. Boston: Beacon Press.

Wittman, Carl 1992: A gay manifesto. In Karla Jay and Allen Young (eds), *Out of the Closets: Voices of Gay Liberation*, London: Gay Men's Press, 330–42. (1st published 1972.)

Wolf, Alexa 2000: *Shocking Truth*. Stockholm: Mother Superior Films.

Woods, Chris 1995: *State of the Queer Nation: A Critique of Gay and Lesbian Politics in 1990s Britain*. London: Cassell.

Young, Ian 1995: *The Stonewall Experiment: A Gay Psychohistory*. London: Cassell.

Zimmerman, Bonnie 1997: 'Confessions' of a lesbian feminist. In Dana Heller (ed.), *Cross Purposes: Lesbians, Feminists, and the Limits of Alliance*, Bloomington, Ind.: Indiana University Press, 157–68.

Index

polygyny 76
pornography: body
  modification 112–13; child
  sexual abuse 29, 79–80;
  defence of 28, 82;
  feminism 15, 78, 79–80;
  Gonzo 99–100; male
  dominance 28, 79; male
  models 93, 94–9;
  mutilation 113; queer
  theory 78–9; rape 79–80;
  sadomasochism 81–3, 85–6;
  Sex Panic 78–9; *see also* gay
  pornography; lesbian
  pornography
post-structuralism 33, 35, 38, 46,
  51–2
postmodern lesbians 38–9, 145,
  158–9
Power, Lisa 10, 16–17, 18
Preston, John 81–3, 102, 103–4
professional dominators 104
promiscuity 59, 62, 94, 95, 149
prostitution: boys 99; child
  sexual abuse 29, 99; defence
  of 69; feminism 15; gay 67,
  70, 71–2, 94, 96, 98; male
  dominance 28; sexual
  abuse 99
public nuisance 71–2
public/private 8, 58, 148, 156–7;
  see also personal/political
public sex: AIDS epidemic 60, 67;
  defended 66–9; gay male
  theorists 61–6;
  Hocquenghem 34; lesbians 57,
  68–9; male dominance 72;
  photography 69; pre-
  Stonewall 57–8;
  promiscuity 94; Sex
  Panic 154–5; sexual
  freedom 161–2; sexually-
  transmitted diseases 64;

transgression 42, 68;
  women 77
public space: *see* appropriation of
  public space

Queer Nation 54, 68
queer politics 4; bisexuals 35;
  capitalism 32–3; lesbian
  feminism 2, 9, 35–6;
  lesbians 53–4; masculinity 30;
  neoliberalism 32;
  outsiderhood 37; performing
  gender 55; post-
  structuralism 35;
  sadomasochism 11, 37; sexual
  freedom 33–4;
  transgenderism 44–5;
  transsexualism 44–5, 143;
  Walters 34–5; woman-
  loving 21
Queer Power 37
queer theory: gay male theorists 37;
  lesbian critique 51–6;
  Murray 42–3;
  performance 137;
  pornography 78–9; post-
  structuralism 33, 38;
  promiscuity 149;
  Sedgwick 40–2; sexual
  freedom 33–4, 149, 153–6;
  transsexualism 45–6, 123,
  133–4

race factors 5, 77, 92–3
radical feminists 146–7; anti-
  pornography 78;
  gender 43–4; lesbians 23, 34;
  men's sexuality 74; sex
  wars 15, 34
Radically Speaking 52
Ramakers, Micha 85, 86, 87
rape 74–5, 79–80, 91
Rauch, Jonathan 150

CPSIA information can be obtained
at www.ICGtesting.com
Printed in the USA
LVOW10s1513061216
516057LV00009B/1225/P